ATLAS OF
WORLD CHRISTIANITY

2000 YEARS

PETER BRIERLEY AND HEATHER WRAIGHT

Publishers Since 1798

THOMAS NELSON PUBLISHERS
NASHVILLE

contents

The Church Past and Present

27   Church Growth

37   Missionary Activity

51   Major World Religions

61   Comparative Material

contents

The Church and the Future

Dr Tom Sine

We are at the threshold of a new millennium in a world which is changing at blinding speed. Incredibly the church seeks to carry out the mission of Christ as though our world is stuck in a time warp. Virtually every church and mission organization does long-range planning as though the future is simply going to be an extension of the present.

Changing Global Context

Global population is projected to almost double from 5.8 billion today to over 11 billion by halfway through the next century. While growing numbers in the Third World are joining the middle class, globally the gap between poor and rich is widening. The numbers of poor are likely to increase dramatically, and in some places such as Haiti, Nepal and Bangladesh, the increase in population could result in ecological collapse.

"Population growth is outstripping church growth"

But that is not the whole story. Bryant Myers, the Executive Director of MARC World Vision, states that global population growth is taking place at a more rapid rate than the growth of the church. The graphs on page 14 show what he means: as we enter the third millennium, there will be fewer Christians as a percentage of the total global population. In other words, global population growth is outstripping the best efforts to complete the task of world evangelization.

"The gap between rich and poor is widening globally"

Changing Western Context

The widening gap between rich and poor is happening not only in the Third World but also in western countries. In most western countries human needs indicators are going up while at the same time social benefit programs are being cut back. The church is moving into a future of escalating human need both at home and abroad.

"The character of religion is changing"

Changes in the global economy impact the middle class as well as the poor. People who are in employment in the west are working longer hours and as a consequence those who are Christians have less time to be involved in the church and its mission than 10 years ago. The indications are that the situation will only get worse in the future. For example, those aged under 30 have to pay a significantly higher share of their income for everything from education to housing than their parents did. This means they are likely to have even less time and money available for the mission of the kingdom of God than their parents' generation.

The character of religion is changing in all western nations. Firstly, religion is becoming both more pluralistic and more privatized. The question for people is no longer which brand of Christianity to select, but which of a broad selection of religious options to embrace.

"The needs challenges and opportunities of the Third World are mounting"

Secondly, virtually all traditional church denominations in the West are declining numerically, and at the same time they have a higher proportion of older people than the general population. Pentecostal, charismatic and evangelical churches in the west are enjoying some growth, but it does not offset the aging and decline of the old denominations. Furthermore, the charismatic movement has plateaued. To this is added the discovery that the generation of those aged under 30 is almost entirely missing in the western church.

"Praying"

So while the needs, challenges and opportunities of the Third World are mounting, the capacity of the western church to increase its response is in serious question.

Implications for the Church and its Mission

What are some of the implications for the church as it seeks to carry out the ministry of Christ in this dramatically changing context?

"Listening"

1 If the western church is to start growing again it must strategically target those aged under 30. We must find creative new ways to reach, mentor and move a new generation into leadership and mission.

"Understanding"

2 To expand the church's mission so as to address the escalating physical and spiritual needs in our world will need more resources, especially of people. Clergy cannot do it all without lay people, but it will take a major educational effort to enable laity to reorder their lifestyles and timetables. The extent to which western Christians can free themselves from the seductions of the modern consumer culture and put God's purposes first will be the extent to which time and money can be freed up for the mission of the church.

"Discerning"

3 The church worldwide will need to create some whole new approaches to Christian community and Christian mission to more effectively engage the challenges of a new millennium.

All that we attempt must be deeply rooted in prayer, listening to our God, understanding those we are called to serve and discerning the winds of change blowing through our world.

Tom Sine is a consultant in futures research and planning for both Christian and secular organizations. He also helps Christian missions and relief and development organizations to develop a theology of mission. He is an Adjunct Professor of Fuller Theological Seminary in Seattle, Washington, USA.

Some Christian organizations do plan for change. The British relief and development organization, Tear Fund, is a good example. Before they did long-range and strategic planning recently they did "contextual forecasting". They asked how the context in which they do mission in Africa, Asia and Latin America is likely to change in the next ten years. They wanted to anticipate new needs, challenges and opportunities that are likely to be a part of tomorrow's world. As a result their long-range planning not only addresses today's needs but also tomorrow's opportunities.

First published in the United States of America in 1998 by Thomas Nelson, Inc.,
Publishers, Nashville, Tennessee.

Copyright © 1998 Hunt & Thorpe

Text copyright © 1998 Peter Brierley and Heather Wraight

Co-published by Christian Research and Hunt & Thorpe.

A CIP catalogue record for this book is available from the U.S. Library of Congress.

ISBN: 0-7852-0991-3 (Thomas Nelson, Inc.)
     1-85608-313-6 (Hunt & Thorpe)
     1-85321-128-1 (Christian Research)

Printed in Singapore

1 2 3 4 5 -- 02 01 00 99 98

NOTES

1. The basis of this volume is the *World Churches Handbook,* which was itself based on Patrick Johnstone's *Operation World* database. For details of these and all other sources, see Bibliography on page 140.

2. All the countries of the world are included on pages 77-127 of this volume. However, only those geographically large enough to show in color on the maps are included in the Tables on pages 128 to 139.

3. a) The church statistics used throughout are in the same 10 denominational groupings as the *World Churches Handbook.* These are: Anglican, Baptist, Catholic, Indigenous, Lutheran, Methodist, Orthodox, Pentecostal, Presbyterian and Other Churches. "Catholic" is mostly Roman Catholic but includes a few others. "Indigenous" churches are individual churches especially following the culture of a particular country, which do not always group together into recognized denominations and rarely form congregations outside their own locality. "Other Churches" are the smaller denominations (Salvation Army, Mennonites, Christian Brethren, etc., and including Independent Churches) which often occur in more than one country.

b) These 10 groups (which together are the Trinitarian Churches) have been further combined into 4 groups for the individual country graphs on pages 77-127: Catholic, Orthodox, Protestant Institutional (Anglican, Baptist, Lutheran, Methodist and Presbyterian), and Protestant Non-Institutional (Indigenous, Pentecostal and Other Churches).

c) The Non-Trinitarian Churches are not included in the totals used elsewhere in this volume. For definition see page 26.

4. n/a = not known or not available.

5. The term Third World has been used for simplicity throughout this volume. It is recognized that some users may have preferred either Developing World, Two-Thirds World or non-Western World.

The Church Past & Present

The Growth of the Christian Church

Professor Andrew Walls

The growth of Islam has been progressive; a story of geographical spread from its original center. Generally speaking, lands and peoples that have accepted Islam have remained Islamic. The growth of Christianity, however, has been serial, with periods of recession as well as of advance. Its history has been marked by decline in the areas of its greatest apparent strength accompanied by unexpected new growth at or beyond its margins. Christian history is a story of interaction between the gospel and a series of local cultures.

Christian history may be seen as a succession of cross-cultural movements.

Judaic Christianity

The first believers were Jewish by birth and conviction, seeing their faith in terms of Jewish history and hope. They saw the work of Jesus in terms of his Messiahship, looked for the salvation of the nation of Israel (Acts 1:6), and kept the observances of Law and Temple. Some Gentiles on the fringe of Judaism (like Cornelius), were brought to faith, but there seems to have been no systematic attempt to reach Gentiles until an outburst of violence drove one group of believers to the Syrian metropolis of Antioch. There they talked to Greek-speaking pagans about Jesus, using the term (Lord, Kyrios) that Hellenistic people used of their cult divinities. The outcome was a mixed community of Jewish and Gentile believers in Jesus; they were called Christians (Acts 11:26).

"Cross-cultural diffusion of the faith"

Barnabas and Paul planted a chain of churches westward from Antioch across Cyprus, Asia Minor and Greece. These churches became the bedrock of Hellenistic Christianity. Other Jewish Christians, of whom much less is known, moved east, to establish early Arab Christianity. When Jerusalem was destroyed by the Romans in A.D. 70, the original believing community scattered. The cross-cultural diffusion of the faith of Jesus had taken place just in time.

Hellenistic Roman Christianity

The church had early decided (Acts 15) that the new Gentile believers did not have to follow the culture and lifestyle of Jewish believers. Over the centuries Christianity spread throughout the Roman Empire. It interacted with and was shaped by the Greek intellectual heritage and the Roman traditions of law and organization. It also penetrated the social, family and religious traditions of the dominant Hellenistic culture, born of the fusion of Greek and Eastern influences. Christians adopted Greek intellectual categories and methods in theology, Hellenistic and Roman structures in their church organization.

The Christian impact was earliest and deepest in the eastern part of the Empire–Syria, Egypt, Asia Minor. In North Africa, Christianity seems to have been rooted more strongly in some ethnic groups than in others. Early vernacular translations of the Bible show that Christianity reached into various sub-cultures.

"Triumph in the Roman Empire"

It was more an urban than a rural movement. Opponents sneered that it was also a lower-class movement of slaves and uneducated proletarians, but there is evidence of learned, and well-off Christians. At first locally and spasmodically, then systematically, the Roman state tried to limit and eventually to exterminate Christianity. By 313, however, a new emperor, Constantine, realized that the Empire must accommodate the church, and persecution ended. Under his successors, Christianity progressed from favor to establishment, becoming the official religion of the Empire.

Arab and African Christianity

However, the first state in which Christianity became dominant was probably Edessa on the border between Roman and Persian spheres of influence. From there, Christianity spread through the Euphrates Valley. This was Arab Christianity, using the Syriac language and maintaining some of the Semitic features of the early church that Hellenistic Christianity abandoned.

"Within the Persian Empire it was a suffering church"

When, following the great theological controversies of the 5th century, the church in the Roman Empire adopted the creed of Chalcedon as orthodox, these Eastern Christians, like most of their kinsfolk in Syria and Egypt, chose the alternative Nestorian or "Monophysite" forms of theology.

Within the Persian Empire it was a suffering church: 16,000 Christians were put to death by the Persians between 339 and 379. But it was also a missionary church. Churches were formed in South Arabia, in Malabar and other parts of India (Indian Christians claim the Apostle Thomas as their first missionary), in Sri Lanka and along the Central Asian trade routes. There were Christians among many of the peoples bordering China proper; and in 635, a Nestorian bishop reached the court of the Emperor of China. Armenia also became a Christian state, some years before Constantine's accession.

"Rude shocks from the 7th century onwards"

The faith spread beyond the Roman boundaries in Africa. Around 316 two young Syrian Christians were shipwrecked on the coast of Axum, in the horn of Africa. They began a church which, following the conversion of King Ezana, became the nucleus of Ethiopian Christianity. This developed on its own lines within an expanding Christian kingdom in the heart of Africa. Meanwhile, churches grew in Nubia (in modern Sudan) which, as archaeology makes plain, lasted for many centuries.

The Great Recession

Christianity, after apparently triumphing in the Roman Empire, suffered rude shocks from the 7th century onwards. In the West, civil society collapsed in dissension under the incursions of tribal peoples. Some Christian communities–the Latin-speaking Christians of North Africa, for instance–dwindled or faded away. In the East, the Arab armies appeared, empowered by their new found faith of Islam. The Christian populations of Egypt and Syria at first welcomed them as liberators from Roman oppression. Under Islamic rule Christianity became inconvenient and expensive to profess. In the territories with the most glorious Christian history, Christianity slowly eroded; and as Muslims occupied further territories of the Roman Empire the story was repeated.

"Asian Christianity was overwhelmed"

In China, the Mongol dynasty, which had protected the Christians, was driven out; we hear nothing of Nestorian Christianity in China after about A.D. 900. Most of the Mongol and Turkic peoples chose Islam rather than Christianity, and as their populations rolled westward, central Asian Christianity was overwhelmed. The fall of Constantinople, "the Second Rome," to the Ottoman Turks in 1453 brought about the eclipse of Hellenistic-Roman Christianity and established a Muslim presence in the Balkans.

Barbarian Christianity

While this story of erosion was in progress, a parallel Christian advance was taking place among the peoples north of the imperial frontiers whom Romans called "barbarians". The chief missionary among the Goths on the Danube, Wulfila (died around 381) and Patrick, apostle of Ireland in the following century, came from prisoner of war stock. Sometimes the pagan conquerors of Christian peoples were attracted to the faith (and culture) of their subjects. Sometimes they responded to organized missions, such as that sent by Pope Gregory in 596 to the Saxon kingdom of Kent; sometimes the missionaries came through local effort or personal vision.

"Christendom was identified with Europe"

Sometimes strong rulers insisted on the baptism of their subjects. More often the process was consensual, whole communities taking Christianity into their system of tribal or communal law and custom. Thus over several centuries, Christendom emerged, territory under the rule of Christ, all its peoples belonging to one church. The tribal peoples of the North and West took over with the Christian faith something of the culture of the Roman Empire. This included Latin, its language for worship, the Scriptures and learning. Christianity was transposed into a new key. Once the faith of an urban literary and technologically advanced civilization, it was now the religion of peasant cultivators and military adventurers.

In Eastern Europe a similar process took place, but with a difference. Wulfila had translated the Scriptures into Gothic; missionaries from the Eastern Empire followed that example and introduced worship in the vernacular. The 9th century Greek missionary brothers Cyril and Methodius laid the foundation of Christian literature in Slavonic languages. In or about 987, Vladimir, Prince of Kiev was baptized. Christianity now actively spread in Russia, though it took centuries to penetrate the countryside to any depth. The Mongol conquest of Russia in the 13th century did not destroy, but rather strengthened, the growth of the church there, so that when Constantinople fell in 1453, Moscow became the effective center of Christianity in the East— "the Third Rome."

European Christianity and the Non-Western World

The center of gravity of Christianity thus shifted from the Mediterranean northward. By 1500 Europe had become more Christian and Christianity more European than ever before. Most of the remaining pagan peoples in the North and in the Baltic accepted the faith; the power of Islam in southern Spain was broken.

"A corps of dedicated workers— the missionary movement"

The eclipse of Christianity in the East meant the remaining Christians there were all under Muslim rule, save those in South India and Ethiopia, of whom Europeans knew little or nothing. "Christendom," Christian territory, was identified with Europe, and existed in two forms: one Latin, from the Atlantic to the Carpathians, and the other Slavic, from the Balkans to the Urals. The Protestant Reformation modified the concept only by bringing about distinctive national, vernacular churches in Northern Europe.

At this point, new exploits at sea brought Western Christians into contact with new worlds in the Americas, in Africa and Asia. Portugal and Spain, Catholic powers, began with the idea of extending Christendom by conquest, the idea that had underlain the Crusades against the Muslims. The Spaniards imposed Christianity on the populations of Mexico, Peru and the Philippines, using the religious orders of Franciscans and Dominicans, and later the Jesuits, to provide Christian instruction. The Portuguese had similar ideas, but smaller resources, and met stiffer resistance from other faiths.

"Recession in the former Christendom"

Where conversion through conquest proved impossible, Western Christianity produced a new corps of dedicated workers whose function was to explain, commend, and demonstrate the Christian faith without the power of coercion—in other words, the missionary movement. The religious orders provided the workers, and took the faith into the great empires of China, Japan and the Moghuls of India. Generally results were modest or even minimal, but there were occasional encouragements, notably in Japan, until ruthless persecution drove the small remnants of the church there underground.

Protestant consciousness of the non-Western world came with English settlements in North America and Dutch acquisition of an empire in Southeast Asia. Serious, organized, Protestant missionary activity however began only in the early 18th century. The Moravian and Pietist movements in Germany and Central Europe first provided a supply of dedicated people, as the religious orders had done for

Catholic Christianity, and found structures to deploy them. In the late 18th century British, and in the early 19th American, Protestants became involved, both empowered by the Evangelical Revival and equipped, through the new device of the voluntary society, with a flexible structure for recruiting, maintaining and supervising missionaries. By this time, Catholic missionary effort had faded, to revive by the middle of the 19th century.

"Christian profession has expanded rapidly"

While the missionary movement reached its peak in the period of Western imperial expansion, 1880-1914, the relationship between the two is very complex: missions sometimes preceded, sometimes followed colonial expansion. Some of the most dramatic Christian expansion was in the United States. Not a vigorously Christian community at the time of independence, it was swept by new modes of evangelism among the vast increasing populations of its westward moving frontier, and its new cities. Meanwhile Eastern Christianity steadily spread among many of the Asian peoples of the Russian Empire, and over into Alaska.

The Twentieth Century: Recession and Advance

The 20th century has seen both a substantial recession from Christianity and a great Christian advance. The recession has centered in the former Christendom. Even in the 19th century, the industrial cities of Europe were never evangelized. In the 20th, explicit anti-Christian (or anti-church) activity was often associated with Communist regimes; but abandonment of Christian allegiance by intellectuals and the general erosion of Christian practice has been a feature of the open, liberal regimes of Western Europe. Immigration from Asia has also produced there a substantial minority with active allegiance to other faiths. North America has felt the same influences to a lesser degree.

"The center of gravity moving southward"

Meanwhile, Christian profession has expanded rapidly in sub-Saharan Africa, throughout a period of major political and social change. While missions from the West were vital in initiating this process, Africans have throughout been the main agents of the propagation of the faith in Africa.

Nineteenth century missions saw entire populations turn to Christianity only in some Pacific islands. The process has continued in Oceania with the continuing Christian penetration of Melanesia.

In Asia, the response to the Christian message has been on a smaller scale, but still statistically important. There are significant numbers of Indian Christians; few indeed, in parts of north India, but in some northeastern provinces forming a majority of the population. Both in India and Southeast Asia "tribal" communities have responded more than those more deeply influenced by Hindu or Buddhist culture. Korea, however, despite the influence of historic East Asian religions has seen dramatic church growth during the century and is now a major source of missionaries. Nepal, until recently closed to Christianity, has a significant church. Despite periods of severe religious repression, China clearly has a much larger Christian community than before Western missionaries were excluded. There are also active overseas Chinese Christian communities in Singapore and elsewhere in Asia; and substantial Christian communities in parts of Indonesia.

The third Christian millennium dawns with the center of gravity of Christianity moving strongly southward, towards Africa, Latin America, and parts of Asia. We may expect to see new expressions of Christianity characteristic of these areas as well as a long process of Christian interaction with the ancient cultures of Africa and Asia, parallel to that which earlier centuries saw with those of Greece and Rome and tribal Europe.

Andrew Walls OBE is an historian and missiologist who has worked in different parts of Africa and has written widely on his subjects. He was Professor of Religious Studies at the University of Aberdeen before becoming the founder Director of the Centre for the Study of Christianity in the Non-Western World at the University of Edinburgh. He has been Visiting Professor of World Christianity at Yale University and has taught at universities on three continents.

Denominations across the World

Dr Peter Brierley

Many of the maps in this volume were created from data in the *World Churches Handbook*. The *Handbook* contains thousands of Tables covering all the major denominations in every country in the world. So that this vast amount of information may be handled more easily it is totalled in the *Handbook* in two ways.

Firstly, by using six continental groups — Africa, North America, South America, Asia, Europe and Oceania. Secondly, by using ten broad denominational groupings: Anglican, Baptist, Catholic, Indigenous, Lutheran, Methodist, Orthodox, Pentecostal, Presbyterian and Other Churches. Non-Trinitarian churches like the Jehovah's Witnesses are listed in the Handbook but are excluded from the main totals. This section of the book draws on the data from the Handbook and concentrates on its two major axes of six continents and ten denominations.

The Handbook gives information on the size of the church community, the number of church members and the number of congregations from 1960 through to 2010. Most of the data from 1995 onwards is forecast. The primary date used in this volume is 1990, so the comments below use that date and focus especially on the church community, or adherents.

Continental Comparison

The number of Christian people by continent in 1990 was as follows:

Continent	Community	% of population	% of total
Africa	220,900,000	34%	15%
North America	323,700,000	76%	21%
South America	282,900,000	97%	19%
Asia	207,100,000	7%	14%
Europe	459,500,000	58%	30%
Oceania	17,900,000	67%	1%
Total	1,512,000,000	*29%	100%

This Table shows us that just under a third of Christendom (30%) are in Europe, followed by a fifth in each of North and South America, with about a seventh in each of Africa and Asia. The Table also shows that the proportion of a continent's population which are Christian varies very greatly. Virtually everyone in South America would say they are Christian, and over three-quarters of those in North America, followed by two-thirds in Oceania. Europe comes next with almost three in five, followed by a third of the African peoples. It is in Asia, where 59% of the world's population live, that the Christian percentage is lowest, and therefore where the priority of missions could be expected.

The proportion of Christendom in the different continents is changing. In 1960 and 2010 the respective percentages are: Africa 7% and 17%, North America 23% and 22%, South America 16% and 20%, Asia 7% and 18%, Europe 46% and 22%, Oceania 1% and 1%. (1% of the Asian increase and European decrease in 2010 is due to the change of definition in putting the ex-USSR countries in Asia.) These figures reveal the plummeting drop of Christianity in Europe and its very rapid advance in both Africa and Asia, due in part to their rapidly increasing population. * This figure is lower than that of DR. David Barrett. The churches in these continents are sending increasing numbers of missionaries to Europe!

Denominational Comparison

The number of Christian people by denomination in 1990 was as follows:

Denomination	Community	% of population	% of total
Anglican	51,600,000	1%	3%
Baptist	62,800,000	1%	4%
Catholic	865,500,000	17%	57%
Indigenous	30,900,000	0%	2%
Lutheran	84,900,000	2%	6%
Methodist	25,000,000	0%	2%
Orthodox	131,900,000	2%	9%
Pentecostal	88,600,000	2%	6%
Presbyterian	46,900,000	1%	3%
Other Churches	123,900,000	2%	8%
Total	1,512,000,000	29%	100%

This Table shows that four in every seven Christian people are Catholics, mostly Roman Catholics. The Orthodox groups account for a further 9% or 1 person in every 11, followed by 6%, or 1 person in 16, of both Lutheran and Pentecostal. The Catholic proportion amounts to well over half the Christian total (57%) and to 17% of the world's population, or 1 person in every 6.

Just as the proportions in each continent are changing, so are the proportions of each denomination. For 1960 and 2010 respectively the percentages were: Anglican 4% and 3%, Baptist 4% and 4%, Catholic 61% and 56%, Indigenous 1% and 3%, Lutheran 9% and 4%, Methodist 3% and 2%, Orthodox 10% and 7%, Pentecostal 1% and 8%, Presbyterian 3% and 3%, and Other Churches 4% and 10%. The denomination which is growing fastest is the Pentecostal which has increased dramatically in the 50 years 1960 to 2010, from 12 million in 1960 to an estimated 154 million by 2010. Indigenous churches are also increasing, as are the Other Churches, largely due to the emergence of many new denominations in this category. The Lutherans and Orthodox have declined most proportionately, though the Catholics have also lost out. The Baptists and Presbyterians have held their own, the first by their growth in the United States, the second by their growth in South Korea.

For a population comparison see page 15.

The Christian presence in the world is slowly declining, although it is still approximately twice the proportion of the next largest religion, Islam. Nevertheless, it is changing within itself and may yet prove that the elements of growth will outweigh those of decline.

Peter Brierley is a statistician who has been researching the church in Britain and around the world for the past 30 years. He founded and directed MARC Europe and is now Executive Director of Christian Research. He helps churches and Christian organizations to gather and interpret data in order to develop vision and plan for the future.

Christian Community by Population
Strengths, 1960, 2000; Changes 1960-1980, 1980-2000

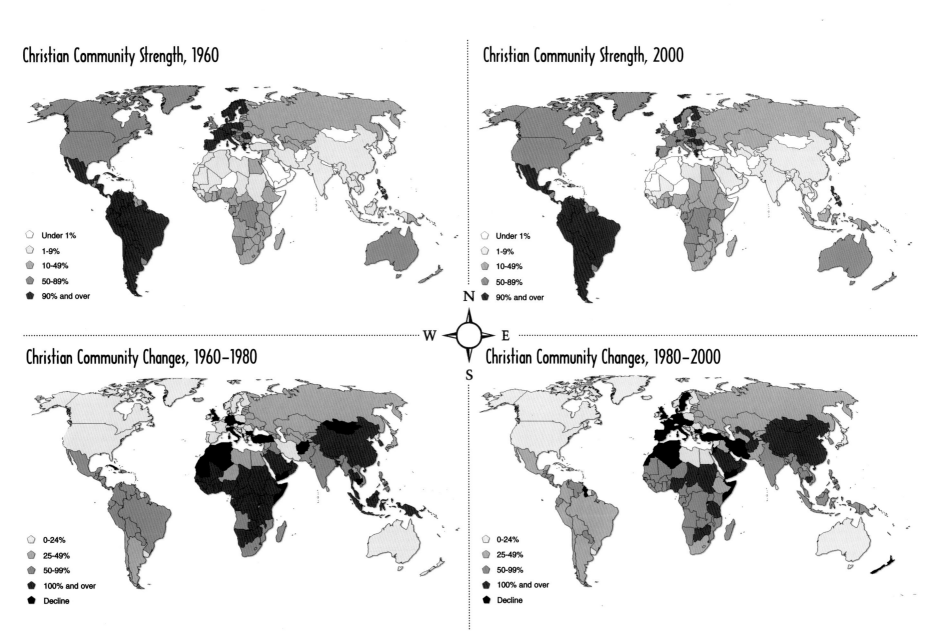

Christian Community Strength, 1960

- Under 1%
- 1-9%
- 10-49%
- 50-89%
- 90% and over

Christian Community Strength, 2000

- Under 1%
- 1-9%
- 10-49%
- 50-89%
- 90% and over

Christian Community Changes, 1960–1980

- 0-24%
- 25-49%
- 50-99%
- 100% and over
- Decline

Christian Community Changes, 1980–2000

- 0-24%
- 25-49%
- 50-99%
- 100% and over
- Decline

N
W E
S

Source: World Churches Handbook

Christian Community

Total Christian Community Compared with World Population, 1960–2010

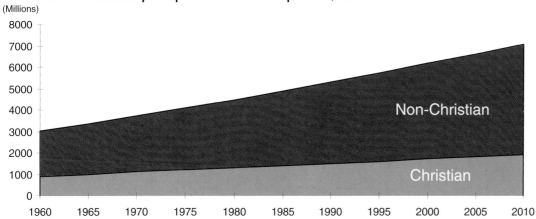

(Millions)

Non-Christian

Christian

Net Average Number of People Joining the Church Every Day, 1960–2010

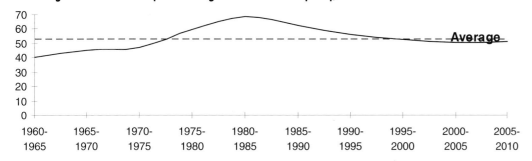

Average

Total Christian Community as a Percentage of Population, 1900–2010

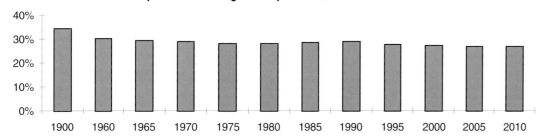

Source : World Churches Handbook

Population Comparison

In 1990, the world's population stood at 5.3 billion people. The total Christian community then was 1.5 billion, or 29% of the population. This means that two people in every seven would in some sense have called themselves Christian in 1990. In 1960 the proportion was 30% so the growth of the church has not matched the growth in the general population. It is forecast to fall even further behind by the year 2010, when it will be just 27%, or slightly more than one person in four. The top graph shows this comparison: although the number of Christians is growing, the number of non-Christians is growing more quickly.

These figures are lower than those given in the table published annually in the International Bulletin of Missionary Research. The Christian proportion did however increase between 1980 and 1985: virtually every country worldwide saw the size of its Christian community grow in that period.

The second graph here shows the net average number of people joining the church every day in each five-year period. It shows very clearly the dramatic increase from 1975 to 1985. A glance at the individual country bar charts from page 90 onwards shows this sudden upward leap, above the expected trend in many countries. If revival is an unexpected increase in the number of Christian people, then the world had a revival then!

Anglican Community by Population
Strengths, 1960, 2000; Changes 1960–1980, 1980–2000

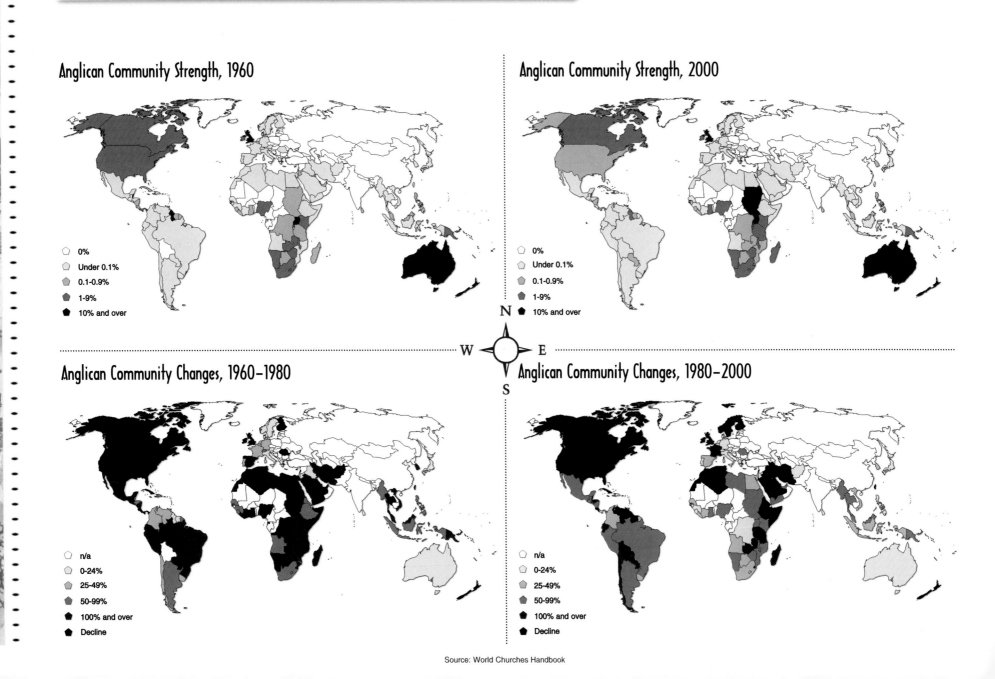

Anglican Community Strength, 1960

- ⬠ 0%
- ⬠ Under 0.1%
- ⬠ 0.1-0.9%
- ⬠ 1-9%
- ⬠ 10% and over

Anglican Community Strength, 2000

- ⬠ 0%
- ⬠ Under 0.1%
- ⬠ 0.1-0.9%
- ⬠ 1-9%
- ⬠ 10% and over

Anglican Community Changes, 1960–1980

- ⬠ n/a
- ⬠ 0-24%
- ⬠ 25-49%
- ⬠ 50-99%
- ⬠ 100% and over
- ⬠ Decline

Anglican Community Changes, 1980–2000

- ⬠ n/a
- ⬠ 0-24%
- ⬠ 25-49%
- ⬠ 50-99%
- ⬠ 100% and over
- ⬠ Decline

Source: World Churches Handbook

Baptist Community by Population
Strengths, 1960, 2000; Changes 1960–1980, 1980–2000

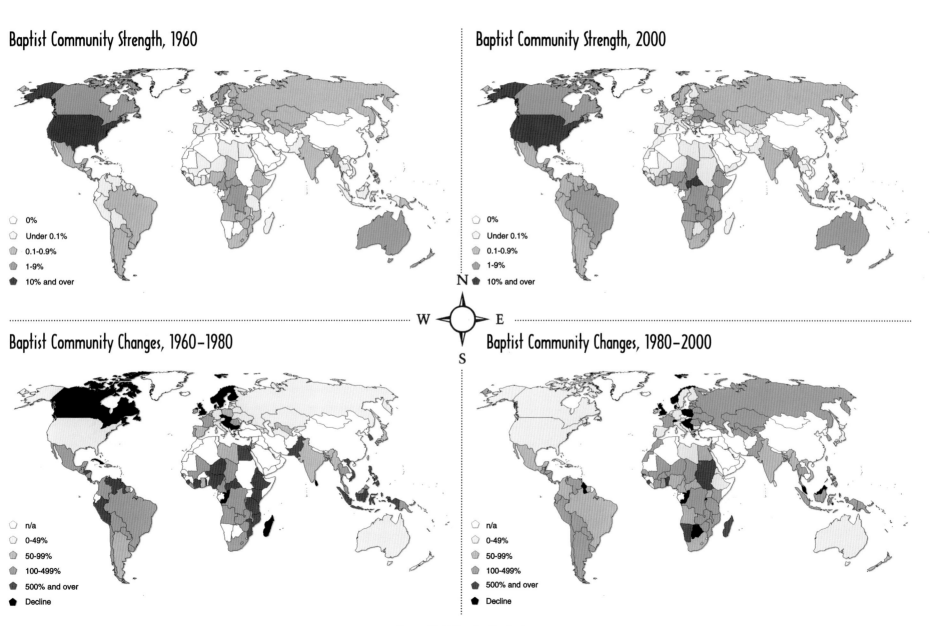

Baptist Community Strength, 1960

- 0%
- Under 0.1%
- 0.1-0.9%
- 1-9%
- 10% and over

Baptist Community Strength, 2000

- 0%
- Under 0.1%
- 0.1-0.9%
- 1-9%
- 10% and over

Baptist Community Changes, 1960–1980

- n/a
- 0-49%
- 50-99%
- 100-499%
- 500% and over
- Decline

Baptist Community Changes, 1980–2000

- n/a
- 0-49%
- 50-99%
- 100-499%
- 500% and over
- Decline

W · N · E · S

Source: World Churches Handbook

Catholic Community by Population
Strengths, 1960, 2000; Changes 1960–1980, 1980–2000

Catholic is mostly, but not exclusively, Roman Catholic

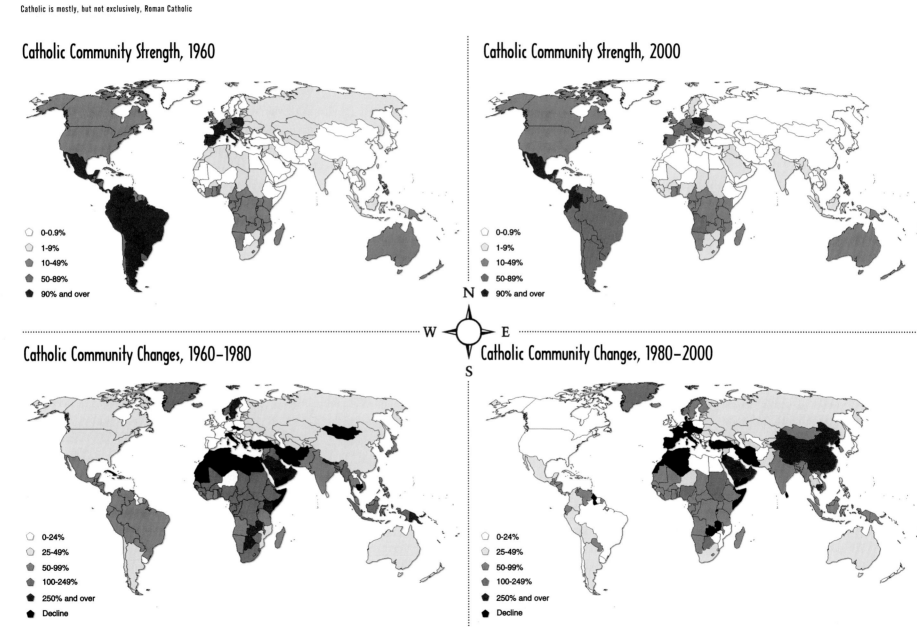

Catholic Community Strength, 1960

- 0-0.9%
- 1-9%
- 10-49%
- 50-89%
- 90% and over

Catholic Community Strength, 2000

- 0-0.9%
- 1-9%
- 10-49%
- 50-89%
- 90% and over

N
W E
S

Catholic Community Changes, 1960–1980

- 0-24%
- 25-49%
- 50-99%
- 100-249%
- 250% and over
- Decline

Catholic Community Changes, 1980–2000

- 0-24%
- 25-49%
- 50-99%
- 100-249%
- 250% and over
- Decline

Source: World Churches Handbook

Indigenous Churches Community by Population
Strengths, 1960, 2000; Changes 1960–1980, 1980–2000

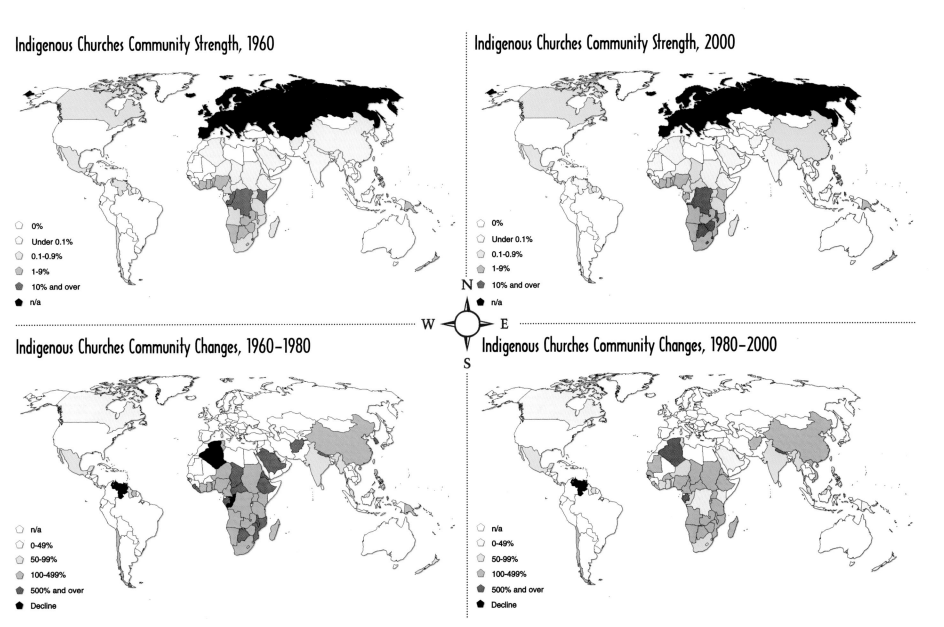

Indigenous Churches Community Strength, 1960

- 0%
- Under 0.1%
- 0.1-0.9%
- 1-9%
- 10% and over
- n/a

Indigenous Churches Community Strength, 2000

- 0%
- Under 0.1%
- 0.1-0.9%
- 1-9%
- 10% and over
- n/a

Indigenous Churches Community Changes, 1960–1980

- n/a
- 0-49%
- 50-99%
- 100-499%
- 500% and over
- Decline

Indigenous Churches Community Changes, 1980–2000

- n/a
- 0-49%
- 50-99%
- 100-499%
- 500% and over
- Decline

N
W E
S

Source: World Churches Handbook

Lutheran Community by Population
Strengths, 1960, 2000; Changes 1960–1980, 1980–2000

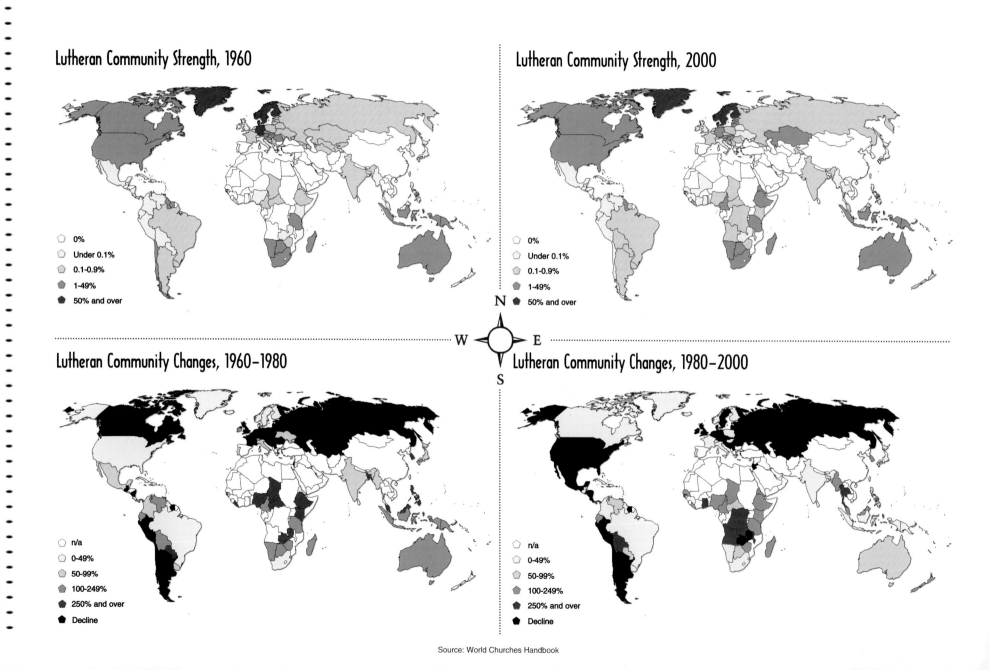

Lutheran Community Strength, 1960

- 0%
- Under 0.1%
- 0.1-0.9%
- 1-49%
- 50% and over

Lutheran Community Strength, 2000

- 0%
- Under 0.1%
- 0.1-0.9%
- 1-49%
- 50% and over

Lutheran Community Changes, 1960–1980

- n/a
- 0-49%
- 50-99%
- 100-249%
- 250% and over
- Decline

Lutheran Community Changes, 1980–2000

- n/a
- 0-49%
- 50-99%
- 100-249%
- 250% and over
- Decline

N
W E
S

Source: World Churches Handbook

Methodist Community by Population
Strengths, 1960, 2000; Changes 1960–1980, 1980–2000

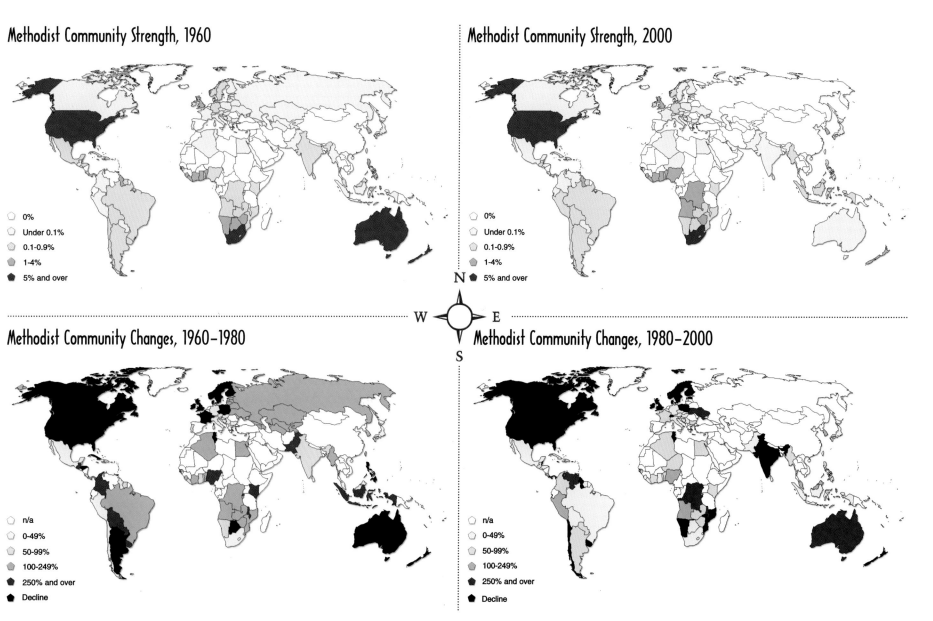

Methodist Community Strength, 1960

- 0%
- Under 0.1%
- 0.1-0.9%
- 1-4%
- 5% and over

Methodist Community Strength, 2000

- 0%
- Under 0.1%
- 0.1-0.9%
- 1-4%
- 5% and over

Methodist Community Changes, 1960–1980

- n/a
- 0-49%
- 50-99%
- 100-249%
- 250% and over
- Decline

Methodist Community Changes, 1980–2000

- n/a
- 0-49%
- 50-99%
- 100-249%
- 250% and over
- Decline

N
W E
S

Source: World Churches Handbook

Orthodox Community by Population
Strengths, 1960, 2000; Changes 1960–1980, 1980–2000

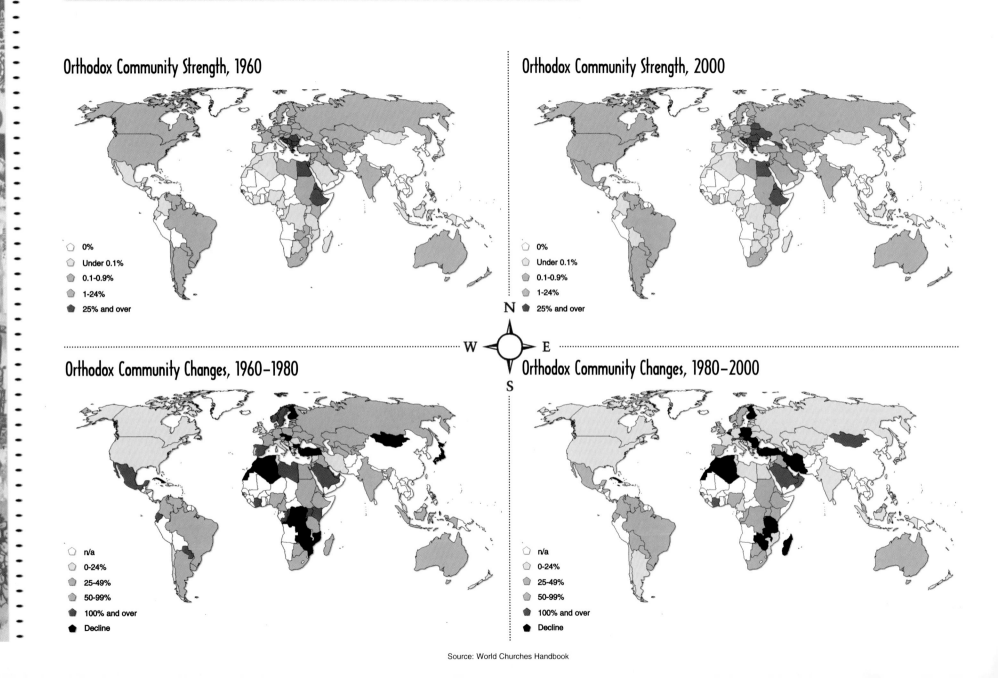

Orthodox Community Strength, 1960

- 0%
- Under 0.1%
- 0.1-0.9%
- 1-24%
- 25% and over

Orthodox Community Strength, 2000

- 0%
- Under 0.1%
- 0.1-0.9%
- 1-24%
- 25% and over

Orthodox Community Changes, 1960–1980

- n/a
- 0-24%
- 25-49%
- 50-99%
- 100% and over
- Decline

Orthodox Community Changes, 1980–2000

- n/a
- 0-24%
- 25-49%
- 50-99%
- 100% and over
- Decline

Source: World Churches Handbook

Pentecostal Community by Population
Strengths, 1960, 2000; Changes 1960–1980, 1980–2000

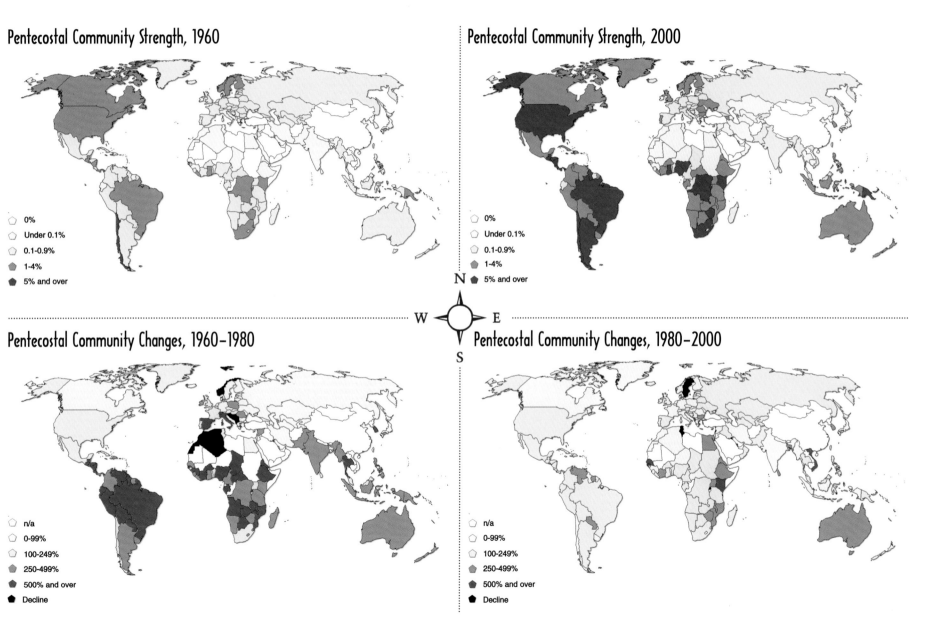

Pentecostal Community Strength, 1960

- 0%
- Under 0.1%
- 0.1-0.9%
- 1-4%
- 5% and over

Pentecostal Community Strength, 2000

- 0%
- Under 0.1%
- 0.1-0.9%
- 1-4%
- 5% and over

Pentecostal Community Changes, 1960–1980

- n/a
- 0-99%
- 100-249%
- 250-499%
- 500% and over
- Decline

Pentecostal Community Changes, 1980–2000

- n/a
- 0-99%
- 100-249%
- 250-499%
- 500% and over
- Decline

N
W E
S

Source: World Churches Handbook

Presbyterian Community by Population
Strengths, 1960, 2000; Changes 1960–1980, 1980–2000

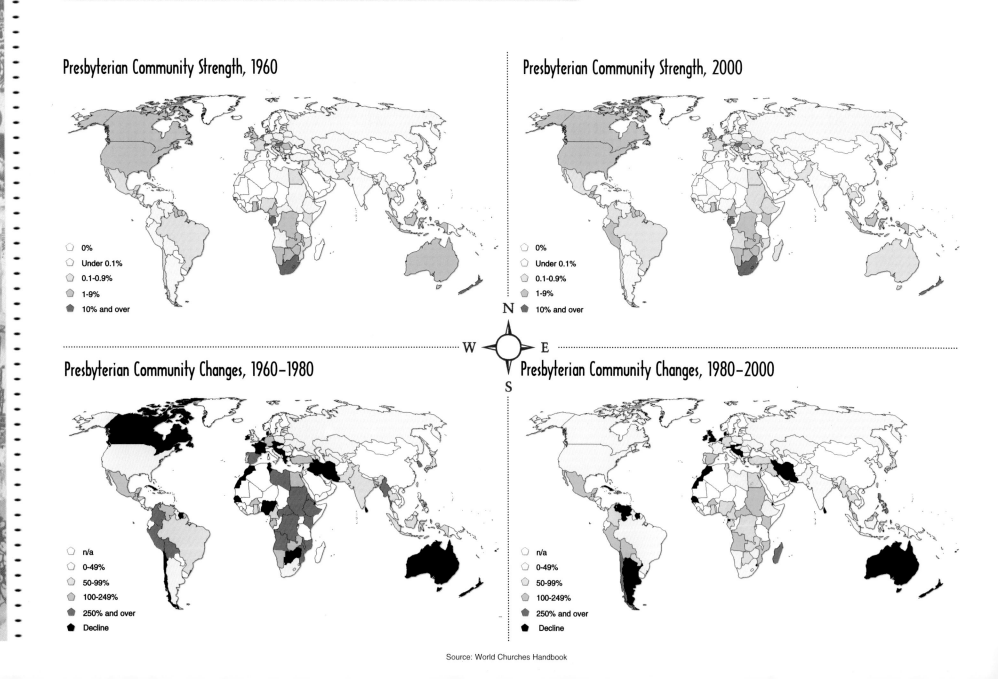

Presbyterian Community Strength, 1960

- 0%
- Under 0.1%
- 0.1-0.9%
- 1-9%
- 10% and over

Presbyterian Community Strength, 2000

- 0%
- Under 0.1%
- 0.1-0.9%
- 1-9%
- 10% and over

Presbyterian Community Changes, 1960–1980

- n/a
- 0-49%
- 50-99%
- 100-249%
- 250% and over
- Decline

Presbyterian Community Changes, 1980–2000

- n/a
- 0-49%
- 50-99%
- 100-249%
- 250% and over
- Decline

N W E S

Source: World Churches Handbook

Other Churches Community by Population

Strengths, 1960, 2000; Changes 1960–1980, 1980–2000

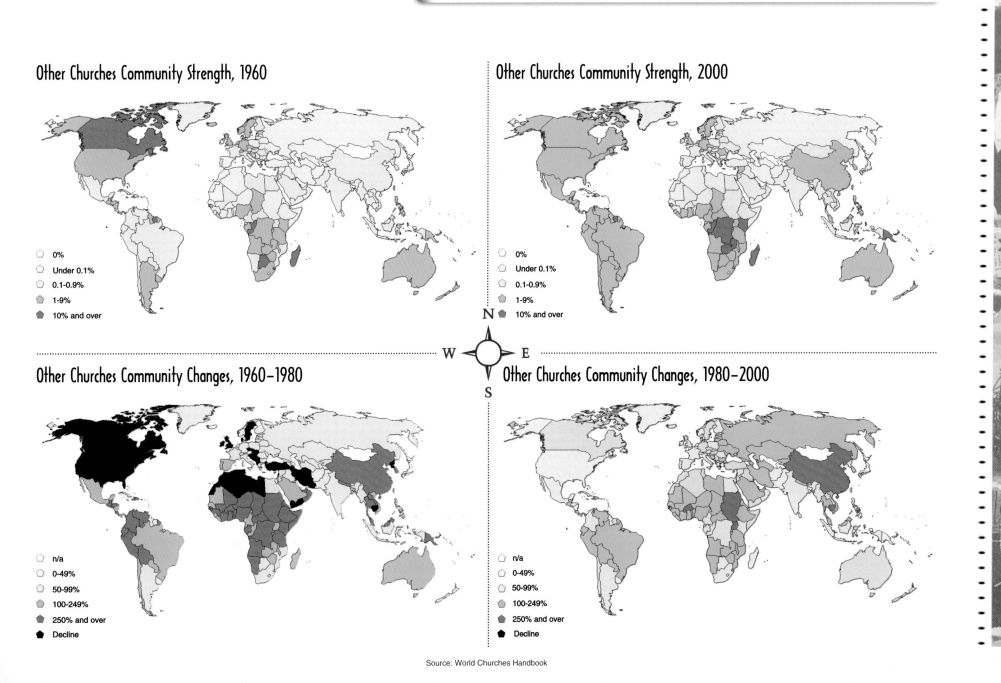

Other Churches Community Strength, 1960

- 0%
- Under 0.1%
- 0.1-0.9%
- 1-9%
- 10% and over

Other Churches Community Strength, 2000

- 0%
- Under 0.1%
- 0.1-0.9%
- 1-9%
- 10% and over

Other Churches Community Changes, 1960–1980

- n/a
- 0-49%
- 50-99%
- 100-249%
- 250% and over
- Decline

Other Churches Community Changes, 1980–2000

- n/a
- 0-49%
- 50-99%
- 100-249%
- 250% and over
- Decline

N
W — E
S

Source: World Churches Handbook

Non–Trinitarian Churches Community by Population
Strengths, 1960, 2000; Changes 1960–1980, 1980–2000

Non-Trinitarian churches include Jehovah's Witnesses, Mormons and others which do not accept the historic formulary of the Godhead as the three eternal persons, God the Father, God the Son and God the Holy Spirit, in one unchanging Essence. These churches are not included in the Christian totals used elsewhere in this volume.

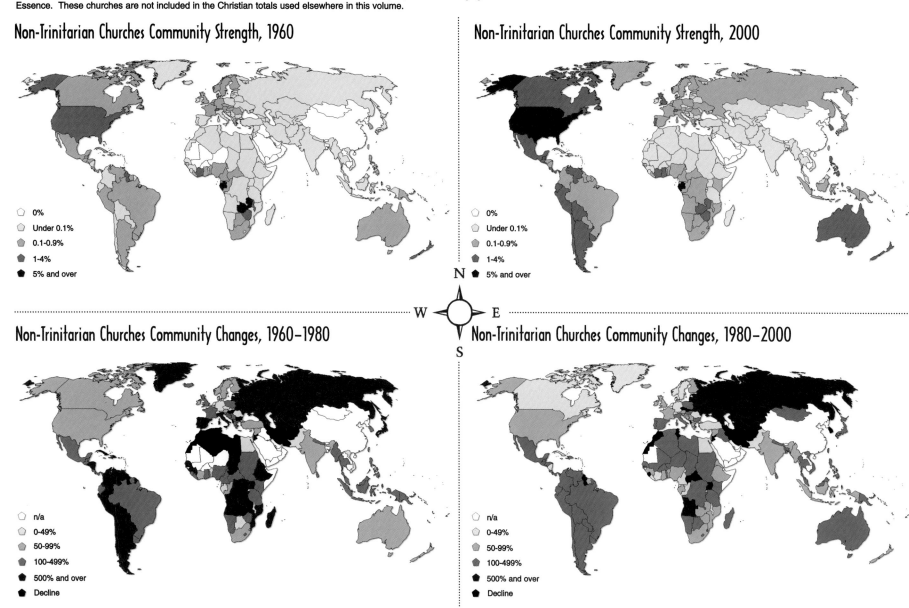

Non-Trinitarian Churches Community Strength, 1960

- 0%
- Under 0.1%
- 0.1-0.9%
- 1-4%
- 5% and over

Non-Trinitarian Churches Community Strength, 2000

- 0%
- Under 0.1%
- 0.1-0.9%
- 1-4%
- 5% and over

Non-Trinitarian Churches Community Changes, 1960–1980

- n/a
- 0-49%
- 50-99%
- 100-499%
- 500% and over
- Decline

Non-Trinitarian Churches Community Changes, 1980–2000

- n/a
- 0-49%
- 50-99%
- 100-499%
- 500% and over
- Decline

N
W E
S

Source: World Churches Handbook

Church Growth

Political Change and Christianity

Rev Canon Dr Michael Bourdeaux

In the last decade or so, many parts of the world have experienced political cataclysms, while the democracies of the Western world have been peaceful and relatively passive bystanders.

Political "Certainties"

People in their sixties or younger grew up in the knowledge of two political certainties in the world: communism and racism. The world was divided between the communist and non-communist blocs, "east and west." South Africa was perceived as the greatest stain on the human rights record of the world while communist atrocities received much less attention.

"Political certainties vanish"

Since the late 1980s both these certainties have vanished, without the massive bloodshed which might have been predicted. Yet the world does not seem to be a happier place. The murderous aftermath of communism in Chechenya and Bosnia has been far worse than the former straitjacket, and similar evil could befall other places. Terrorism or guerilla wars continue to take their toll in societies where democracy or good government should be making progress, such as Colombia, Northern Ireland, Israel, Peru, Spain, Sri Lanka, East Timor and even the USA. The rise of Islamic fundamentalism has hindered the evolution of the "new world order" which some commentators predicted when most of communism suddenly ceased to be.

The Role of the Church

Where totalitarian rule has collapsed over the last ten years, it is astonishing how significant and active a role Christianity has played. This fact has been missed, even by many political commentators. Ask a politically literate person about this, and most would instantly reply, "Oh yes, of course, Archbishop Desmond Tutu in South Africa," but then fall silent, unable to remember another name.

"The murderous aftermath of communism"

The brave or dangerous role played by others is less well known. The late Archbishop Julijonas Steponavičious in Lithuania or Patriarch Volodymyr Romanyuk in Ukraine both served a major portion of their Christian ministry as political prisoners, but ended it as church leaders in a free society. A controversial area is the way that humanitarian agencies and international Christian organizations have often been a focus for the activities of those who wished to see political change in societies other than their own. Has there ever been a time in history since the deeds of "These who have turned the world upside down" (Acts 17:6), when Christians have been more at the forefront of political change?

East and West

1989 was a watershed year, for it was then that the European order was utterly transformed after hardly changing for over forty years. Two years later the disintegration of the Soviet Union followed as the very pillars of Marxist society were renounced, and it temporarily seemed as if the communist regime in China would go the same way.

Political commentators analyzed every conceivable reason for this cataclysm: political, economic, historical, ethnic and demographic. Most totally ignored the religious factor. Yet it really does not take very subtle analysis to see the election of Pope John Paul II in 1978 as the most significant single event in uniting Poland in opposition to communism. It was that opposition which eventually destabilized Eastern Europe.

"The rise of Islamic fundamentalism"

In the Soviet Union itself tiny Lithuania, just as dedicated to Catholicism as its Polish neighbor, played a role out of all proportion to its size, in demanding secession from the Soviet Union. In the Ukraine the rise of nationalism was largely motivated by Christian activists in the west of the country, who instigated demands which were originally alien to the more russianized people of the east.

"The active role of Christianity"

North and South

The North-South divide (prosperity versus deprivation) is less susceptible to dramatic change than that between East and West, but even there the church has been involved. In the 1970s Salvador Allende moved Chile fast towards Marxism before being toppled with American involvement and a shower of world criticism. He was replaced by the right-wing dictator General Pinochet, who fell in 1989 and was succeeded by a democratic regime. The Roman Catholic Church was heavily and positively involved in this process.

It is almost inconceivable that the white regime in South Africa should have relinquished its hold on power without major bloodshed. Such a calamity would have befallen the country without the ceaseless calls for peaceful change from Archbishop Tutu, joined later by Nelson Mandela, and

eventually by many whites too, both Christians and others.

The Future

Conflicts between atheist totalitarianism and Christian democracy may be almost a thing of the past. Nevertheless there are still religious tensions, mainly between Islamic nations and the rest of the world. We also see increasing ethnic and tribal strife. In this world of turmoil, there should be no conflict which is impervious to the reasoned intervention of religious leaders.

Michael Bourdeaux is the founder and director of the Keston Institute in England, which specializes in research and information on religion in the previously communist countries, mainly in Eastern Europe and the former USSR.

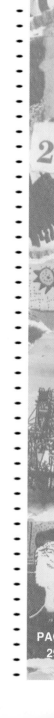

Denominations per Country

Denominations per Country, 1975

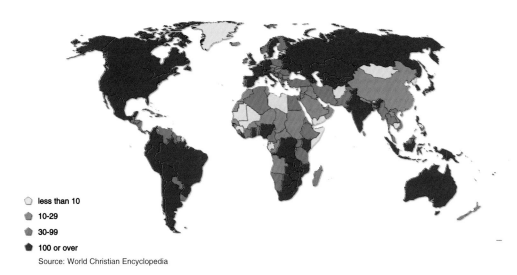

○ less than 10
● 10-29
● 30-99
● 100 or over

Source: World Christian Encyclopedia

Denominations per Country, 2000

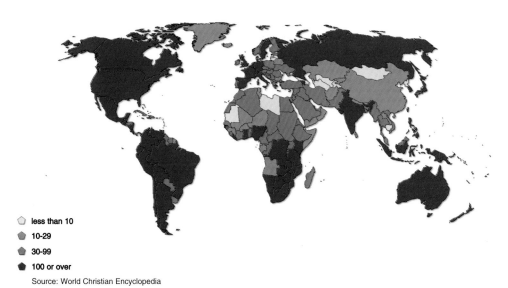

○ less than 10
● 10-29
● 30-99
● 100 or over

Source: World Christian Encyclopedia

Members per Church, 1995 (Average Worldwide)

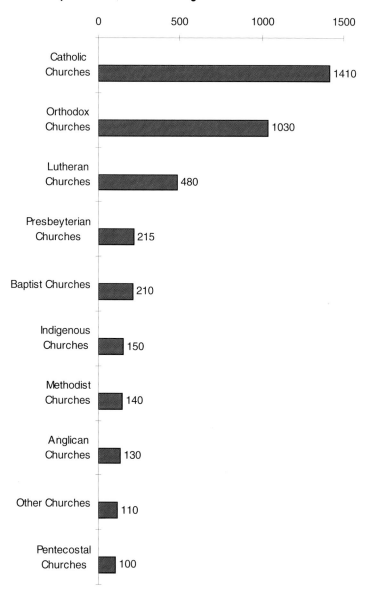

Church	Members
Catholic Churches	1410
Orthodox Churches	1030
Lutheran Churches	480
Presbeyterian Churches	215
Baptist Churches	210
Indigenous Churches	150
Methodist Churches	140
Anglican Churches	130
Other Churches	110
Pentecostal Churches	100

Source: World Churches Handbook

Number of Churches by Continent, 1960–2010

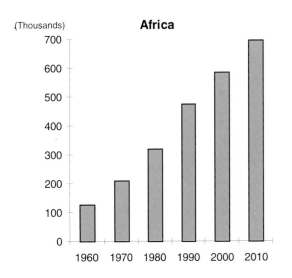

Africa (Thousands)

Year	Value
1960	125
1970	210
1980	320
1990	475
2000	585
2010	700

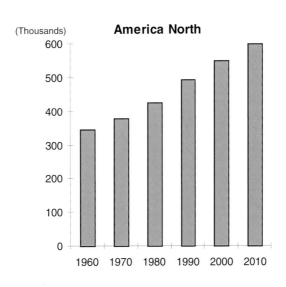

America North (Thousands)

Year	Value
1960	345
1970	380
1980	425
1990	495
2000	550
2010	600

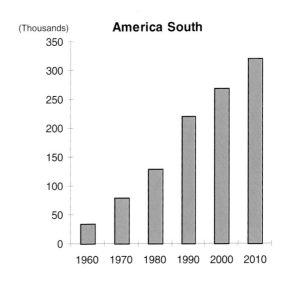

America South (Thousands)

Year	Value
1960	35
1970	80
1980	130
1990	220
2000	270
2010	320

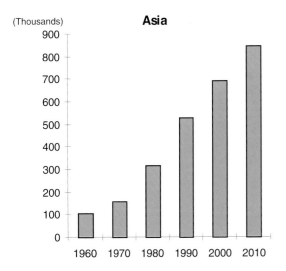

Asia (Thousands)

Year	Value
1960	105
1970	160
1980	315
1990	530
2000	690
2010	850

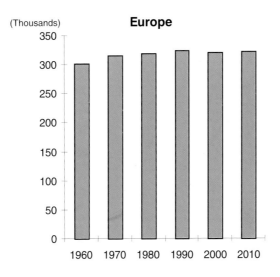

Europe (Thousands)

Year	Value
1960	300
1970	315
1980	320
1990	325
2000	320
2010	322

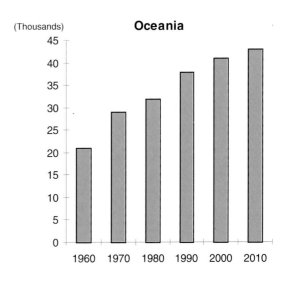

Oceania (Thousands)

Year	Value
1960	21
1970	29
1980	32
1990	38
2000	41
2010	43

Source: World Churches Handbook

Restrictions to Church Growth, 1970, 1995

1970

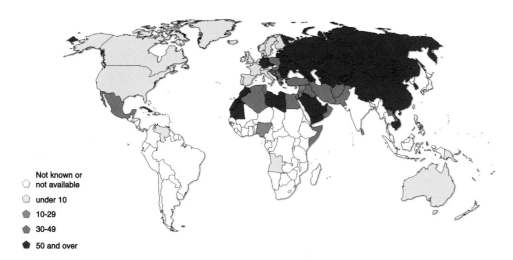

Not known or not available

under 10

10-29

30-49

50 and over

1995

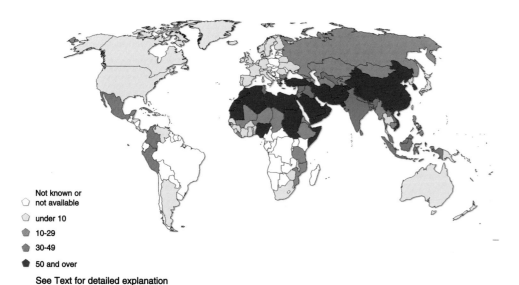

Not known or not available

under 10

10-29

30-49

50 and over

See Text for detailed explanation

Freedom of Religion for Christians

The freedom that Christians have to practice their religion varies in a wide range of ways. Open Doors have developed a scale which tries to take account of all these variations. It includes factors such as legal restrictions on meeting for worship and on church buildings; opposition in the media; personal restrictions of movement, educational or employment opportunities, etc. On this scale, under 10 is considered to be freedom of religion for Christians, even though everything may not be as free as practicing believers would like it to be! Over 50 on the scale is very restrictive indeed.

The map for 1970 contains many gaps, mainly because of the enormous political changes taking place at the time. In Southeast Asia, Vietnam, Laos and Cambodia were entangled in Civil War, but not yet under communist control. Africa was in the process of decolonization, and although there was much Marxist activity, they had not yet taken power anywhere.

In recent years the rise of fundamentalism in non-Christian religions has often resulted in less freedom for Christians.

Another factor is that in many countries there is considerably more freedom for Christians from one tradition than from others. In the former Soviet Union the Orthodox Church is the main church in most countries, and other traditions may find themselves under pressure. In Latin America it is the Roman Catholic Church which often holds the power.

Source: Open Doors

Revivals (Protestant)

Places Where Revival has Occurred (Protestant)

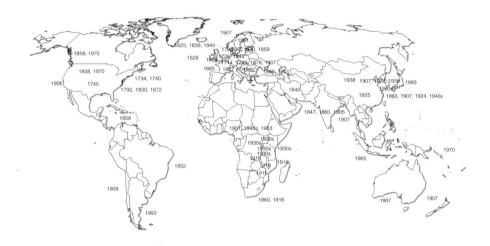

Dates in Which Revival has Occurred

1625	Scotland	1858	Canada, USA, Jamaica	1907	Korea (North & South)	1940s	China
1628	Ireland	1859	England, Scotland,		Myanmar, China	1949	Scotland, Hebrides
1685	France		Wales, Northern Ireland	1909	Chile	1952	Brazil
1714	Holland	1860	India, Lebanon, Armenia	1910	Malawi	1953	Central Africa
1722	Germany		China, South Africa	1915	Zimbabwe	1965	Indonesia
1734	USA, New England	1861	Sweden	1916	Mozambique	1970	USA, Canada
1739-90	UK (Not Ireland)	1872	Eastern USA		South Africa, Zambia	1970	Pacific Islands
1740	USA, New England	1878	Holland	1924	China	1980s	Korea, South
1745	USA, Midwest	1883	Japan	1925	South China	1990	Hungary
1749	Holland	1901	Armenia, Central Africa	1927	Korea	1993	Argentina
1792	Eastern USA	1904	Wales	1930s	Uganda, Rwanda		
1830	UK, Eastern USA	1905	India		Burundi, Kenya		
1839	Scotland	1906	USA West		Eastern Zaire		
1840	Iran	1907	England, Scandinavia	1938	Korea (North & South)		
1844	Germany		Holland, Switzerland		North China		
1847	India		Australia, New Zealand	1940s	Central Africa		

Revivals

The word "revival" with a specifically Christian meaning was first used in 1702. Historically it has been used to refer to "mass conversions to the Christian faith ...; a rapid extension of monastic orders and to a surge in crowds attending a shrine ...; a series of meetings which have an evangelistic aim..."

The "revivals" marked on these maps were an event or series of events in which a large number of people experienced an extraordinarily powerful sense of the reality and presence of God. At the same time they felt an overwhelming conviction of the need for a personal relationship between themselves and God, or for a renewal of an already existing relationship. This experience may or may not have been accompanied by dramatic physical manifestations, but always had an effect on other people in the neighborhood.

Some revivals last only a brief time, others for many months as in East Africa in the 1930s, a few continue for years as in 18th Century England during the time of John and Charles Wesley and George Whitefield. Some are very localized such as in Sunderland (England) in 1907, others are almost worldwide and are referred to as General Awakenings. The long-term effect of revival varies: the Wesley's revival is commonly agreed to have saved England from something similar to the French Revolution; the Azusa Street Revival of Los Angeles in 1906 brought to birth the Pentecostal Churches; while the long-term effect of the Welsh Revival of 1904 is seen when crowds attending a Rugby Football game in Wales sing hymns before the match!

There is some disagreement as to whether the "Toronto Blessing" of 1994, which was experienced in many parts of the world, can be called a revival in the sense used here. For that reason it has not been included.

Sources: Revival - God's Spotlight; Signs of Revival; Great Revivals; Revival Fire; Evangelical Awakenings in Southern Asia; ... in Eastern Asia; ... in Africa.

Total Christian Membership, 1960–2010

By Denominational Groupings

Catholic, 1960–2010
(Millions)

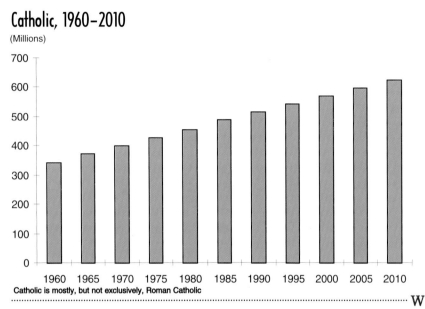

Catholic is mostly, but not exclusively, Roman Catholic

Protestant Institutional Denominations, 1960–2010
(Millions)

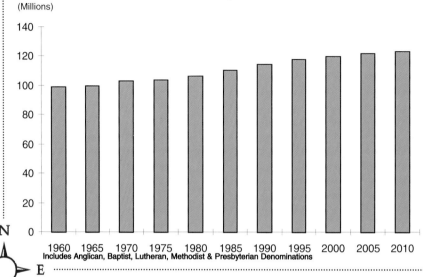

Includes Anglican, Baptist, Lutheran, Methodist & Presbyterian Denominations

Protestant Non-Institutional Denominations, 1960–2010
(Millions)

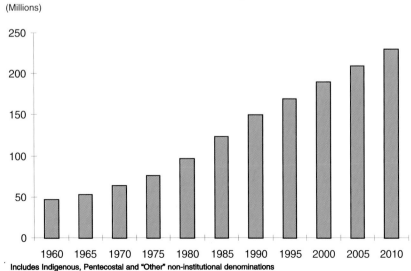

Includes Indigenous, Pentecostal and "Other" non-institutional denominations

Orthodox, 1960–2010
(Millions)

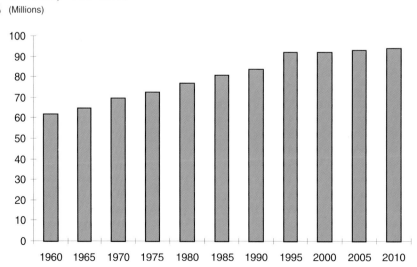

N
W — E
S

Source: World Churches Handbook

Total Christian Community, 1960–2010
By Denominational Groupings

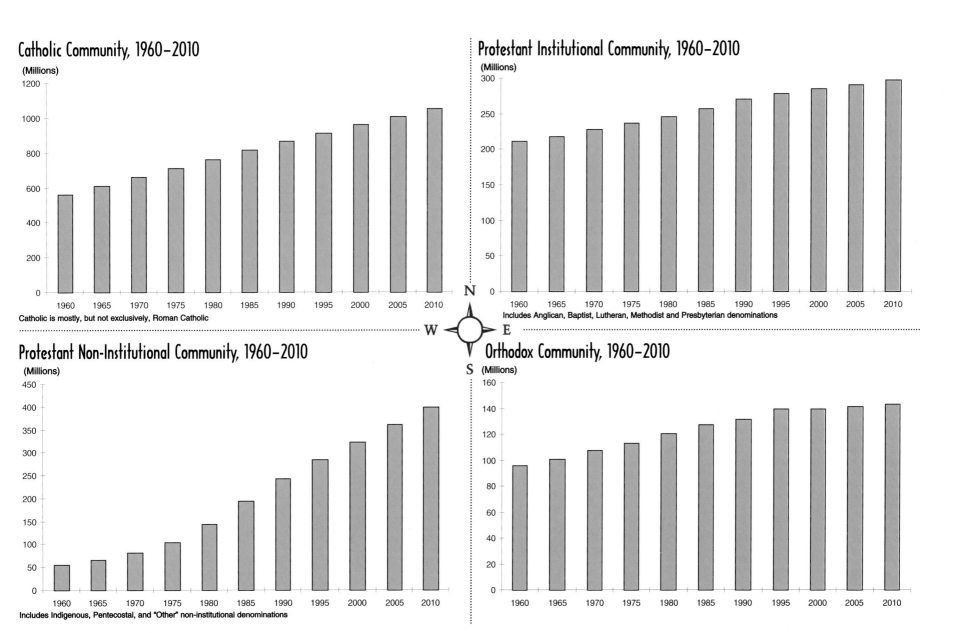

Catholic Community, 1960–2010

(Millions)

Catholic is mostly, but not exclusively, Roman Catholic

Protestant Institutional Community, 1960–2010

(Millions)

Includes Anglican, Baptist, Lutheran, Methodist and Presbyterian denominations

Protestant Non-Institutional Community, 1960–2010

(Millions)

Includes Indigenous, Pentecostal, and "Other" non-institutional denominations

Orthodox Community, 1960–2010

(Millions)

N
W   E
S

Source: World Churches Handbook

Distribution of Evangelicals, 1960–1990

As Percentage of Population

less than 1%   1-4%   5-9%   10-14%   15% and over

Distribution of Evangelicals, 1960

Distribution of Evangelicals, 1970

Distribution of Evangelicals, 1980

Distribution of Evangelicals, 1990

N
W E
S

Source: Operation World Database

Missionary Activity

Trends in Contemporary Ministry

Dr Vinay Samuel

Developing Understanding

The understanding of ministry that developed in the later New Testament period is reflected in the pastoral epistles of Timothy and Titus. Leaders were appointed and ordained to provide a service of Word and Sacrament to Christian congregations. An ordained ministry of those specially called and set apart to serve local churches became widespread.

"Priest who performed sacramental functions"

In medieval times the understanding of the ordained leader as a priest who performed sacramental functions became dominant. The Protestant Reformation of the 16th century emphasized the priesthood of all believers, that is that each Christian is called to ministry and gifted to engage in acts of service towards God and others.

The growth of missions broadened Christian service in the world to include educational, medical and social work along with preaching the gospel and teaching the Bible to converts. Christian ministry was seen as how the church served its members and Christian mission as how the church served the world. The 20th century has seen an increasing integration of the two, especially for Protestants, as the focus has shifted to God's mission in the world. All that God does in the church and the world is His mission and the church is His prime instrument of action.

"Ministry designed to meet particular needs"

Theological Developments

A variety of theological themes have strongly influenced contemporary understanding of Christian ministry. A foundational theme is the calling of every Christian to ministry and mission. The Reformation recovery that every Christian's work is a vocation from God has enabled contemporary Christians of all denominations to express their discipleship and witness through their daily work.

The experience of cross-cultural missions strengthened the idea of the universal body of Christ which includes a diversity of cultures. This has led to an increasing concern to learn from the global church, a globalization of theological training, and a recognition that cross-cultural ministry is no longer from the western churches to the rest but from everywhere to everywhere.

Holistic mission accepts that ministry is not just a "cure of souls" but includes all areas of life: public and private, individual and community, spiritual and social.

Holistic Ministry

Holistic ministry has developed in two directions. One is to address specific groups and areas with ministry designed and developed to meet those particular needs. So for example the desperate plight of poor children in industrial Britain resulted in the setting up of Sunday schools in the 19th century and children's ministry grew rapidly. Focus on university students at the beginning of the 20th century fueled the rapid growth of student and youth ministries.

"Programs to equip churches and individual Christians"

Since the Second World War, ministry to poor communities particularly in the non-western world has expanded dramatically. Such ministries address economic, social and political needs of the poor while sharing the good news of the kingdom of God. Inner-city ministries in large cities of the North and South tend to be holistic, addressing most needs of local communities.

The other direction in which holistic ministry has developed is the recognition that ministry belongs to the local congregation which gathers to worship regularly. In the past an ordained minister, priest or pastor was expected to have all the necessary skills to build up his congregation. While some churches continue to function in that mode, increasingly training programs have developed to equip churches and individual Christians in a variety of ministries: educational, media, children, literature, disabled, etc. In such areas the growth of parachurch specialist ministries provides opportunities for many more Christians to be engaged in ministry today. Also, there is growth in training programs which reflect an inclusive understanding of ministry by equipping any Christian through extension education. This inclusiveness extends to gender. The ordination of women is now a reality in historic Protestant churches, while in the Roman Catholic and Orthodox Churches which do not ordain women, there is nevertheless a recognition that women have access to many ministries.

The Context of Ministry

The increasing importance of the market as the social mechanism that shapes daily life means that people are defined as consumers of services and products, who are offered choices which they allegedly have the space freely to make. This forces ministry activities increasingly to treat church members as consumers, the gospel as a product, and ministry as a market place, which requires effective strategies and wise management.

"Transforming contexts"

The contemporary context also focuses on the individual person as self. Post-modern influences undermine the stability of the self in individuals and stress the role of experience. This has led to an exponential growth in ministries which focus on the therapy of the self. Resources are drawn from psychology, psychiatry, and counseling to address the needs of individuals struggling to reconstitute themselves.

In the context of poverty where more than half of the world's population are excluded from the possibility of economic, social and political security in this life, ministries focus on transforming contexts by bringing the hope of the gospel. While on an earth which is increasingly threatened with environmental degradation and destruction, some ministries focus primarily on the care of the earth and the environment.

Ministry is always shaped by the context, and the current context of modernity and post-modernity continue to shape the nature of contemporary ministry, just as much as previous historical and social contexts shaped earlier understandings of ministry.

Dr Vinay Samuel is a theologian who was born in India and lived and worked there until 1992, apart from five years of study at Cambridge University. He is now Executive Director of both the Oxford Centre for Mission Studies and the International Fellowship of Evangelical Mission Theologians. He is a prolific writer, and continues to be involved regularly in ministry in Asia.

The Spread of Missionaries

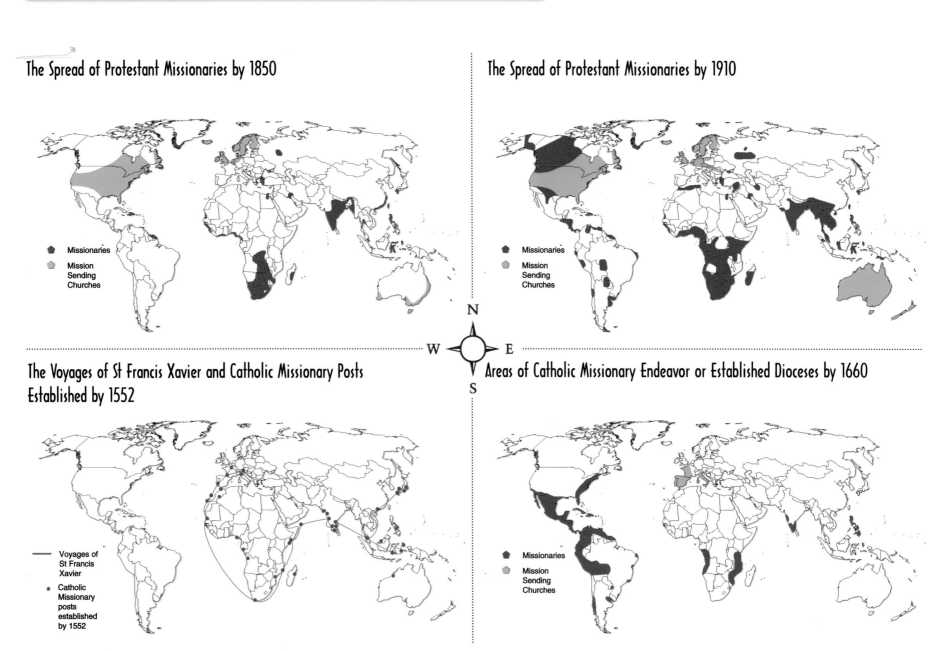

The Spread of Protestant Missionaries by 1850

Missionaries

Mission Sending Churches

The Spread of Protestant Missionaries by 1910

Missionaries

Mission Sending Churches

The Voyages of St Francis Xavier and Catholic Missionary Posts Established by 1552

— Voyages of St Francis Xavier

• Catholic Missionary posts established by 1552

Areas of Catholic Missionary Endeavor or Established Dioceses by 1660

Missionaries

Mission Sending Churches

N
W — E
S

Source: Operation World, Catholic Central Library and Information Centre, London

Current Missionary Force, 1990

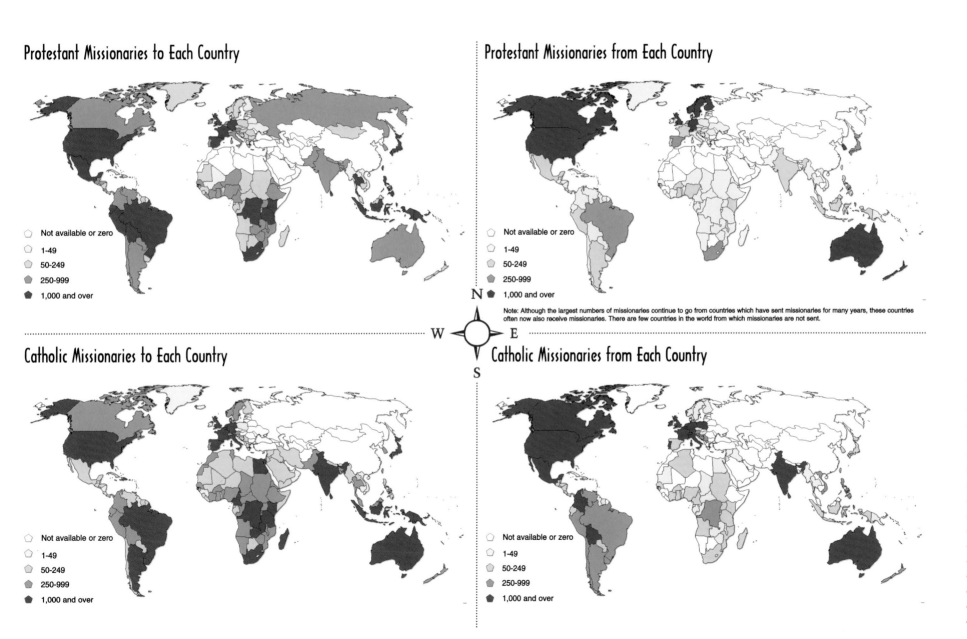

Protestant Missionaries to Each Country

- ⬠ Not available or zero
- ⬠ 1-49
- ⬠ 50-249
- ⬠ 250-999
- ⬟ 1,000 and over

Protestant Missionaries from Each Country

- ⬠ Not available or zero
- ⬠ 1-49
- ⬠ 50-249
- ⬠ 250-999
- ⬟ 1,000 and over

Note: Although the largest numbers of missionaries continue to go from countries which have sent missionaries for many years, these countries often now also receive missionaries. There are few countries in the world from which missionaries are not sent.

Catholic Missionaries to Each Country

- ⬠ Not available or zero
- ⬠ 1-49
- ⬠ 50-249
- ⬠ 250-999
- ⬟ 1,000 and over

Catholic Missionaries from Each Country

- ⬠ Not available or zero
- ⬠ 1-49
- ⬠ 50-249
- ⬠ 250-999
- ⬟ 1,000 and over

N / W / E / S

Source: Operation World Database

Parachurch Agencies and World Wealth
Percentages, per Continent

1995 Figures

1975 Figures

Number of Parachurch agencies per continent

Total: 14,100 23,200

Percentage of world wealth by continent 1995

Bar charts on each continent show its percentage of parachurch agencies

Sources: World Population Data Sheet, World Christian Encyclopedia

Least Evangelized People, 1995
As Percentage of Population

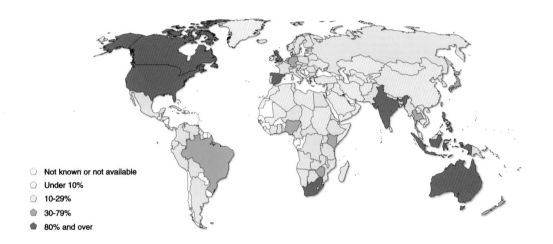

- ○ Not known or not available
- ⬠ Under 10%
- ⬠ 10-29%
- ⬠ 30-79%
- ⬠ 80% and over

Least Evangelized People

What or who are Least Evangelized People? The AD2000 & Beyond Movement defines them as people groups that are less than 2% Christian, have insufficient access to the gospel, are adoptable for prayer and mission and are most in need of a church planting movement.

The AD2000 & Beyond Movement's goal is "a church for every people by the year 2000" and to accomplish this their priority is to establish "a pioneer church planting movement within every country of the world by December 31, 2000." For the Global Consultation on World Evangelization in Seoul, Korea, in 1995 they compiled a "Key List of Priority Least Evangelized Peoples."

The list contains 2,500 people groups with 10,000 or more individuals. It is sorted by country and language. (People groups should not be confused with individual people.) To create this map the groups in each country have been aggregated and the combined number of least evangelized individuals in each country has been coded as a percentage of the population. This shows that the greatest number of such persons are in Asia and parts of North Africa.

Source: The Least Evangelized Peoples of the World

Theological Institutions and Seminaries

Roman Catholic Seminaries, 1970

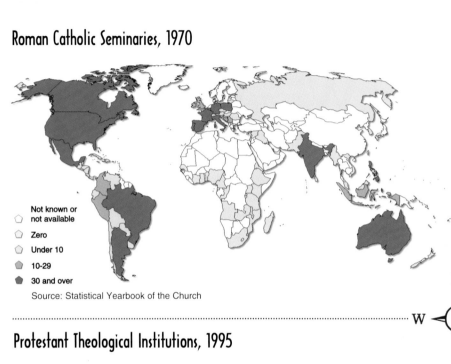

Not known or not available
Zero
Under 10
10-29
30 and over

Source: Statistical Yearbook of the Church

Roman Catholic Seminaries, 1993

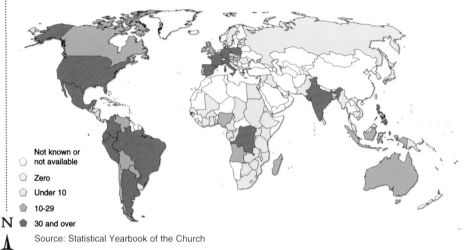

Not known or not available
Zero
Under 10
10-29
30 and over

Source: Statistical Yearbook of the Church

Protestant Theological Institutions, 1995

Not Known or not available
Zero
Under 10
10-29
30 and over

Source: World Directory of Theological Institutions

Training Institutions by Continent

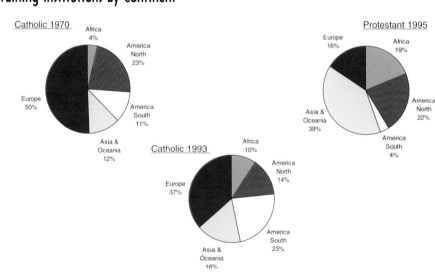

Catholic 1970
Africa 4%
America North 23%
America South 11%
Asia & Oceania 12%
Europe 50%

Catholic 1993
Africa 10%
America North 14%
America South 23%
Asia & Oceania 16%
Europe 37%

Protestant 1995
Europe 16%
Africa 19%
America North 22%
America South 4%
Asia & Oceania 39%

Bible Translation—Percentage of Population with the Bible or New Testament in Their Own Language

Under 25%   26-49%   50-74%   75-94%   95% and over

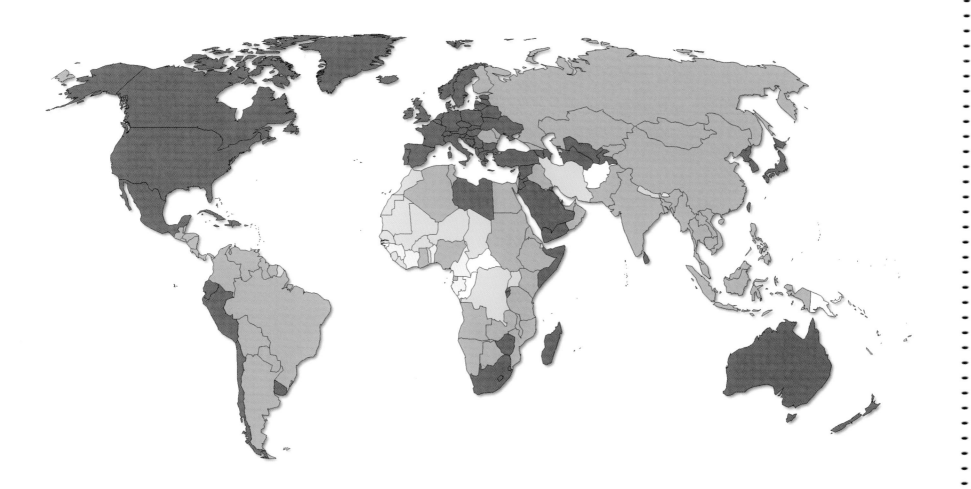

Not allowing for the 25% of the World's Population who cannot read. See page 69 for Literacy.

Source: United Bible Societies and SIL Ethnologue

Christian Radio Broadcasting

International Christian Radio Broadcast Hours per Head of Population, 1996 (Hours per Week per Million People)

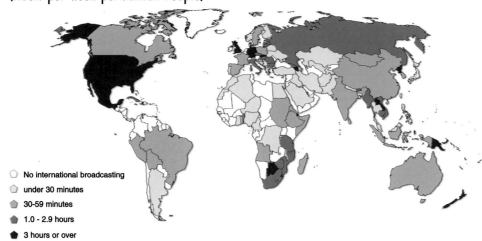

- ○ No international broadcasting
- ○ under 30 minutes
- ○ 30-59 minutes
- ● 1.0 - 2.9 hours
- ● 3 hours or over

Degree of Freedom for Christian Radio Broadcasts

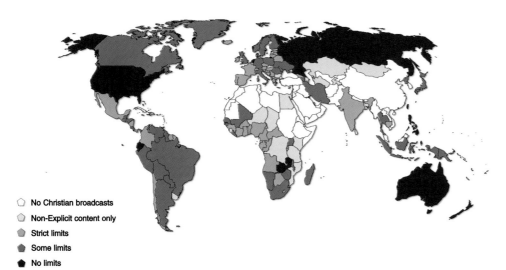

- ○ No Christian broadcasts
- ○ Non-Explicit content only
- ◐ Strict limits
- ● Some limits
- ● No limits

Christian Broadcast Hours

Around the world there are hundreds of radio stations owned and/or run by Protestant, Roman Catholic or Seventh Day Adventist Christians. The largest and best known of these are international stations broadcasting on short wave (SW) or sometimes medium wave (MW) frequencies. Many of their broadcasts are in international languages such as English, others in trade languages such as Swahili for east Africa, but the majority are in mother-tongue languages (a person's first language, usually the one they speak at home). The major Protestant broadcasters are working together on the *World by 2000 Project* which aims to have broadcasts in all mother-tongue languages with over 1 million speakers (mega-languages) by the year 2000.

The top map shows the extent of broadcasts by all international Christian stations. All speakers of a language are considered potential listeners, whether or not they have access to a radio receiver. Domestic broadcasts are not included as information is less available both as to the amount of broadcasting and what proportion of a language group can potentially hear broadcasts on geographically limited local stations. Many countries especially in North and South America have access to domestic broadcasts. Listeners also tune in to programs not specifically broadcast to them (e.g., English language programs are listened to in virtually every country).

The lower map shows how much freedom there is for Christian broadcasts within a country. The worst scenario is where no Christian programs are allowed at all. Some countries allow only non-explicit Christian programs to be made by Christians e.g., on health or community development. The next level allow explicit Christian content but with strict limits e.g., only by one denomination or only at major Christian festivals. Others impose some restrictions, usually to do with program content, such as no proselytizing or no criticism of other religions, while the freest countries impose no restrictions at all.

Source: Frank Gray, FEBC Radio International and World by 2000 Project

Languages in the *World by 2000 Project*, 1986

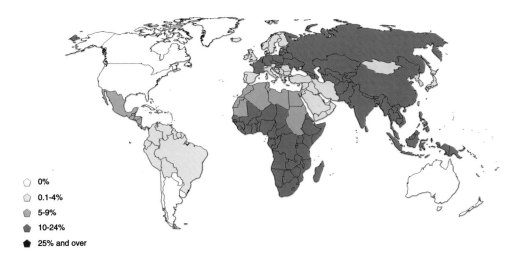

- ○ 0%
- ○ 0.1-4%
- ◓ 5-9%
- ◑ 10-24%
- ● 25% and over

Languages in the *World by 2000 Project*, 1996

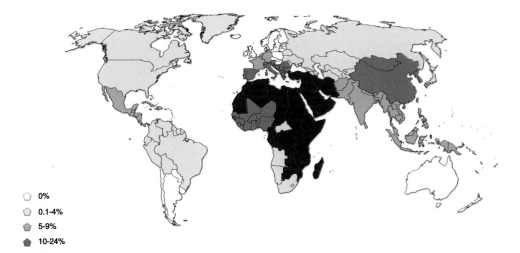

- ○ 0%
- ○ 0.1-4%
- ◓ 5-9%
- ◑ 10-24%
- ● 25% and over

See text for detailed explanation

Languages Covered by Christian Broadcasts

The aim of the *World by 2000 Project* is to provide broadcasts in every language which has more than 1 million speakers. The first research for the project was done in 1986, and set out to identify those regions of the world which were most in need of new language broadcasts. A first attempt was also made to identify the specific languages in question, but data at that time was very incomplete. The maps on this page therefore indicate the size of the broadcasters' task in 1986 and 1996. They show the percentage of a country's population which speak mega-languages and which did not have Christian radio broadcasts in 1986 or 1996. Minority language groups have not been taken into account since in most instances they do little to change the picture.

In many places language groups spill across political boundaries so are not tied to the statistics of any one country e.g., there are Azeri speakers in Azerbaijan and in Iran. In some regions the figures appear worse for 1996 rather than better in spite of more than seventy new language services having been added worldwide! This is for a number of reasons: at least one major Christian international station (Radio ELWA) has ceased broadcasting because of political unrest, a large number of mega-languages have been discovered as research has become more refined, and some large language groups (such as Arabic) have been broken down into regional dialects.

Source: Frank Gray, FEBC Radio International and World by 2000 Project

Relief and Development

Relief and Development

    Almost all branches of the Christian church are involved in relief and development in the Third World, as well as in social action in their own country. The range of projects undertaken is enormous, both short and long term. All Christian aid agencies do some or all of the following major types of work:

- emergency and disaster relief
- reconciliation
- community development
- education
- health
- disease prevention
- aid to or sponsorship of children
- small business projects sometimes including local banking or co-operatives
- intermediate technology.

These maps feature the countries in which some of the key Christian agencies are working, three from the USA on this page and four from the UK opposite.

Catholic Relief Services

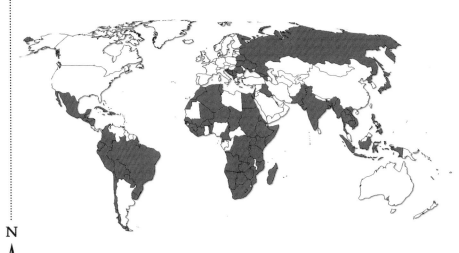

Lutheran World Relief

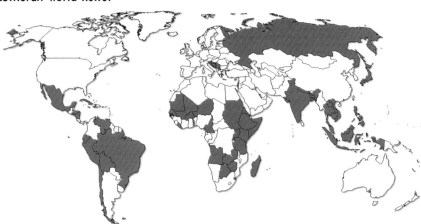

World Vision

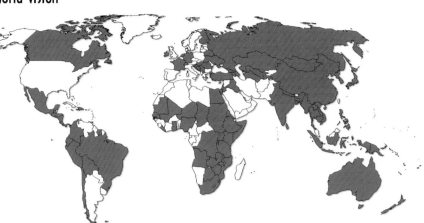

Sources: Catholic Relief Service, Lutheran World Relief, and World Vision

Relief and Development
UK Relief and Development Agencies—Countries Involved With

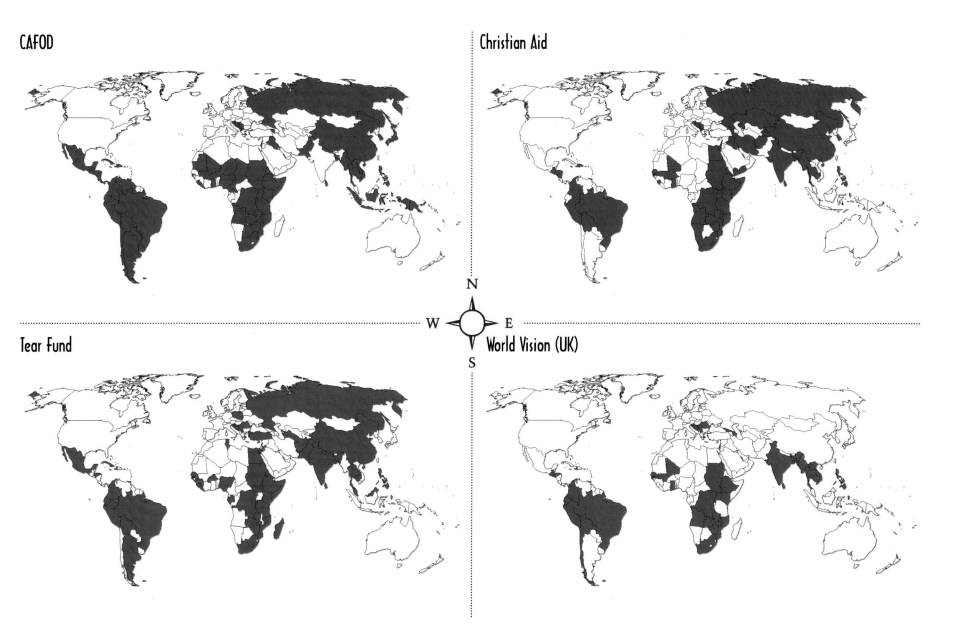

CAFOD

Christian Aid

Tear Fund

World Vision (UK)

N
W — E
S

Sources: CAFOD, Christian Aid, Tear Fund, and World Vision (UK)

Short-Term Missionaries, 1990
Percentage of all Missionaries

Percentage of Protestant Missionaries which Are Short-Term, 1990

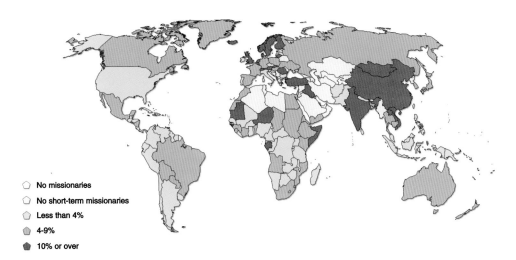

- ⬠ No missionaries
- ⬠ No short-term missionaries
- ⬠ Less than 4%
- ⬠ 4-9%
- ⬠ 10% or over

Percentage of Catholic Missionaries which Are Short-Term, 1990

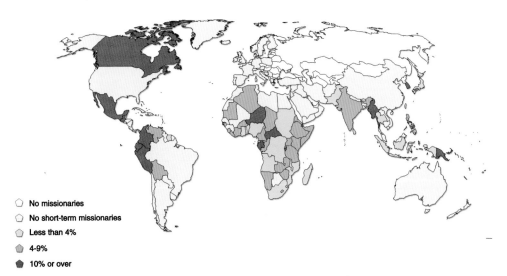

- ⬠ No missionaries
- ⬠ No short-term missionaries
- ⬠ Less than 4%
- ⬠ 4-9%
- ⬠ 10% or over

Percentage of Missionaries Who Are Short-Term

Until international air travel developed the concept of short-term missionary service was a practical impossibility–it might take many months on a sea voyage followed by weeks of overland travel to arrive at one's destination. Short-term missionaries are accepted to serve less than a full period of service, which is usually considered to be 4 years. Since the 1970s the percentage of short-term missionaries has been growing. In Britain it was 5% in 1976, reached a peak of 30% in 1982 and in 1995 was 15%.

There is considerable variation on what length of missionary service is considered short-term, with anything from a short visit of two weeks up to four years being counted in different countries or by certain Mission Sending Agencies.

The definitions fall into three groups: less than 4 months, 4 months to 2 years, over 2 years. The figures for these maps were taken from Operation World which defines short-term as 2 years or less.

The maps show that the distribution of short-term missionaries is not the same for Catholics and Protestants. Far fewer countries with Catholic missionaries have any short-term workers, though in those which do, the percentages are roughly similar to the Protestant ones.

Source: Operation World Database

Major World Religions

Islamic Expansion and Encounter

Professor Lamin Sanneh

"Scripture," "church," etc. in this article relate to Muslim, not Christian, use of these terms.

Origin and Expansion

Islam began as a world-conquering faith and remains today a world-embracing religion. In the earliest preaching of the Prophet Muhammad in Mecca from about A.D. 610 we find a call to ethical responsibility. Believers are deemed accountable to God for their behavior and conduct and will be accordingly judged at the Last Day.

Such accountability became vested in the person of the Prophet himself after he subdued Medina in A.D. 622 and returned soon thereafter to Mecca.

- **In Mecca he was a private citizen, in Medina he became supreme magistrate.**
- **In Mecca he was a subject, in Medina he ruled.**
- **In Mecca he preached, in Medina he practised.**

Thus at his hands Islam became a religion and a government, a church and a state combined. Political power was deployed to advance the religious cause.

As Islam spread beyond the Arabian peninsula it came into contact with different cultures and civilizations which interpenetrated the Islamic worldview, producing complex responses and reactions. Byzantine and Sasanid political ideas and structures were adopted as a framework for the sprawling Muslim empire. Military organization and the administration of justice were readjusted in the light of the new materials and influences. Islamic theology was transfused from Greek sources, with Greek scientific ideas flowing in to shape the Muslim conception of the physical universe, although the relationship between revelation and reason was a new problem for believers. Similarly, Islamic legal jurisprudence was developed to deal with the vexing issues of divergent practices, sectarian splits, divisive rituals and observances, and conflicting interpretations of the canonical sources of Scripture and tradition.

"A religion and a government"

There were impressive intellectual achievements in these early Islamic centuries. However, by the second half of the 10th century breakaway states and fiefdoms had virtually destroyed the cohesiveness of the Pax Islamica. Only in Andalusian Spain could one speak of a continuous tradition of caliphal authority, though even there there was the pressure of the reconquista.

Encounter and Challenge

In its meteoric rise and expansion Islam faced two kinds of challenges. One was that of internal assimilation and adaptation, in which Islam yielded important ground on the content of life. Nevertheless it continued to provide the political framework and was still able to maintain the unifying influence of the Arabic of Scripture, liturgy and law. On the religious level, Sufism represents the flexible synthesis of code and piety. On the canonical level, a blend of norms and principles was introduced to rehabilitate and modernize the Shar¡'ah, the legal code. Such eclectic use breaches the autonomy normally enjoyed by the four orthodox legal schools, but the advantage is to allow for new formulations without abandoning Islamic standards.

"The unifying influence of the Arabic of Scripture, liturgy and law"

From its encounter with civilizations with a strong political and economic base, a new and different challenge to Islam arose. This affected its infrastructure and self-image, precipitating a crisis of identity. The Muslim encounter with the modern West was a challenge with hidden benefits for Islam. The Western colonial advance weakened the opposition that Islamic rule had aroused and fed among indigenous populations in its frontier districts, from northern India to Nigeria, from East Java to northern Ghana. The willingness of colonial administrators to placate Muslim community leaders with state concessions made it easier to acknowledge, and even reconcile with, the authority of an infidel Western power.

"A challenge with hidden benefits"

Responses

Both of these challenges helped to change Islam, the one toward a syncretist cultural convergence with non-Islamic materials, and the other toward a secular Western accommodation. As a consequence Islam has been molded by this rhythm of cultural expansion and secular retrenchment. Thus on the one hand the religion leaves its imprint on internal patterns of local religious and social life, while on the other it absorbs from without the effects of a relentless Western secularization.

By all appearances, the period of Islam's spectacular numerical and territorial expansion is over. Today it is replaced with issues facing all religions: national identity, human rights, women's rights, minority rights, the information revolution, and environmental security. There does not yet seem to be any corresponding interest in inter-faith issues, though ecumenical efforts are continuing, such as programs of the Vatican Office for inter-religious relations and of the department with similar responsibility in the World Council of Churches.

The Future

The future for Islam seems to lie in the extent to which its important birthmark of joining church and state can survive the cauterizing effects of an equally resilient tradition of the modern West which insists on separation of the two. Thus, the new social radicalism of women and youth, guided by postmodernist social criticism, is combining with the fundamentalist challenge to unsettle received authority. This signals upheaval and uncertainty on an unprecedented scale.

"The cauterizing effects of the modern West"

No religion is immune to these forces, but in its failure to break decisively with the tradition of religion having a right to state sponsorship, and vice versa, Islam is exposed to a particularly truculent form of the challenge.

Lamin Sanneh was educated on four continents and has taught at several universities, including Harvard and Yale where he is the D Willis James Professor of Missions and World Christianity and Professor of History. He is a prolific writer and for his academic work he was made Commandeur de l'Ordre National du Lion, Senegal's highest national honor.

Total Growth of Christianity and Other Major World Religions, 1900-2000

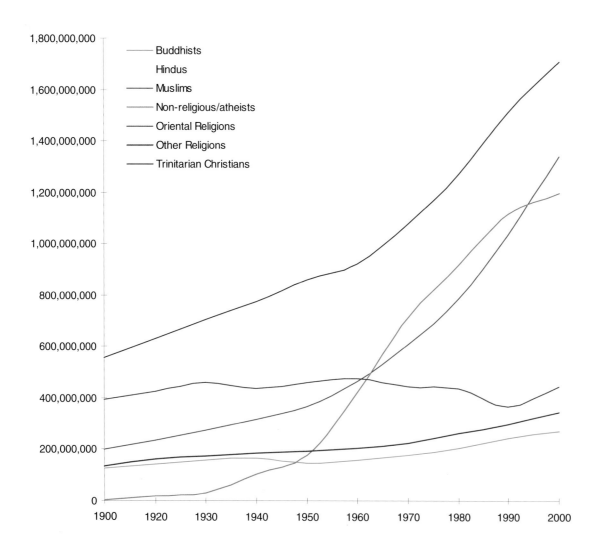

Legend:
- Buddhists
- Hindus
- Muslims
- Non-religious/atheists
- Oriental Religions
- Other Religions
- Trinitarian Christians

1900

Buddhists	127,159,000
Hindus	203,033,300
Muslims	200,102,200
Non-religious/atheists	3,148,900
Oriental Religions	394,020,000
Other Religions	134,367,100
Trinitarian Christians	558,056,300
TOTAL	1,619,886,800

1950

Buddhists	147,500,000
Hindus	320,800,000
Muslims	368,800,000
Non-religious/atheists	176,820,000
Oriental Religions	459,785,000
Other Religions	192,195,000
Trinitarian Christians	860,100,000
TOTAL	2,526,000,000

2000

Buddhists	272,950,000
Hindus	865,565,000
Muslims	1,340,743,000
Non-religious/atheists	1,200,143,000
Oriental Religions	444,745,000
Other Religions	343,397,000
Trinitarian Christians	1,710,454,000
TOTAL	6,177,997,000

Source: Operation World Database

Strength of Buddhism as Percentage of Population, 2000

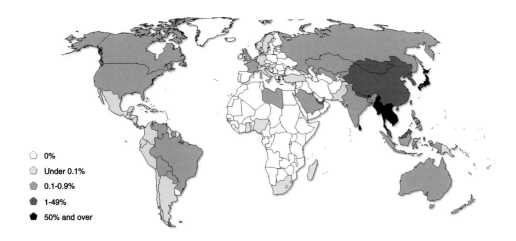

- ○ 0%
- ○ Under 0.1%
- ○ 0.1-0.9%
- ● 1-49%
- ● 50% and over

Growth of Buddhism, by Continent, 1900, 1980, 2000

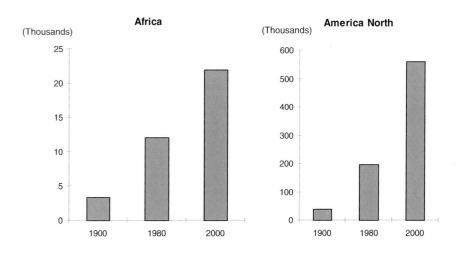

Africa
(Thousands)

America North
(Thousands)

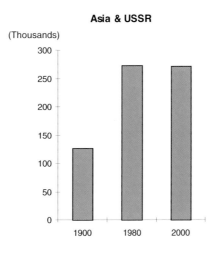

America South
(Thousands)

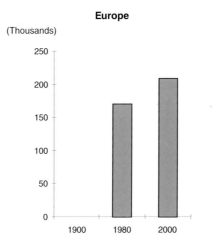

Asia & USSR
(Thousands)

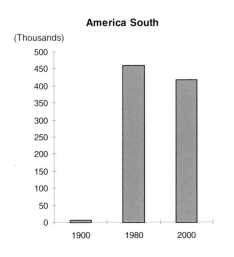

Europe
(Thousands)

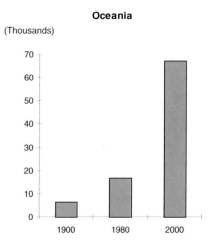

Oceania
(Thousands)

Sources: 1900, 1980, World Christian Encyclopedia; 2000, Operation World Database

Growth of Each Religion, by Continent
Hinduism

Strength of Hinduism as Percentage of Population, 2000

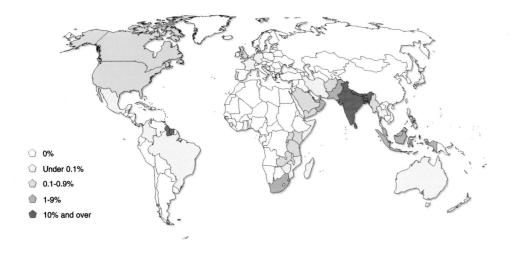

- ⬠ 0%
- ⬠ Under 0.1%
- ⬠ 0.1-0.9%
- ⬠ 1-9%
- ⬠ 10% and over

Growth of Hinduism, by Continent, 1900, 1980, 2000

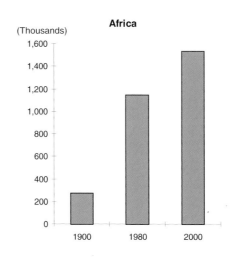

Africa (Thousands)

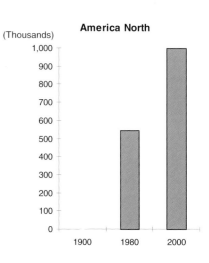

America North (Thousands)

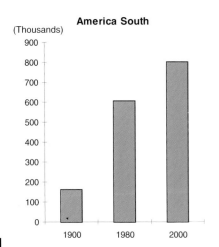

America South (Thousands)

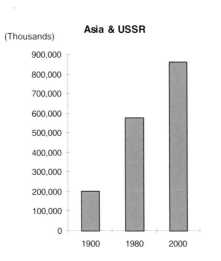

Asia & USSR (Thousands)

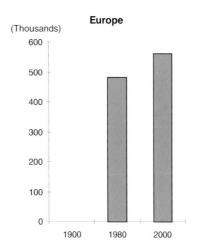

Europe (Thousands)

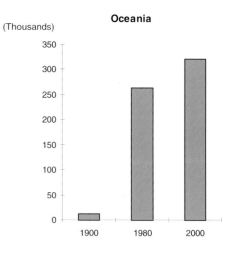

Oceania (Thousands)

Sources: 1900, 1980, World Christian Encyclopedia; 2000, Operation World Database

Strength of Islam as Percentage of Population, 2000

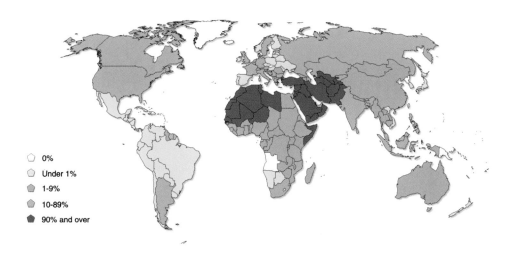

- ○ 0%
- ○ Under 1%
- ◔ 1-9%
- ◑ 10-89%
- ● 90% and over

Growth of Islam by Continent, 1900, 1980, 2000

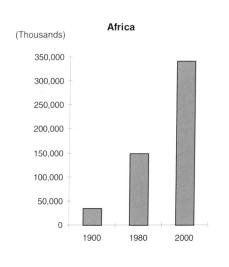

Africa (Thousands)

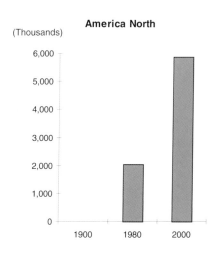

America North (Thousands)

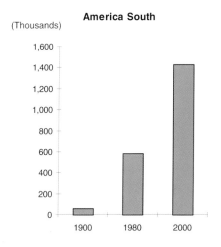

America South (Thousands)

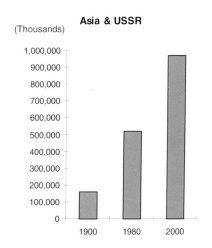

Asia & USSR (Thousands)

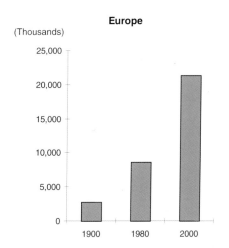

Europe (Thousands)

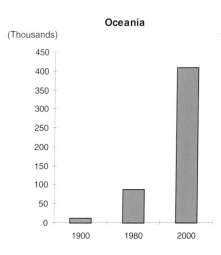

Oceania (Thousands)

Sources: 1900, 1980, World Christian Encyclopedia; 2000, Operation World Database

Growth of Each Religion, by Continent
Oriental Religions

Strength of Oriental Religions as Percentage of Population, 2000

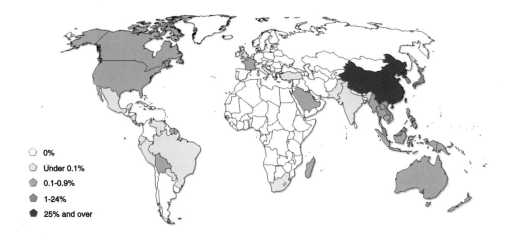

- ○ 0%
- ○ Under 0.1%
- ⬠ 0.1-0.9%
- ⬠ 1-24%
- ⬟ 25% and over

Growth of Oriental Religions by Continent, 1900, 1980, 2000

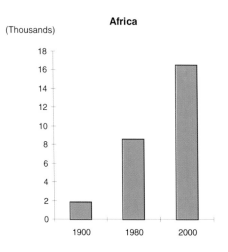

Africa
(Thousands)

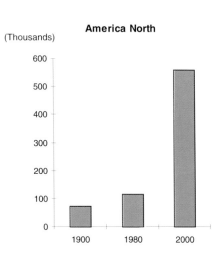

America North
(Thousands)

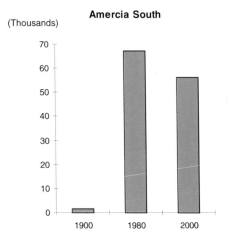

Amercia South
(Thousands)

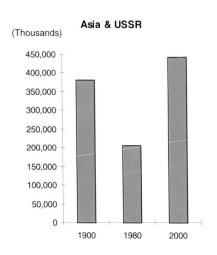

Asia & USSR
(Thousands)

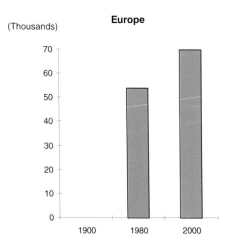

Europe
(Thousands)

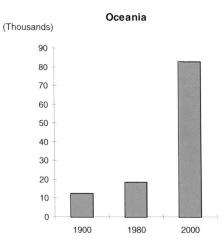

Oceania
(Thousands)

Sources: 1900, 1980, World Christian Encyclopedia; 2000, Operation World Database

Strength of Tribal Religions as Percentage of Population, 2000

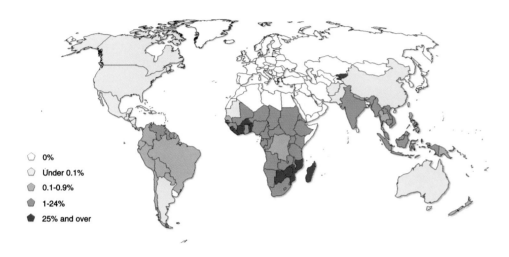

- ○ 0%
- ○ Under 0.1%
- ◓ 0.1-0.9%
- ◓ 1-24%
- ● 25% and over

Growth of Tribal Religions by Continent, 1900, 1980, 2000

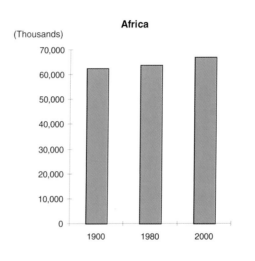

Africa

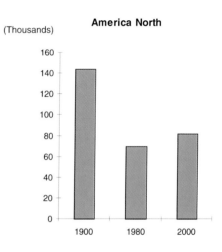

America North

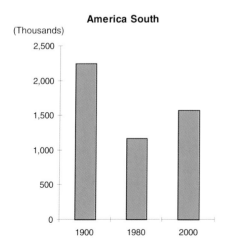

America South

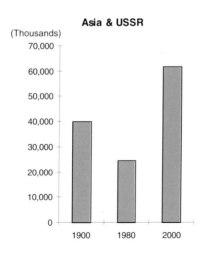

Asia & USSR

Europe

ZERO

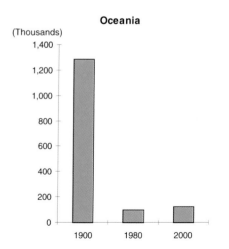

Oceania

Sources: 1900, 1980, World Christian Encyclopedia; 2000, Operation World Database

Communism

Communist and Socialist One Party/Military States, 1980

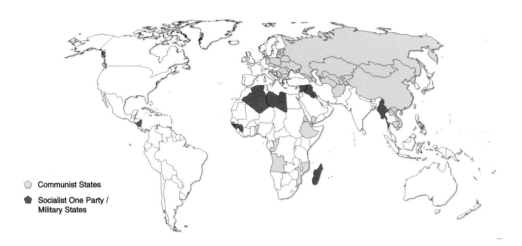

Communist States

Socialist One Party / Military States

Communist and Socialist One Party/Military States, 2000

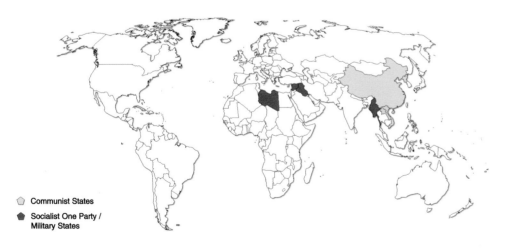

Communist States

Socialist One Party / Military States

See Text for detailed explanation

Communism

"Socialist One Party/Military States" are shown separately from "Communist States" because their status as truly communist regimes is highly contentious.

The definition is also open to debate and different sources list different countries in this category. For example Libya, Iraq and Syria are still regarded as Muslim countries although headed by secular socialist leaders, while some sources would include more of the African republics. From 1960 to 1990 around a third of the world's population was subject to communist rule, and even with the so called "collapse" of Communism in the early 1990s it still remains at around a quarter of the world's population today.

Population Changes, 1960-2000

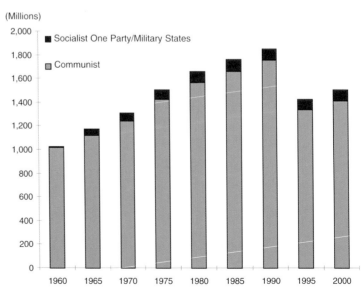

Source: Population figures: World Churches Handbook

Comparative Material

Christianity and Culture

Dr John Wijngaards

Culture is a generic term for the beliefs, values, symbolic systems of meaning, collective fears and expectations that make up the soul of a nation. Culture expresses itself in social institutions, customs, feasts, visual art, literature, drama, etc. If we understand a people's culture, we know its inner life.

Christianity does not create a single, uniform culture. However through the beliefs and values it inspires, Christianity transforms local cultures. This has produced and still produces a myriad of distinct Christian cultures. To see their diversity we could compare the culture of the Copts in Egypt with that of the Syro-Malankara people of Kerala in South India. Or the Orthodox community in the Ukraine with the Christian Zulus in South Africa.

"Christianity transforms local cultures"

Enculturation

The influence of Christianity on a particular culture is known as its "enculturation." It happens to varying degrees, partly depending how long a society has had Christian influence. People groups which have only recently become Christian will exhibit a different degree of enculturation from western Europe which has experienced Christianity for many centuries.

"Thrown into the lion's den"

The gospel has reached a high degree of enculturation in classical English. One example is seen in the many popular sayings which derive from Scripture. We speak of "a wolf in sheep's clothing," of someone being "a Judas," of escaping "by the skin of your teeth," of "being thrown into the lion's den," and so on. Even though people may not realize it, their everyday talk reflects thoughts and images from the Bible.

Cultural History

There is an almost global civilization that covers Europe, North America and the related parts of the world and is spreading elsewhere, particularly through the media. This western culture bears the imprint of 15 centuries of Christian molding. The major historical expressions of this western culture whether in art, literature, architecture, or theatre are thoroughly Christian. Consider the medieval cathedrals, mystery plays, frescoes, or religious poetry that form the heritage of every single European nation.

Yet western civilization owes an even greater debt to Christian thought than this. Modern progress in industry, technology, democracy and human rights was made possible through a radical realization of key Christian principles:

- the belief that the world is good and has been entrusted to humankind for its development
- the value of every single individual
- the importance of freedom
- the demands of personal responsibility for one's actions
- the conviction that good will overcome evil.

"Secular countercurrents"

Secular Culture

Secular countercurrents are nowadays undermining Western culture's links with Christianity. There are no longer any absolute standards which can guide one's conscience. Human reason is seen as the ultimate judge of truth and science is trusted to solve all problems, though some people now question whether it can. Individual success and personal pleasure have become the focus of life. The universe is analyzed from a physical point of view, but has lost an overriding religious meaning.

"No longer any absolute standards"

It is clear that a new Western Secular Culture is emerging which is out of tune with its Christian past. This is not a new phenomenon in history. The civilization of Roman Christianity was swept aside by the migrating pagan nations of Northern Europe from the 4th to the 6th centuries A.D. It took hundreds of years before these nations in turn were sufficiently impregnated with the gospel to create the Christian Middle Ages.

"Christian re-enculturation"

Christianity and Culture

The process of Christian enculturation faces special problems peculiar to our own time. Through improved international contacts and constant immigrations, Western society is becoming pluriform in every respect. Rapid technological changes erode people's sense of stability. The communication media direct the common perception of reality yet are themselves largely dominated by commercial interests. This new secular Western culture needs to be re-enculturated by Christianity.

A dynamic reassessment will need to happen. As with all cultures, Christianity will have to discern the good and valuable in modern secular culture, remedy its excesses and help to create a new Christian soul. It is this "soul" which will eventually give expression to a new cultural identity in the future.

Father John Wijngaards is a theologian who lectured in India for 12 years and was Director General of Amruthavani, a communications center in Andhra Pradesh. From 1976 to 1982 he was Vicar General of Mill Hill Missionary Society in London and is now Director of Housetop, an International Missionary Communications Centre.

Population, 1995

Percentage of Population Under 15

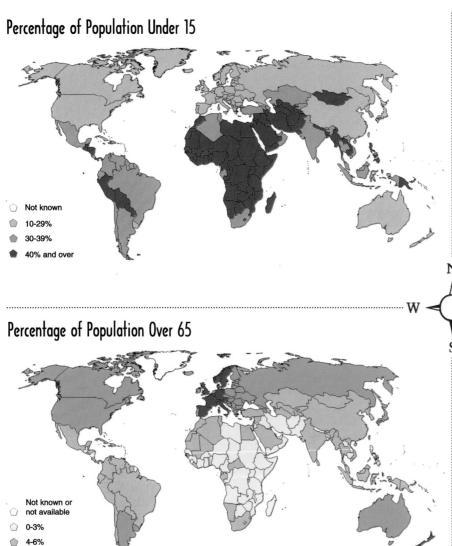

- Not known
- 10-29%
- 30-39%
- 40% and over

Percentage of Natural Increase of Population per Annum

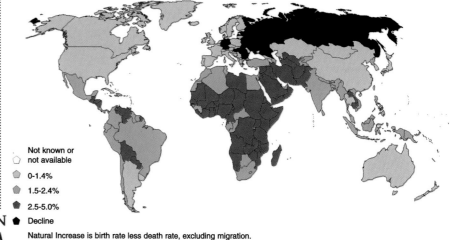

- Not known or not available
- 0-1.4%
- 1.5-2.4%
- 2.5-5.0%
- Decline

Natural Increase is birth rate less death rate, excluding migration.

Percentage of Population Over 65

- Not known or not available
- 0-3%
- 4-6%
- 7-14%
- 15-25%

Doubling Time of Population - In Years at Present Rate

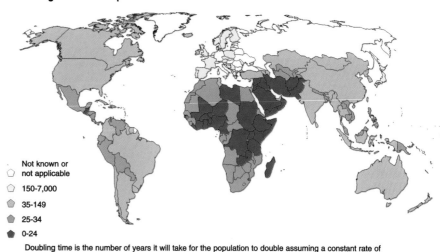

- Not known or not applicable
- 150-7,000
- 35-149
- 25-34
- 0-24

Doubling time is the number of years it will take for the population to double assuming a constant rate of natural increase

N
W E
S

Source: Target Earth, World Population Data Sheet

Urbanization

Urban Population as Percentage of Total Population, 1950

Not known, not available

0 - 29%

30 - 49%

50 - 69%

Over 70%

Source: World Population Prospects

Urban Population as Percentage of Total Population, 1995

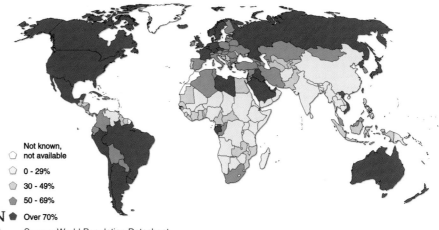

Not known, not available

0 - 29%

30 - 49%

50 - 69%

Over 70%

Source: World Population Datasheet

Urban Population as Percentage of Total Population, 1970

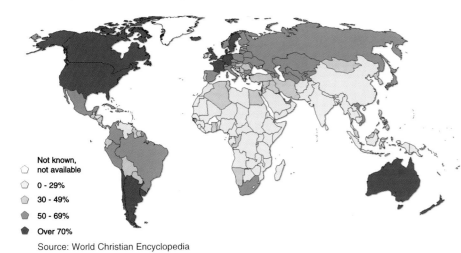

Not known, not available

0 - 29%

30 - 49%

50 - 69%

Over 70%

Source: World Christian Encyclopedia

The World's Largest Cities, 1994 and 2015

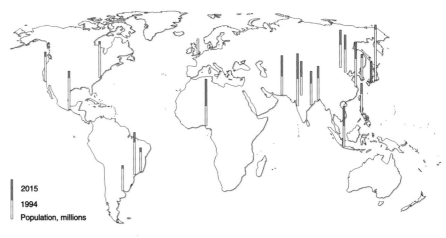

2015

1994

Population, millions

Source: The Independent 30 May 1996

N
W — E
S

Human Development Index, 1992

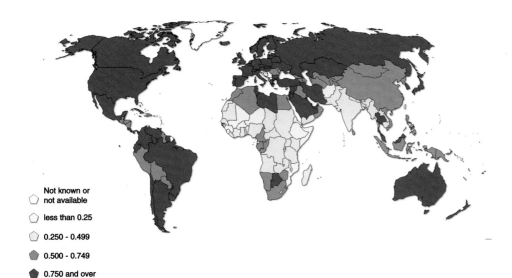

Not known or not available

less than 0.25

0.250 - 0.499

0.500 - 0.749

0.750 and over

Human Development Index

T he three factors considered essential for development are for people:

- to lead a long and healthy life
- to acquire knowledge
- to have access to the resources needed for a decent standard of living.

The Human Development Index (HDI) is therefore produced by combining three indicators:

- life expectancy
- educational attainment
- Gross Domestic Product (GDP–purchasing power parity against dollars).

The HDI is increasingly being used alongside or as an alternative to Gross National Product (GNP) as a measure of the development of a nation. The figure technically ranges from 0 to 1 and the higher the figure, the better the quality of life. In 1992 Canada had the highest Human Development Index (0.950), while Niger had the lowest (0.207). The average for the developing countries was 0.570 and for the industrialized world, 0.916. The overall world figure in 1992 was 0.760.

Source: Human Development Report

Life Expectancy at Birth, 1960

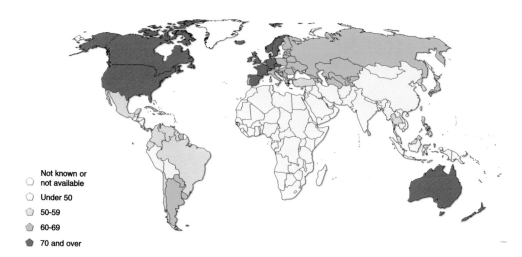

Not known or
not available
Under 50
50-59
60-69
70 and over

Life Expectancy at Birth, 1995

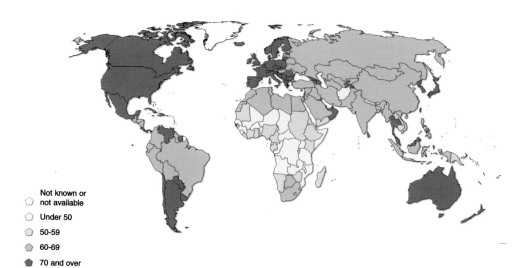

Not known or
not available
Under 50
50-59
60-69
70 and over

Life Expectancy at Birth

How long can a child born today expect to live? Life expectancy varies a great deal across the world, but not nearly as much as it did 30 or 40 years ago. Since 1960 the developing world has seen an increase of 17 years in the average length of life, as medical care has become available to more people. It took the industrialized world about a century to achieve the same increase, though starting from a higher base. Life expectancy is one of the factors measured in the Human Development Index–for an explanation of that see page 66.

Thirty countries in the developing world now have a life expectancy of more than 70 years, and in 24 industrialized countries it is now over 75.

In 1992 the country with the longest life expectancy was Canada with 77.4 years, while the shortest was Niger at 46.5.

Life expectancy has increased mainly for two reasons: improved medical care and better diet. In many countries these are not equally available to everyone. This can result in a significant variation in life expectancy between rural and urban areas, or between various social and ethnic groups.

Primary school children, Nepal

Source: Human Development Report, Third World Guide

Primary, Secondary and University Education

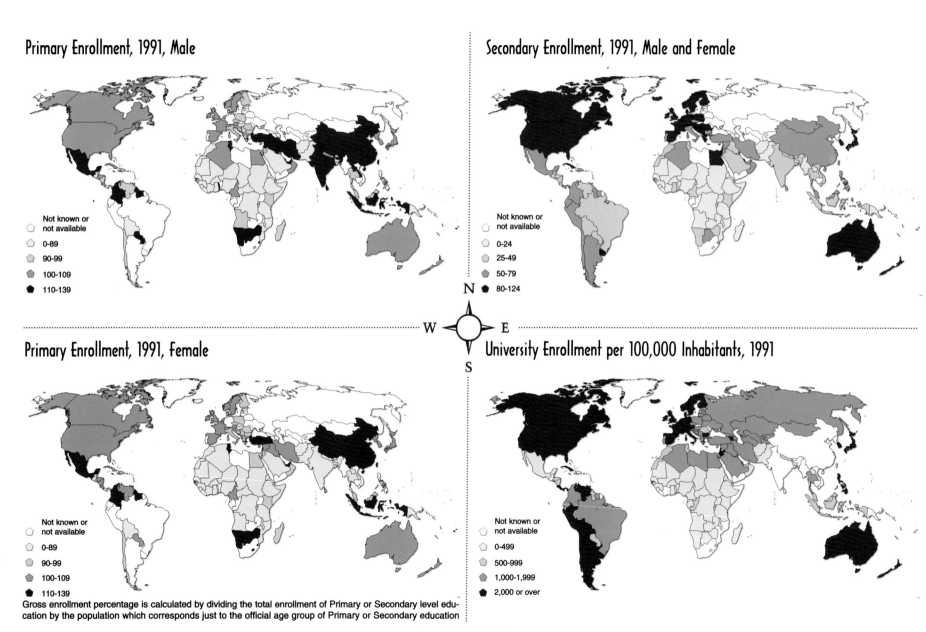

Primary Enrollment, 1991, Male

Not known or not available
0-89
90-99
100-109
110-139

Secondary Enrollment, 1991, Male and Female

Not known or not available
0-24
25-49
50-79
80-124

N
W E
S

Primary Enrollment, 1991, Female

Not known or not available
0-89
90-99
100-109
110-139

University Enrollment per 100,000 Inhabitants, 1991

Not known or not available
0-499
500-999
1,000-1,999
2,000 or over

Gross enrollment percentage is calculated by dividing the total enrollment of Primary or Secondary level education by the population which corresponds just to the official age group of Primary or Secondary education

Source: A Third World Guide

Male and Female Literacy Rates, 1971, 1990
As Percentage of Population

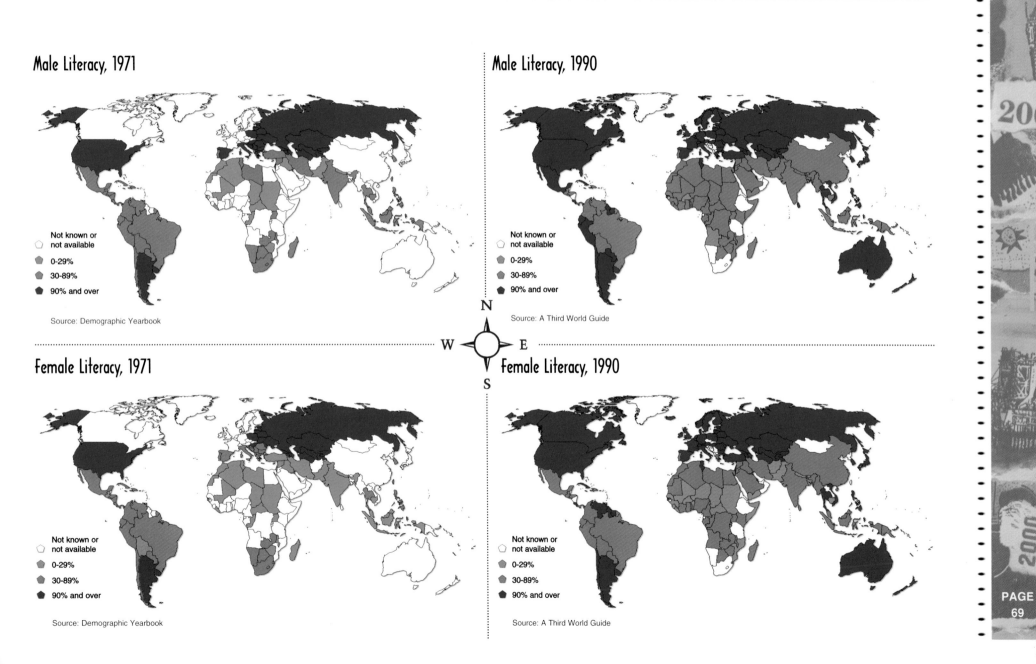

Male Literacy, 1971

Not known or not available
0-29%
30-89%
90% and over

Source: Demographic Yearbook

Male Literacy, 1990

Not known or not available
0-29%
30-89%
90% and over

Source: A Third World Guide

N
W E
S

Female Literacy, 1971

Not known or not available
0-29%
30-89%
90% and over

Source: Demographic Yearbook

Female Literacy, 1990

Not known or not available
0-29%
30-89%
90% and over

Source: A Third World Guide

GNP per Capita and Growth, 1980-1991

GNP per Capita, 1993

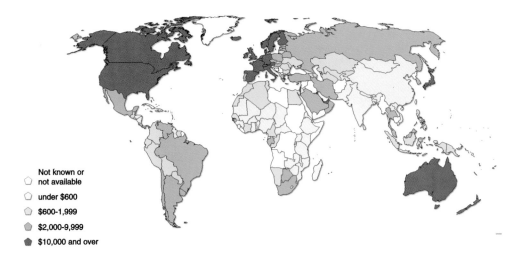

Not known or not available

under $600

$600-1,999

$2,000-9,999

$10,000 and over

GNP Percentage Annual Growth, 1980–1991

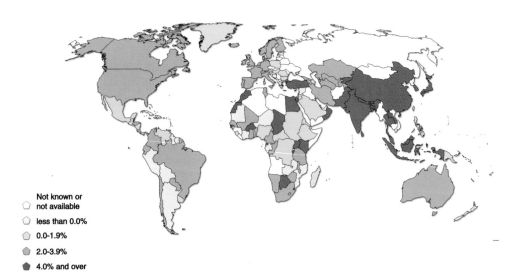

Not known or not available

less than 0.0%

0.0-1.9%

2.0-3.9%

4.0% and over

Source: A Third World Guide

GNP

GNP, or Gross National Product at Factor Cost to give its full name, is "The sum of all incomes earned by national residents in return for contributions to current production that takes place anywhere in the world,"[1] GNP is essentially the total money earned by all the citizens of a country in their country (that is workers from abroad are excluded). The "Factor Cost" means that government taxation is excluded as are any government subsidies to aid production of the goods or services. It therefore reflects the genuine price at which these are produced, which may or may not be the same as the normal retail price.

This figure is usually divided by the population of a country to give "GNP per capita." The average worldwide in 1992 was $4,500. The richest country was Switzerland at $36,400 while the poorest was Mozambique at $80. Half the countries were above $1,630 and half below (the median value).

The top map shows the size of a country's GNP, the second the average annual rate of change 1980-1991. Comparing them shows that many of the the poorest countries became even poorer during the 1980s (their GNP growth was negative), while many of the richest countries became even richer (annual growth at 4% or more).

The Distribution of GNP Across the World[2]

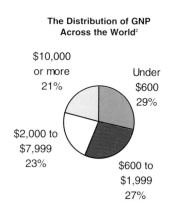

$10,000 or more 21%

Under $600 29%

$2,000 to $7,999 23%

$600 to $1,999 27%

Part of this variation is because it takes different amounts of money to produce similar goods in each country. An alternative measure, Purchasing Power Parity (PPP), corrects this, by defining the United States as 100 and measuring every other country in relation to it.

[1]"The First Principles of Economics," Prof Richard Lipsey and Prof Colin Hanbury, Oxford University Press, 1994

[2]No country had a GNP between $8,000 and $9,999

Infant Deaths per 1000 Live Births, 1960

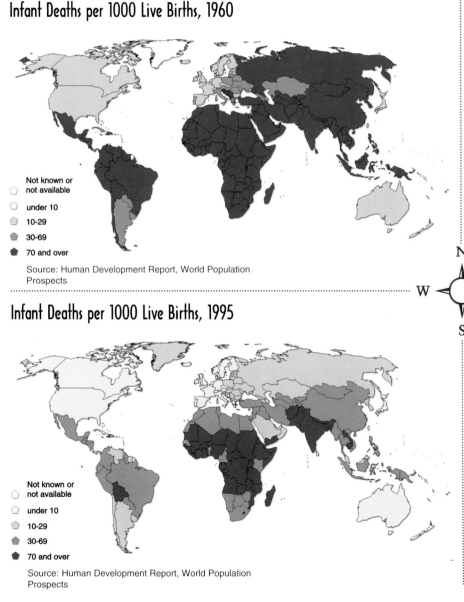

Not known or not available

under 10

10-29

30-69

70 and over

Source: Human Development Report, World Population Prospects

Number of Children per Woman, 1991

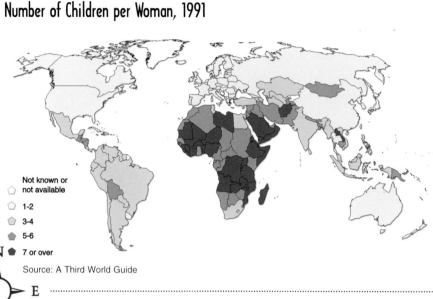

Not known or not available

1-2

3-4

5-6

7 or over

Source: A Third World Guide

Infant Deaths per 1000 Live Births, 1995

Not known or not available

under 10

10-29

30-69

70 and over

Source: Human Development Report, World Population Prospects

Infant Deaths per 1000 Live Births, 1960, 1995

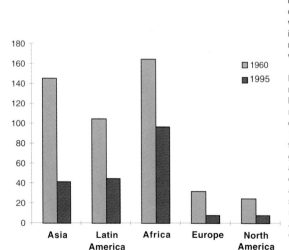

☐ 1960
■ 1995

Asia Latin America Africa Europe North America

Infant mortality is measured by how many babies die at or around the time of birth, compared to every 1,000 which survive. It therefore does not include pregnancies which end in a miscarriage or abortion, nor babies which die in early childhood.

Like other health measures, the infant mortality rate has improved dramatically in the second half of the 20th century. In the developing world it has dropped by more than a half since 1960, and in the industrialized world by three-quarters. However, this does not give a very fair picture, because the actual numbers are much more significant. This bar chart spells out the average numbers, by continents. They show that in the period 1960-92, the rate in Europe has dropped 75% but in Africa it has only fallen by 41%. The other continents are in between.

Prevalence of Leprosy and Population per Doctor

Population per Doctor, 1988–1991

Not known or not available

<500

500-999

1,000-9,999

10,000 and over

Source: Human Development Report, *Third World Guide*

Prevalence of Leprosy and Population per Doctor

Access to a doctor varies enormously across the world, and with it access to medical treatment. One of the most feared diseases has been leprosy. Effective treatment for leprosy began in the early 1950s. In 1982 the World Health Organization (WHO) introduced a new combination of drugs which treats leprosy in 6 months to two years. However, if cases are not detected early permanent damage to the body's nervous system can be the result, and it is this which leads to the deformities so often associated with the disease.

These maps show registered cases. This number is declining, but the number of new cases is not showing such a dramatic fall. In 1988 WHO changed the definition of a case of leprosy. Before then a person who had been affected by leprosy was always defined as a case of leprosy. Since 1988 the number of registered cases includes only people who are on treatment or awaiting treatment. It does not include those cured of the disease but who remain permanently deformed or disabled by its effects, and who therefore may continue to be regarded in their community as having leprosy.

It is mainly for this reason that the second map appears to show a significant decline between 1985 and 1995 in the number of registered cases of leprosy.

Source: World Health Organization, Leprosy Mission International

Registered Cases of Leprosy, 1996–per 10,000 People

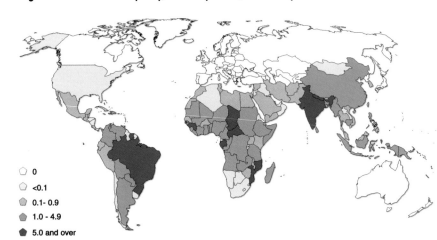

0

<0.1

0.1- 0.9

1.0 - 4.9

5.0 and over

Registered Cases of Leprosy, by Continent, 1985, 1995 –Actual Numbers

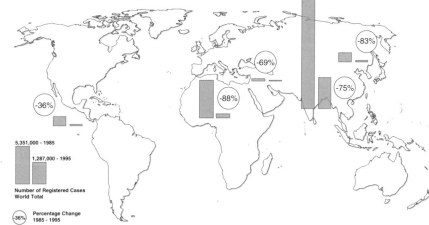

-36%

-69%

-88%

-83%

-75%

5,351,000 - 1985

1,287,000 - 1995

Number of Registered Cases World Total

-36% Percentage Change 1985 - 1995

Source: World Health Organization Weekly Epidemiological Record Number 20 (17th May, 1996)

Growth of AIDS

Average Number of AIDS Cases per Year, 1979–1992

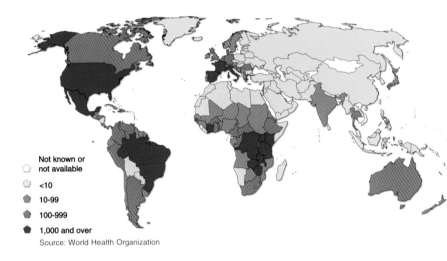

Not known or not available

<10

10-99

100-999

1,000 and over

Source: World Health Organization

World Totals of HIV Infection, 1992, 1995 (Estimated)

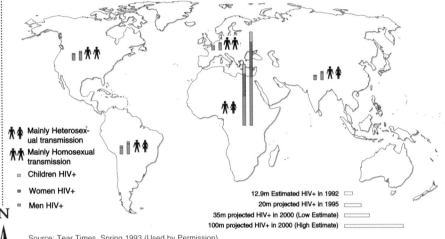

👫 Mainly Heterosex-ual transmission

👬 Mainly Homosexual transmission

▫ Children HIV+

▪ Women HIV+

▪ Men HIV+

12.9m Estimated HIV+ in 1992

20m projected HIV+ in 1995

35m projected HIV+ in 2000 (Low Estimate)

100m projected HIV+ in 2000 (High Estimate)

Source: Tear Times, Spring 1993 (Used by Permission)

N
W — E
S

Average Number of AIDS Cases per Year, 1993–1995

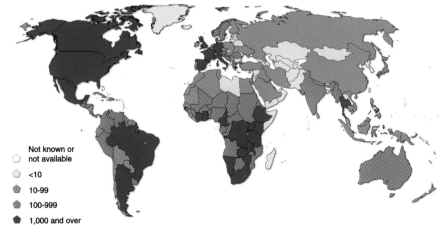

Not known or not available

<10

10-99

100-999

1,000 and over

Global Totals June 1996, AIDS: 1,394,000 HIV:25,500,000 ADULTS, 2,400,000 CHILDREN

Source: World Health Organization

AIDS Cases by Continent, 1979–2010

(Thousands)

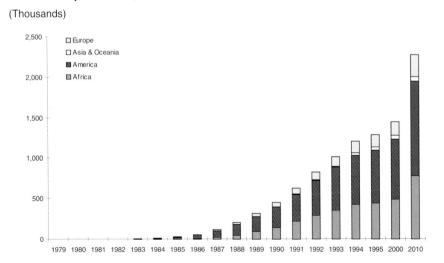

☐ Europe
☐ Asia & Oceania
■ America
■ Africa

2,500

2,000

1,500

1,000

500

0

1979 1980 1981 1982 1983 1984 1985 1986 1987 1988 1989 1990 1991 1992 1993 1994 1995 2000 2010

Source: World Health Organization. (2000, 2010, Estimated)

Newspapers and Periodicals

Number of Newspapers and Periodicals Published, 1970

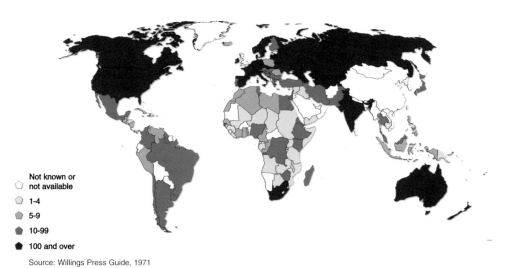

Not known or not available

1-4

5-9

10-99

100 and over

Source: Willings Press Guide, 1971

Number of Daily Newspapers Read, 1992–Copies per 100 People

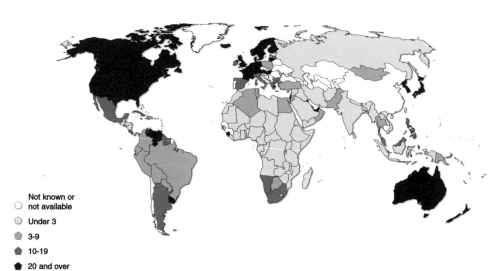

Not known or not available

Under 3

3-9

10-19

20 and over

Source: Third World Guide

Newspapers and Periodicals

These two maps measure different things. The 1970 map shows actual numbers of newspapers and periodicals that were published, information which is not available for about half the countries. The 1992 map is about circulation of daily newspapers, showing how many copies are read per 100 people. The total number of daily newspapers given for 1992 in the Third World Guide is 1,540, with the average number of copies read per 100 people being 12.

Although the figures used and the information shown on the maps are different, it is immediately obvious that the publication and reading of newspapers and periodicals is much higher in industrialized nations than in the developing world. There are three factors that have led to this disparity: literacy, economics and distribution problems. Particularly in the developing world, newspapers and periodicals are mainly distributed in major cities, while rural populations rely much more on radio, and more recently television, as their main source of news and entertainment. (See page 75 for the distribution of radios and televisions.) Each copy of a newspaper has to be distributed to the customer, who has to purchase it, while radio and television provide instant access for a once only purchase of the equipment.

A recent development in the newspaper industry is the electronic publishing of newspapers on the World Wide Web. This makes them accessible via the Internet, and also allows people to search through archives of previously published material.

Radios, Televisions and Video Recorders per 100 Population

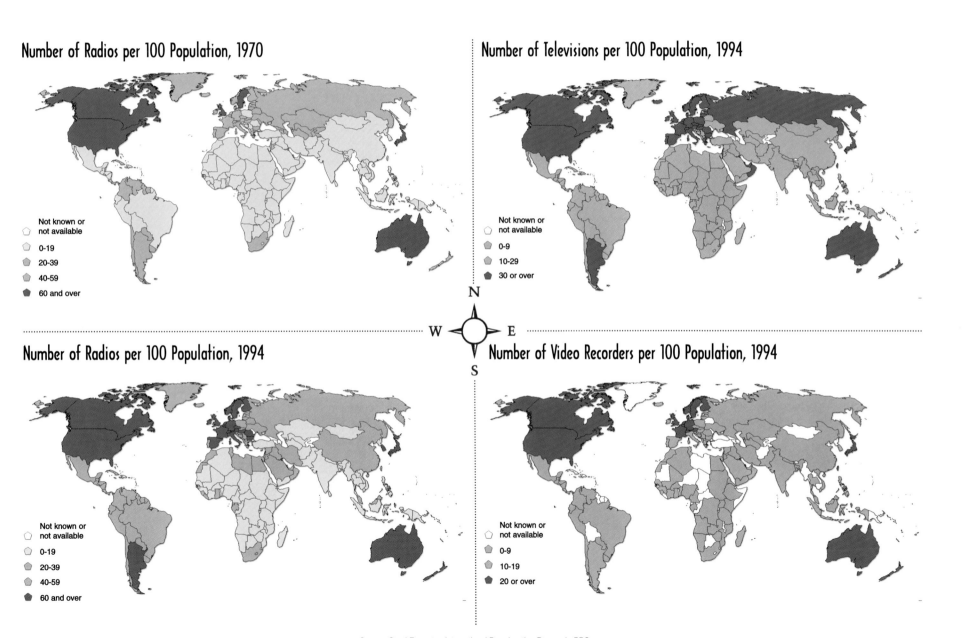

Number of Radios per 100 Population, 1970

Not known or not available
0-19
20-39
40-59
60 and over

Number of Televisions per 100 Population, 1994

Not known or not available
0-9
10-29
30 or over

Number of Radios per 100 Population, 1994

Not known or not available
0-19
20-39
40-59
60 and over

Number of Video Recorders per 100 Population, 1994

Not known or not available
0-9
10-19
20 or over

N
W E
S

Source: Carol Forrester, International Broadcasting Research, BBC

Population Growth by Continent, 1960-2010

For the purposes of these graphs, to show the true trends over the period, the former USSR states, now part of Asia, have been assumed to continue to remain in Europe.

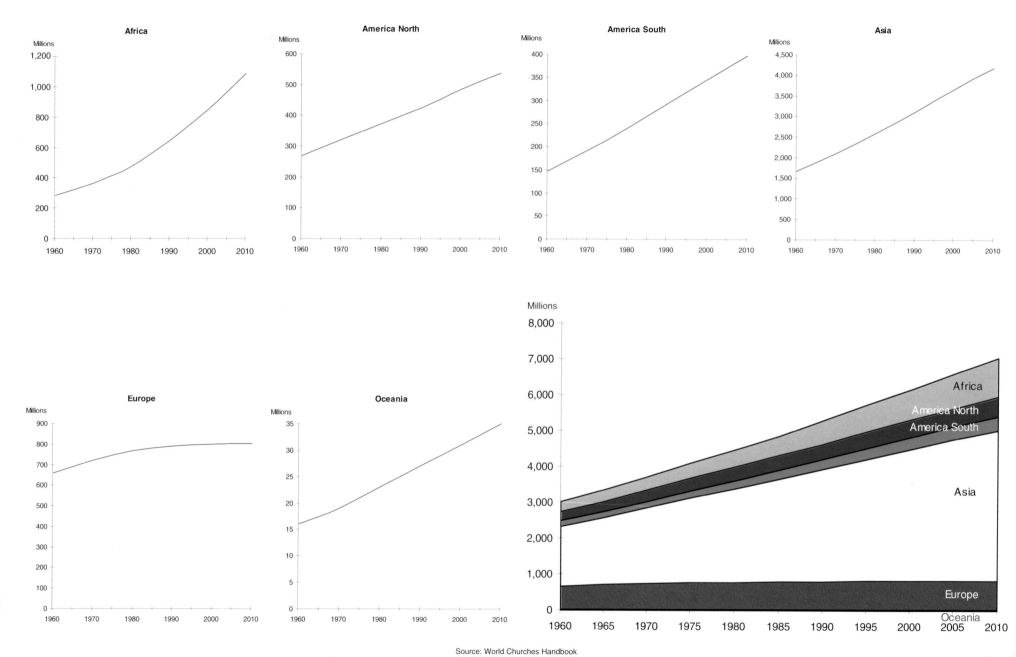

Africa

Millions

America North

Millions

America South

Millions

Asia

Millions

Europe

Millions

Oceania

Millions

Millions

Africa

America North

America South

Asia

Europe

Oceania

Source: World Churches Handbook

Africa

Africa

Political Map

Tunisia
Morocco
Algeria
Libya
Egypt
Western Sahara
Mauritania
Mali
Niger
Chad
Eritrea
Senegal
Sudan
Djibouti
Gm
Guinea Bissau
Guinea
BF
Benin
Nigeria
Ethiopia
Sierra Leone
CD
Gh
Tg
Central African Republic
Liberia
Cameroon
Somalia
Equatorial Guinea
Congo
Uganda
Kenya
Gabon
Democratic Republic of Congo
Rw
Bu
Tanzania
Angola
Zambia
Malawi
Mozambique
Zimbabwe
Namibia
Madagascar
Botswana
Swaziland
Lesotho
South Africa

Algeria
Angola
Benin
Botswana
Burkina Faso (BF)
Burundi (Bu)
Cameroon
Central African Republic
Chad
Congo
Cote d'Ivoire (CD)
Democratic Republic of Congo
Djibouti
Egypt
Equatorial Guinea
Eritrea
Ethiopia

Gabon
Gambia (Gm)
Ghana (Gh)
Guinea
Guinea Bissau
Kenya
Lesotho
Liberia
Libya
Madagascar
Malawi
Mali
Mauritania
Morocco
Mozambique
Namibia
Niger

Nigeria
Rwanda (Rw)
Senegal
Sierra Leone
Somalia
South Africa
Sudan
Swaziland
Tanzania
Togo (Tg)
Tunisia
Uganda
Western Sahara
Zambia
Zimbabwe

Trends in Africa

(numbers in brackets refer to page numbers of the maps)

Africa is a continent of contrasts from a Christian perspective. The denominational maps on pages 16-25 show the church is strong and growing south of the Sahara, but weak and declining to the north. Islam is strong in North Africa and growing rapidly (57) resulting in considerable restrictions to church growth there (32) and also in it being one of the least evangelized parts of the world (43).

All Christian denominations are strong somewhere in sub-Saharan Africa, but there are distinctive features worth noting. Indigenous churches are overwhelmingly an African phenomenon and are still growing rapidly, as are Pentecostal churches. These churches have comparatively small congregations (30), which accounts for the massive increase in the number of churches in Africa between 1960 and 2010 (31). The colonial history of the continent is revealed in the distribution of the institutional denominations (Anglican in the east and south, Nigeria, Ghana, and also Sudan; Catholic in Angola and other former French, Belgian and Portuguese colonies; Lutheran, Methodist and Presbyterian in South Africa). The ancient churches are also present in Africa, with the Orthodox in Egypt and Ethiopia. With strong and growing churches, there has also been strong growth of Evangelicals (36). Central, east and southern Africa have experienced Protestant revival a number of times in the past century or so (33).

Africa has traditionally been regarded as receiving missionaries, who began their work on the coasts and gradually spread inland (40). However, the continent is now sending some (41), which may account for the new parachurch agencies which are springing up (42). There are some training institutions, both Catholic and Protestant, but far fewer than in South America (44). West Africa is the largest land area in the world which still needs significant work on Bible translation (45) and most of the languages needing Christian radio broadcasts are in Africa (47).

The comparative maps show this continent to be young and with a growing population (64), poor (70), and still predominantly rural (65). Education and medical care have improved considerably but overall are still below the rest of the world (67-72). AIDS is a particular problem with more HIV+ women and children than elsewhere (73). It is hardly surprising that all the Relief and Development agencies work in Africa (48, 49). The Human Development Index map (66) sums it up: Africa may be rich spiritually, but it is poor economically and socially.

Population per Head per Church, 1995

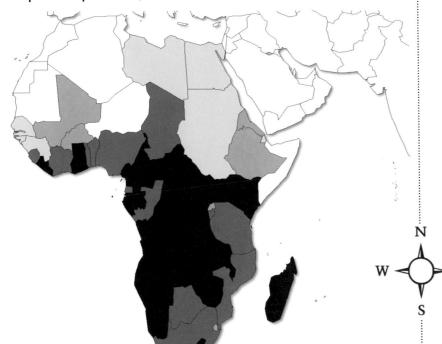

- ⬠ 50,000 and over
- ⬠ 10,000 - 49,999
- ⬠ 2,000 - 9,999
- ⬠ 1,000 - 1,999
- ⬠ Under 1,000

Source: World Christian Encyclopedia

Strongest Religion

- ⬠ Buddhism
- ⬠ Christianity
- ⬠ Hinduism
- ⬠ Islam
- ⬠ Judaism
- ⬠ Traditional/Oriental

Source: World Churches Handbook

N
W ✦ E
S

Church Community by Denomination and Percentages of Population

- ROMAN CATHOLIC
- PROTESTANT NON-INSTITUTIONAL
- PROTESTANT INSTITUTIONAL
- ORTHODOX

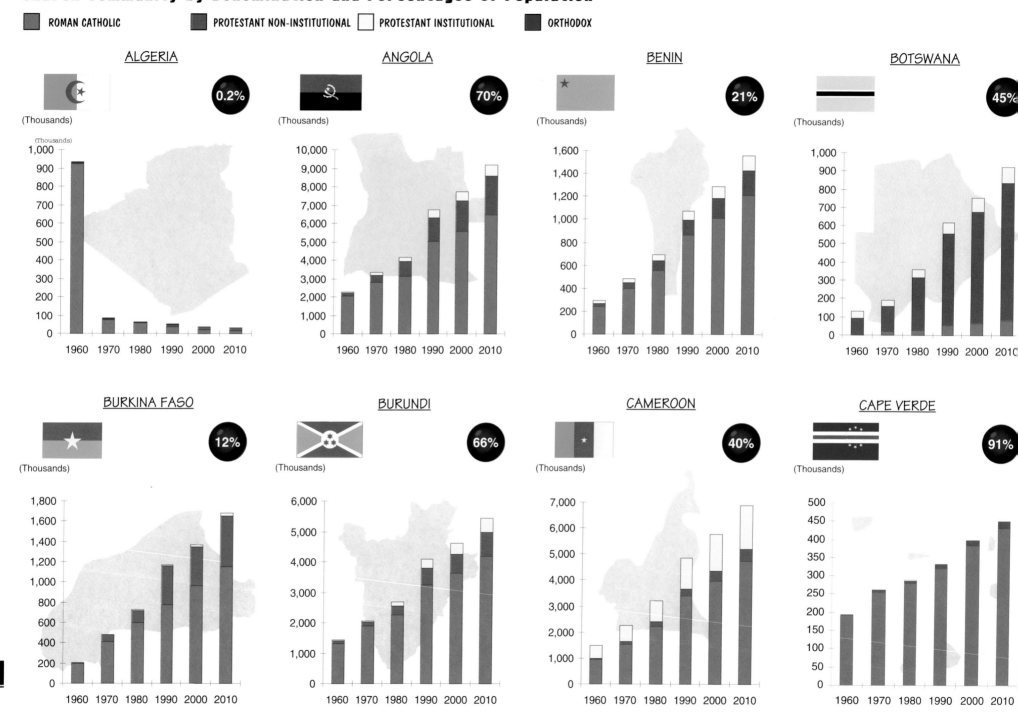

ALGERIA
0.2%
(Thousands)

(Thousands)

ANGOLA
70%
(Thousands)

BENIN
21%
(Thousands)

BOTSWANA
45%
(Thousands)

BURKINA FASO
12%
(Thousands)

BURUNDI
66%
(Thousands)

CAMEROON
40%
(Thousands)

CAPE VERDE
91%
(Thousands)

Church Community by Denomination and Percentage of Population

ROMAN CATHOLIC   PROTESTANT NON-INSTITUTIONAL   PROTESTANT INSTITUTIONAL   ORTHODOX

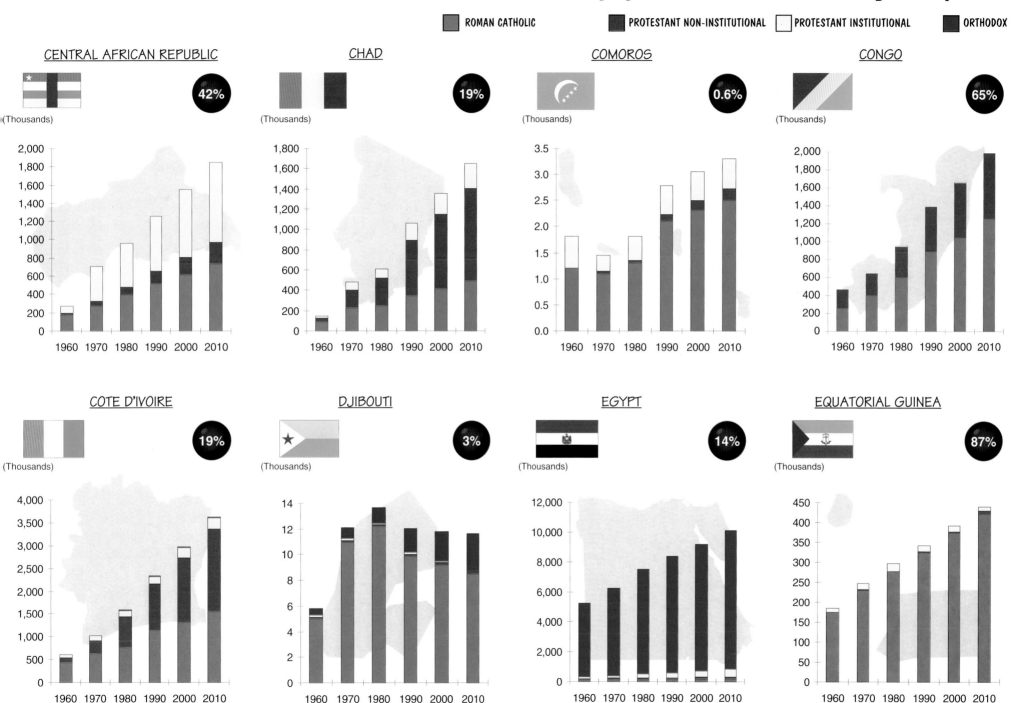

CENTRAL AFRICAN REPUBLIC
42%
(Thousands)

CHAD
19%
(Thousands)

COMOROS
0.6%
(Thousands)

CONGO
65%
(Thousands)

COTE D'IVOIRE
19%
(Thousands)

DJIBOUTI
3%
(Thousands)

EGYPT
14%
(Thousands)

EQUATORIAL GUINEA
87%
(Thousands)

81

Church Community by Denomination and Percentage of Population

■ ROMAN CATHOLIC　　　■ PROTESTANT NON-INSTITUTIONAL　□ PROTESTANT INSTITUTIONAL　■ ORTHODOX

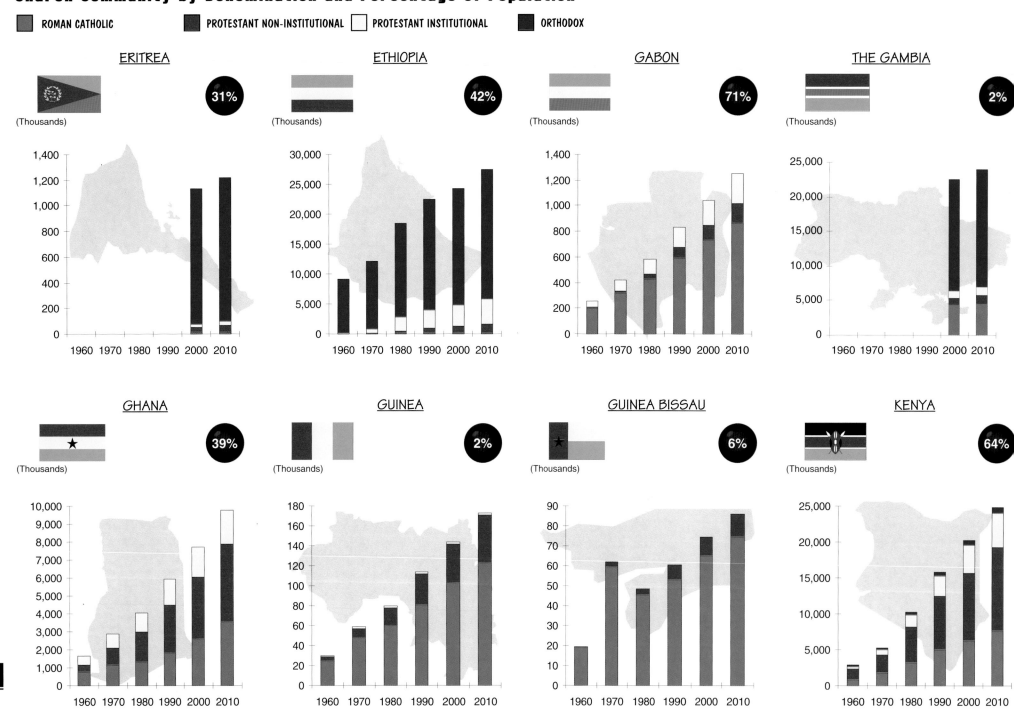

ERITREA
(Thousands) — 31%

ETHIOPIA
(Thousands) — 42%

GABON
(Thousands) — 71%

THE GAMBIA
(Thousands) — 2%

GHANA
(Thousands) — 39%

GUINEA
(Thousands) — 2%

GUINEA BISSAU
(Thousands) — 6%

KENYA
(Thousands) — 64%

82

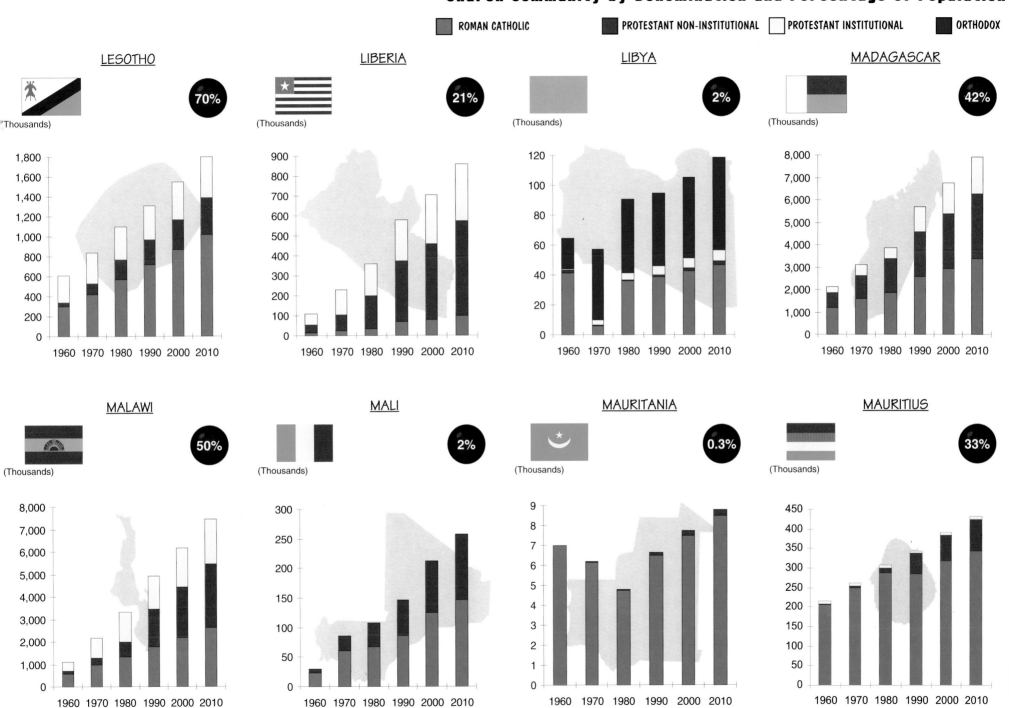

Church Community by Denomination and Percentage of Population

■ ROMAN CATHOLIC   ■ PROTESTANT NON-INSTITUTIONAL   ☐ PROTESTANT INSTITUTIONAL   ■ ORTHODOX

LESOTHO
70%
(Thousands)

LIBERIA
21%
(Thousands)

LIBYA
2%
(Thousands)

MADAGASCAR
42%
(Thousands)

MALAWI
50%
(Thousands)

MALI
2%
(Thousands)

MAURITANIA
0.3%
(Thousands)

MAURITIUS
33%
(Thousands)

Church Community by Denomination and Percentage of Population

- ROMAN CATHOLIC
- PROTESTANT NON-INSTITUTIONAL
- PROTESTANT INSTITUTIONAL
- ORTHODOX

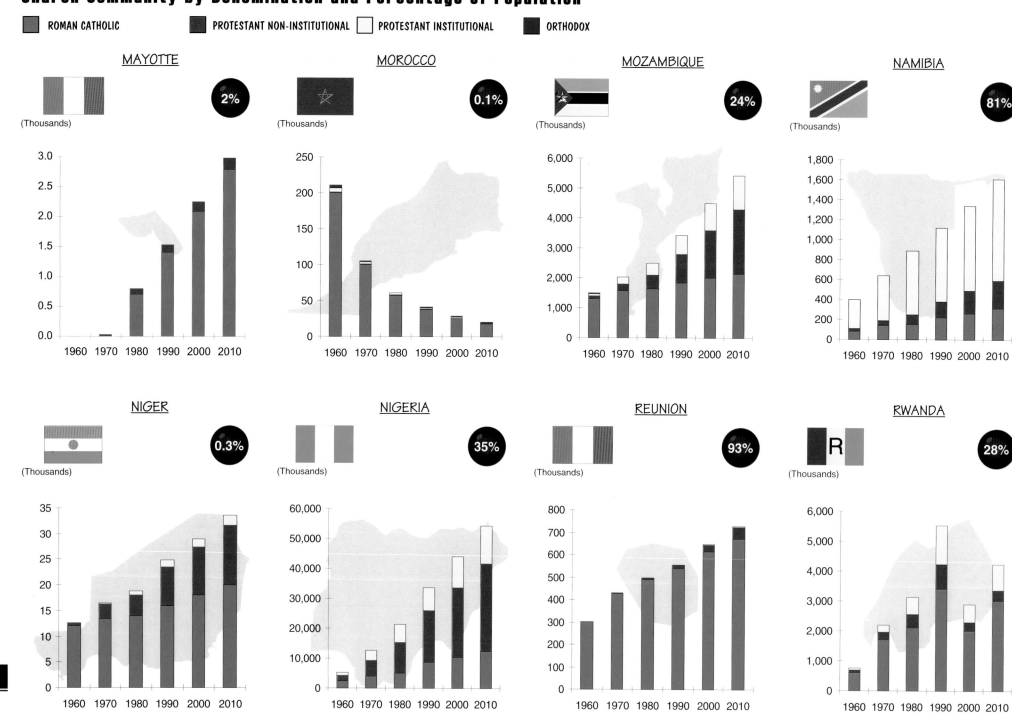

MAYOTTE
2%
(Thousands)

MOROCCO
0.1%
(Thousands)

MOZAMBIQUE
24%
(Thousands)

NAMIBIA
81%
(Thousands)

NIGER
0.3%
(Thousands)

NIGERIA
35%
(Thousands)

REUNION
93%
(Thousands)

RWANDA
28%
(Thousands)

Church Community by Denomination and Percentage of Population

ROMAN CATHOLIC PROTESTANT NON-INSTITUTIONAL PROTESTANT INSTITUTIONAL ORTHODOX

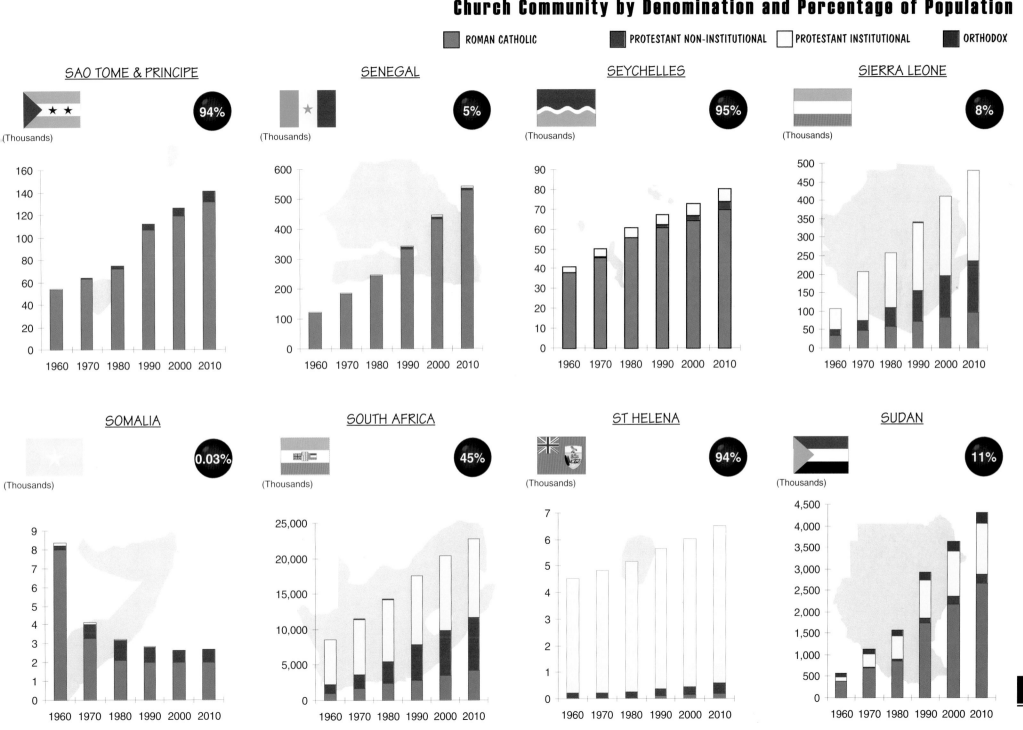

SAO TOME & PRINCIPE — 94% (Thousands)

SENEGAL — 5% (Thousands)

SEYCHELLES — 95% (Thousands)

SIERRA LEONE — 8% (Thousands)

SOMALIA — 0.03% (Thousands)

SOUTH AFRICA — 45% (Thousands)

ST HELENA — 94% (Thousands)

SUDAN — 11% (Thousands)

85

Church Community by Denomination and Percentage of Population

- ROMAN CATHOLIC
- PROTESTANT NON-INSTITUTIONAL
- PROTESTANT INSTITUTIONAL
- ORTHODOX

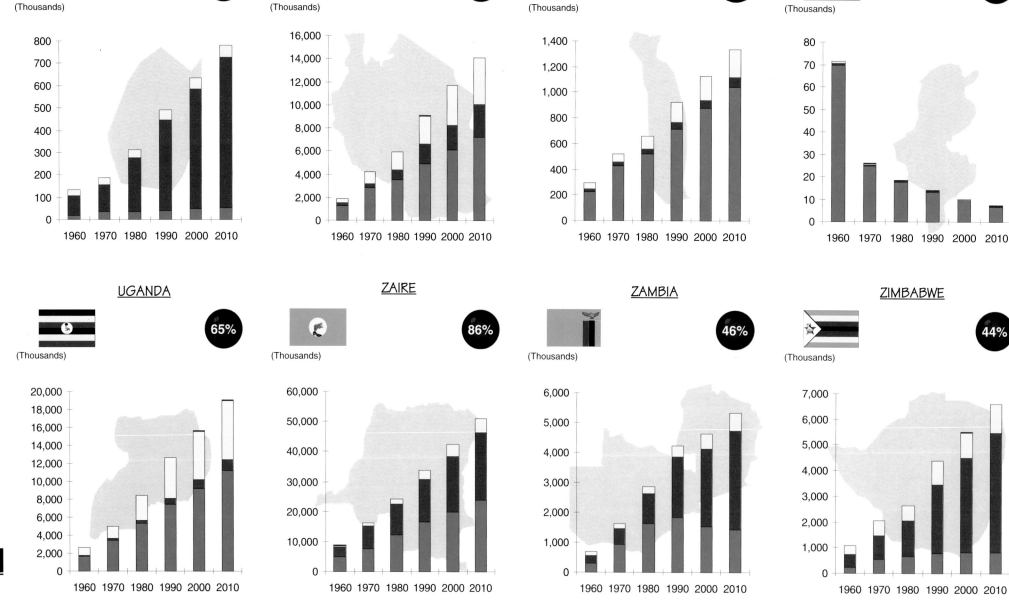

SWAZILAND 66% (Thousands)

TANZANIA 33% (Thousands)

TOGO 25% (Thousands)

TUNISIA 0.1% (Thousands)

UGANDA 65% (Thousands)

ZAIRE 86% (Thousands)

ZAMBIA 46% (Thousands)

ZIMBABWE 44% (Thousands)

NORTH
America

North America

Political Map

Bahamas	El Salvador	Nicaragua
Belize (Bz)	Greenland	Panama
Bermuda	Guatemala	Puerto Rico (PR)
Canada	Haiti	United States
Costa Rica	Honduras (Hn)	
Cuba	Jamaica	
Dominican Republic	Mexico	

Trends in North America

(numbers in brackets refer to page numbers of the maps)

The USA is one of the strongest Protestant churchgoing nations in the world. The denominational maps on pages 16-25 show the USA with strengths in almost every denominational grouping, with both decline (Anglican, Lutheran, Methodist and Other Churches) and some growth (notably among Pentecostals). Baptists stand out as being much stronger in the USA than anywhere else in the world, and there is also great strength of Evangelicals (36). There has been a Protestant revival at least every half century since the early 18th century (33). Non-Trinitarians are strong. The USA sends many missionaries, both Catholic and Protestant (41), but it also receives many, perhaps because it has quite a number of Least Evangelized Peoples (43). The USA is the only major missionary sending country in the top band for both sending and receiving Catholic and Protestant missionaries (40).

The USA's churchgoing characteristics are not necessarily shared by others in this continent: Canada, Central America and the Caribbean. Canada and Mexico both have growing Indigenous Churches, and Canada is one of the strongest in the world for Other Churches. Central America is predominantly Catholic while the Caribbean is a mix, mainly of Catholic and Baptist. There is less freedom of religion in Mexico and Cuba (32) than elsewhere in North America. There are proportionately slightly fewer Evangelicals in Canada than the USA, while in parts of the Caribbean and Central America the proportion has grown significantly since 1960 (36).

In the continent as a whole, the number of churches is expected to have almost doubled in the 50 years from 1960 to 2010 (31). Its share of the world's parachurch agencies dropped dramatically between 1975 and 1995 and is now under 1/3, although this is still a slight increase in actual numbers. It also has 1/3 of the world's wealth (42). There are many training institutions, though the proportion of Catholic seminaries has declined in North America and risen in South America (44). A few countries in Central America still have scope for further Bible translation (45).

The comparative maps show this continent, to be mostly rich (70), urbanized (65) and well educated (68, 69). There are fewer young people than much of the rest of the world (64). Medically it's a good place to live (67, 71, 72), though with many cases of AIDS (73). People who live there can find out all about it by reading one of the many newspapers (74), listening to the radio, or watching TV (75)!

Population per Head per Church, 1995

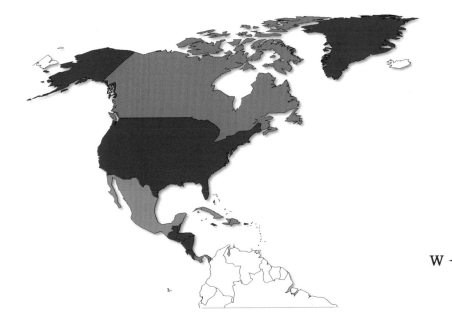

- 2,000 - 9,999
- 1,000 - 1,999
- Under 1,000

Source: World Churches Handbook

Strongest Religion

N
W · E
S

- Buddhism
- Christianity
- Hinduism
- Islam
- Judaism
- Traditional/Oriental

Source: World Christian Encyclopedia

Church Community by Denomination and Percentage of Population

- ROMAN CATHOLIC
- PROTESTANT NON-INSTITUTIONAL
- PROTESTANT INSTITUTIONAL
- ORTHODOX

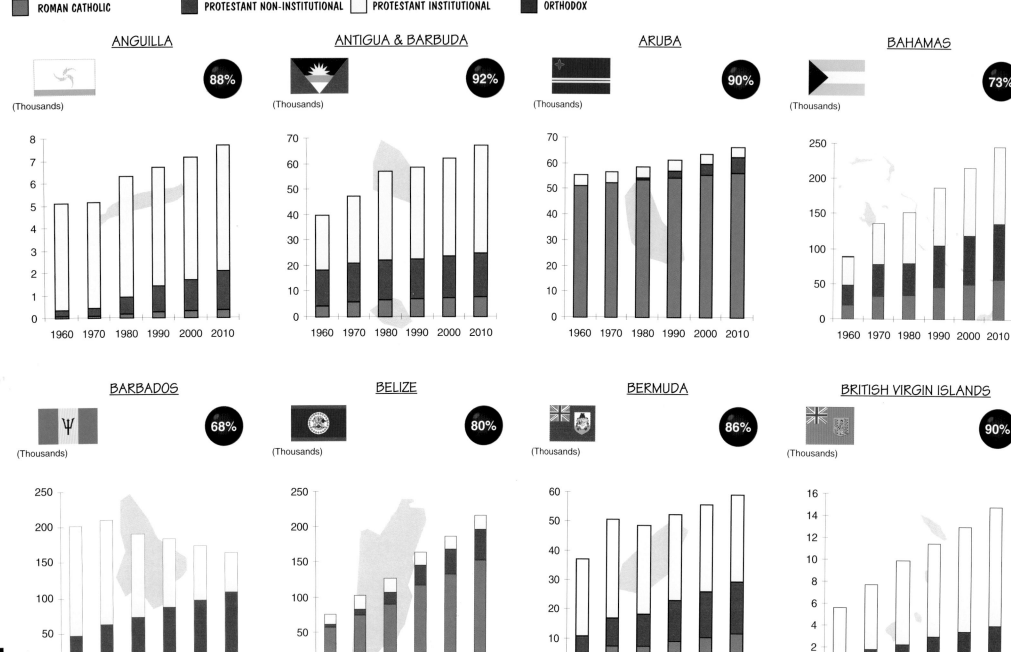

ANGUILLA — 88% (Thousands)

ANTIGUA & BARBUDA — 92% (Thousands)

ARUBA — 90% (Thousands)

BAHAMAS — 73% (Thousands)

BARBADOS — 68% (Thousands)

BELIZE — 80% (Thousands)

BERMUDA — 86% (Thousands)

BRITISH VIRGIN ISLANDS — 90% (Thousands)

Population per Head per Church, 1995

○ 2,000 - 9,999
◍ 1,000 - 1,999
● Under 1,000

Source: World Churches Handbook

Strongest Religion

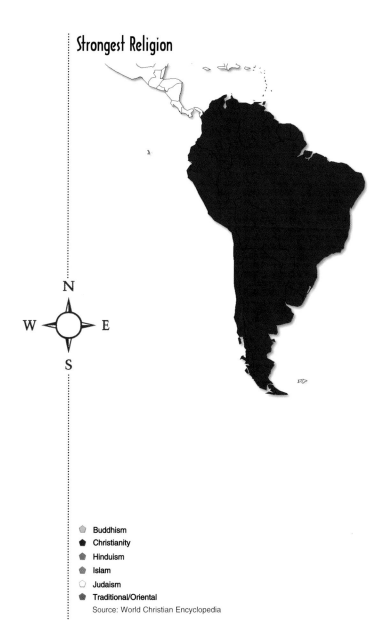

N
W ⊕ E
S

◍ Buddhism
● Christianity
◍ Hinduism
◍ Islam
○ Judaism
◍ Traditional/Oriental

Source: World Christian Encyclopedia

Church Community by Denomination and Percentage of Population

- ■ ROMAN CATHOLIC
- ■ PROTESTANT NON-INSTITUTIONAL
- □ PROTESTANT INSTITUTIONAL
- ■ ORTHODOX

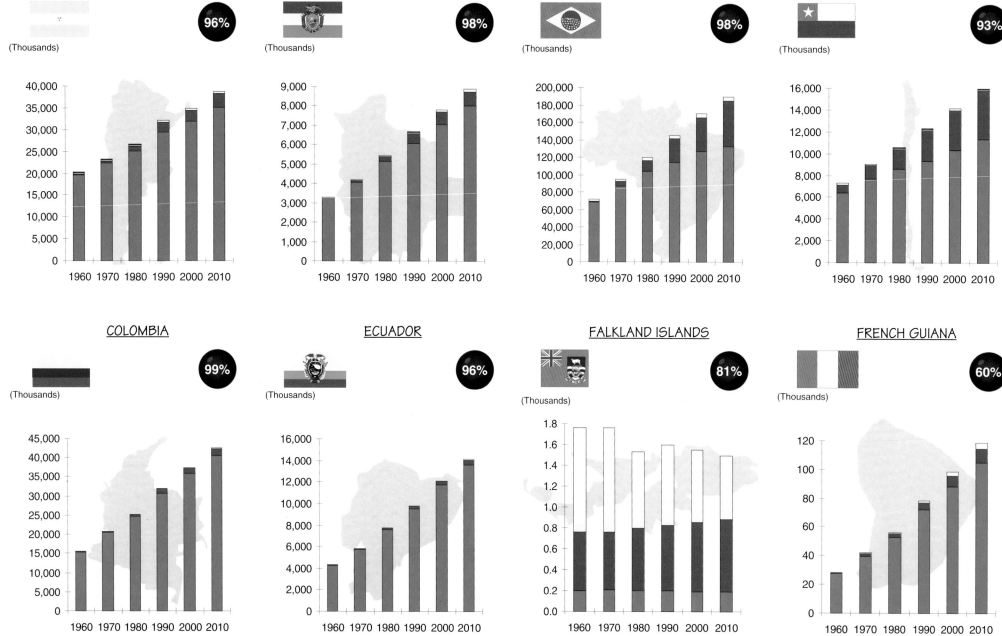

ARGENTINA — 96%
(Thousands)

BOLIVIA — 98%
(Thousands)

BRAZIL — 98%
(Thousands)

CHILE — 93%
(Thousands)

COLOMBIA — 99%
(Thousands)

ECUADOR — 96%
(Thousands)

FALKLAND ISLANDS — 81%
(Thousands)

FRENCH GUIANA — 60%
(Thousands)

98

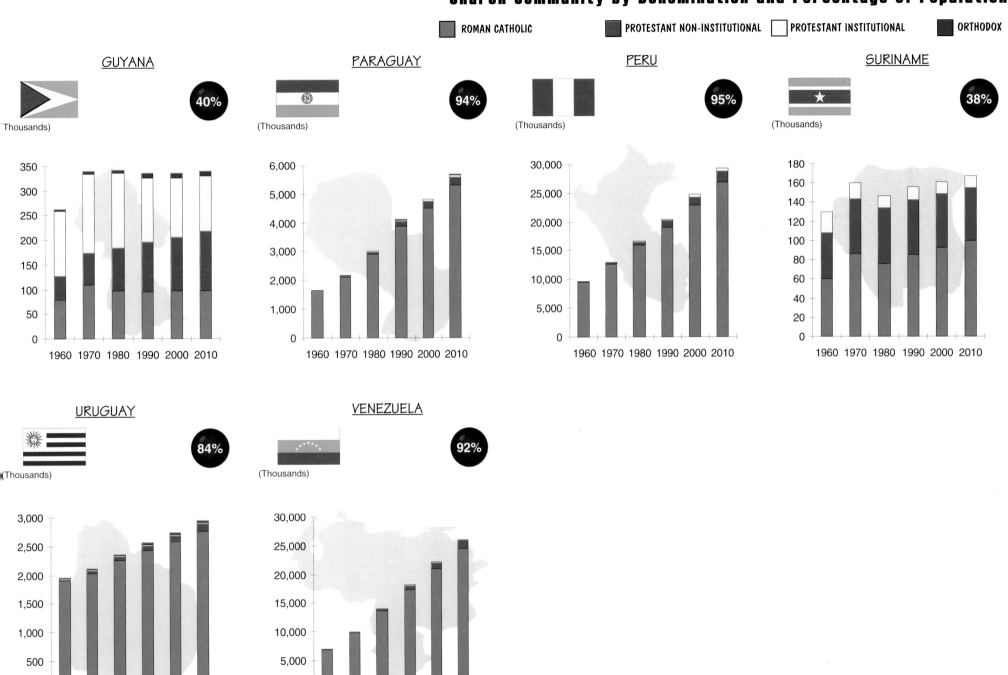

Church Community by Denomination and Percentage of Population

■ ROMAN CATHOLIC ■ PROTESTANT NON-INSTITUTIONAL □ PROTESTANT INSTITUTIONAL ■ ORTHODOX

GUYANA
40%
(Thousands)

PARAGUAY
94%
(Thousands)

PERU
95%
(Thousands)

SURINAME
38%
(Thousands)

URUGUAY
84%
(Thousands)

VENEZUELA
92%
(Thousands)

Christian Community by Denominational Groups

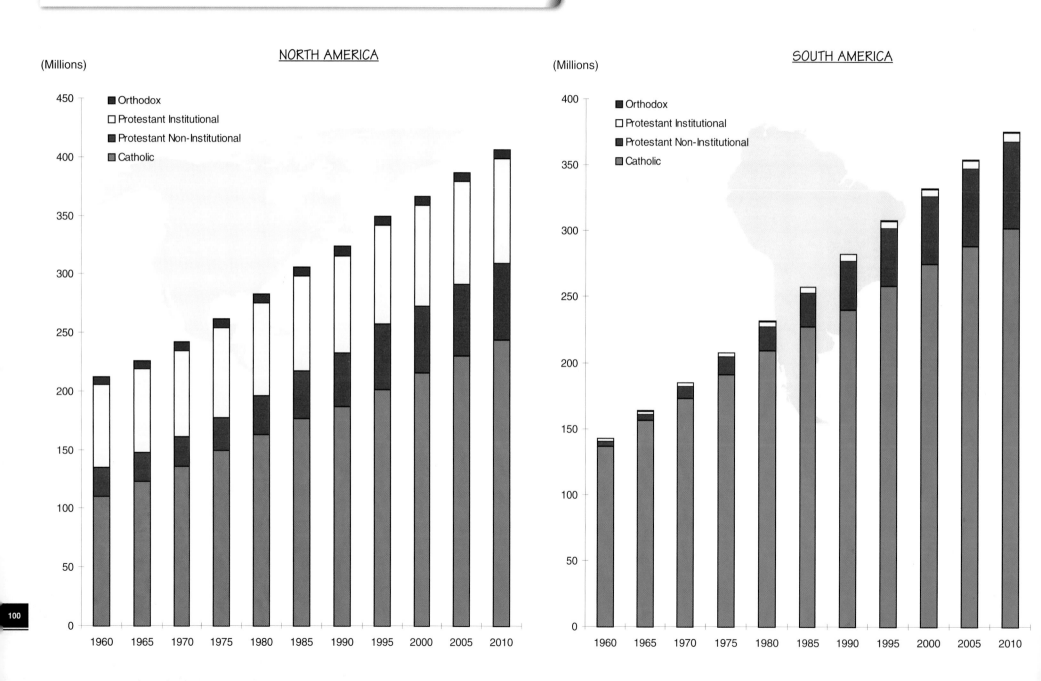

Asia

Asia

Political Map

Afghanistan
Armenia (Ar)
Azerbaijan (Az)
Bahrain (Bh)
Bangladesh
Bhutan (Bt)
Brunei
Cambodia (Cm)
China
Georgia
Hong Kong
India
Indonesia
Iran
Iraq
Israel

Japan
Jordan
Kazakhstan
Korea Dem. People's Rep. (KDR)
Korea, Republic of (KR)
Kuwait
Kyrgyzstan
Laos
Lebanon (Lb)
Malaysia
Mongolia
Myanmar
Nepal
Oman
Pakistan
Philippines

Qatar (Qt)
Saudi Arabia
Singapore
Sri Lanka
Syria
Taiwan
Tajikistan
Thailand
Turkey
Turkmenistan
United Arab Emirates
Uzbekistan
Vietnam
Yemen

Trends in Asia

(numbers in brackets refer to page numbers of the maps)

Asia covers a massive area of the world from the eastern Mediterranean to the Pacific, and there are therefore wide variations in its church life. The church is not strong as a percentage of the population (except in the Philippines), but while it is declining in the west of the area it is growing in the east (14). The denominational maps on pages 16-25 show that no one church dominates across the whole region, but most are strong in at least one country (Baptist - Korea, Myanmar; Catholic - Philippines; Indigenous - China; Lutheran - Indonesia; Methodist - Indonesia, Korea, Malaysia, Myanmar; Orthodox - the Middle East; Pentecostal - Indonesia; Presbyterian - Korea; Other Churches - China). These maps show percentage of population rather than actual numbers, which is why India's numerically large Christian community (105) looks less strong. Across Asia almost all denominations are growing in some countries and declining in others. Asia has seen the largest increase of any continent in the number of churches (31). As in South America, the unexpected "step" in the rate of increase between 1980 and 1990 (13) is evident in many countries in this region and can be seen in the graphs in this section.

Asia is the heartland of all the other major world religions (55-59). This considerably restricts church growth in most of the region (32) and means that the percentage of Least Evangelized Peoples is very high (43). A Protestant revival has occurred in most countries at some time (33). Missionary activity, both Catholic and Protestant started on the coasts and spread inland (40), but is now mainly confined to south and southeast Asia (41). Korea sends many Protestant missionaries and India many Catholics. There is a small but growing number of parachurch agencies (42) and many training institutions— more Protestant ones than in any other continent (44). Most of the region still needs some Bible translation (45) and Christian radio broadcasts (47).

The comparative maps show this continent to be young, with the highest natural population increase in the Muslim countries to the west (64). West Asia is rapidly urbanizing, the east is already urbanized (65), with seven of the "largest cities" (more than any other area in the world). The Human Development Index (66) is high at both the eastern and western ends of the continent, but much lower in between, and this is reflected in the educational, medical and other maps in this section (67-75). The economic prominence of the oil economies of the Gulf and the "Asian Tigers" in the east, which have the most rapidly growing economies in the world, is very obvious (70). Asia is definitely the continent with the most extremes of them all.

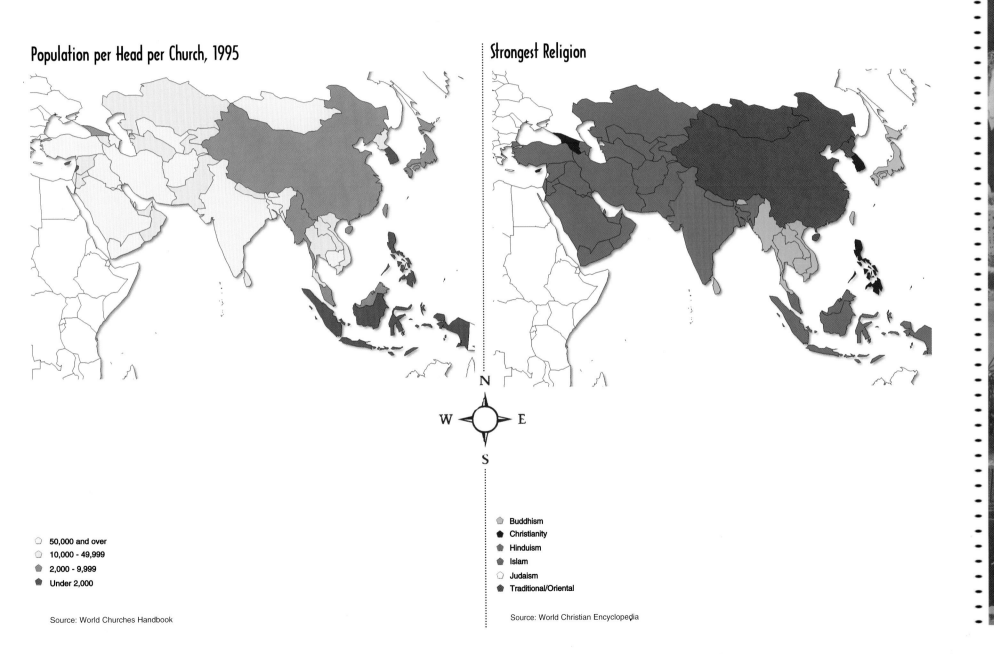

Population per Head per Church, 1995

- ⬠ 50,000 and over
- ⬠ 10,000 - 49,999
- ⬠ 2,000 - 9,999
- ⬠ Under 2,000

Source: World Churches Handbook

Strongest Religion

- ⬠ Buddhism
- ⬠ Christianity
- ⬠ Hinduism
- ⬠ Islam
- ⬠ Judaism
- ⬠ Traditional/Oriental

Source: World Christian Encyclopedia

Church Community by Denomination and Percentage of Population

■ ROMAN CATHOLIC   ■ PROTESTANT NON-INSTITUTIONAL   □ PROTESTANT INSTITUTIONAL   ■ ORTHODOX

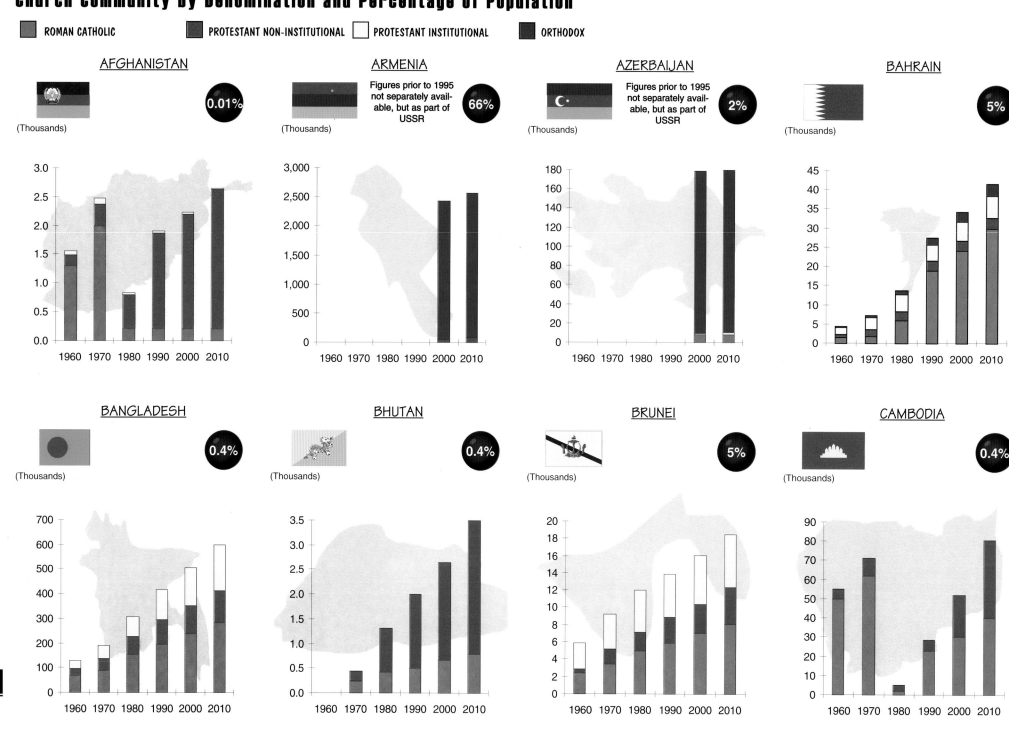

AFGHANISTAN

(Thousands)

0.01%

ARMENIA

Figures prior to 1995 not separately available, but as part of USSR

(Thousands)

66%

AZERBAIJAN

Figures prior to 1995 not separately available, but as part of USSR

(Thousands)

2%

BAHRAIN

(Thousands)

5%

BANGLADESH

(Thousands)

0.4%

BHUTAN

(Thousands)

0.4%

BRUNEI

(Thousands)

5%

CAMBODIA

(Thousands)

0.4%

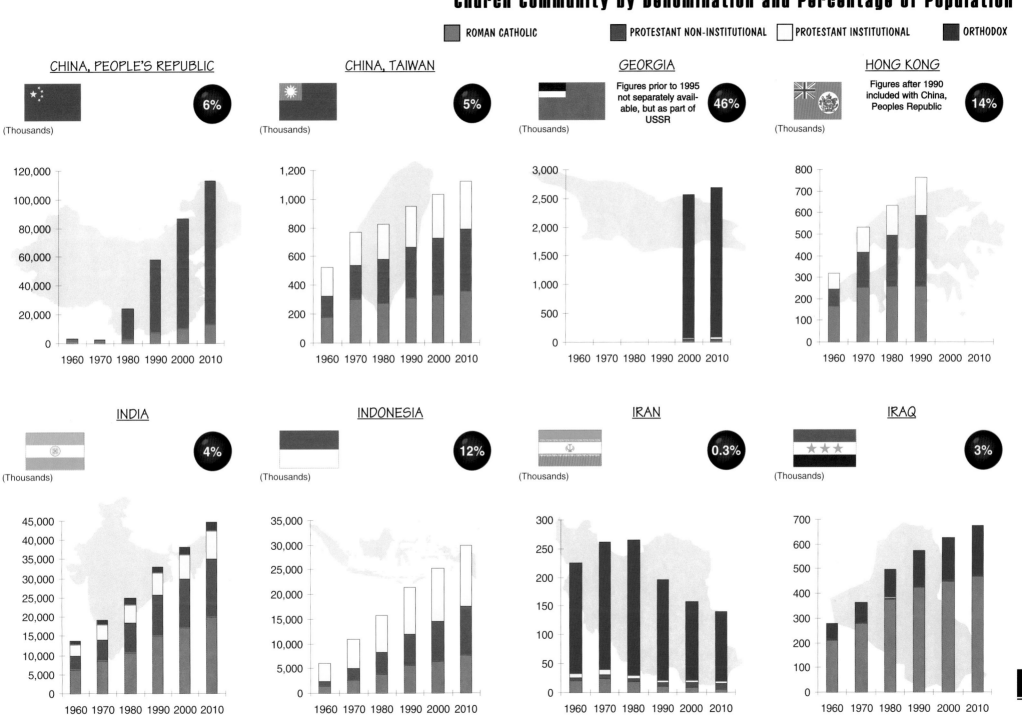

Church Community by Denomination and Percentage of Population

ROMAN CATHOLIC   PROTESTANT NON-INSTITUTIONAL   PROTESTANT INSTITUTIONAL   ORTHODOX

CHINA, PEOPLE'S REPUBLIC
6%
(Thousands)

CHINA, TAIWAN
5%
(Thousands)

GEORGIA
Figures prior to 1995 not separately available, but as part of USSR
46%
(Thousands)

HONG KONG
Figures after 1990 included with China, Peoples Republic
14%
(Thousands)

INDIA
4%
(Thousands)

INDONESIA
12%
(Thousands)

IRAN
0.3%
(Thousands)

IRAQ
3%
(Thousands)

105

Church Community by Denomination and Percentage of Population

- ■ ROMAN CATHOLIC
- ■ PROTESTANT NON-INSTITUTIONAL
- □ PROTESTANT INSTITUTIONAL
- ■ ORTHODOX

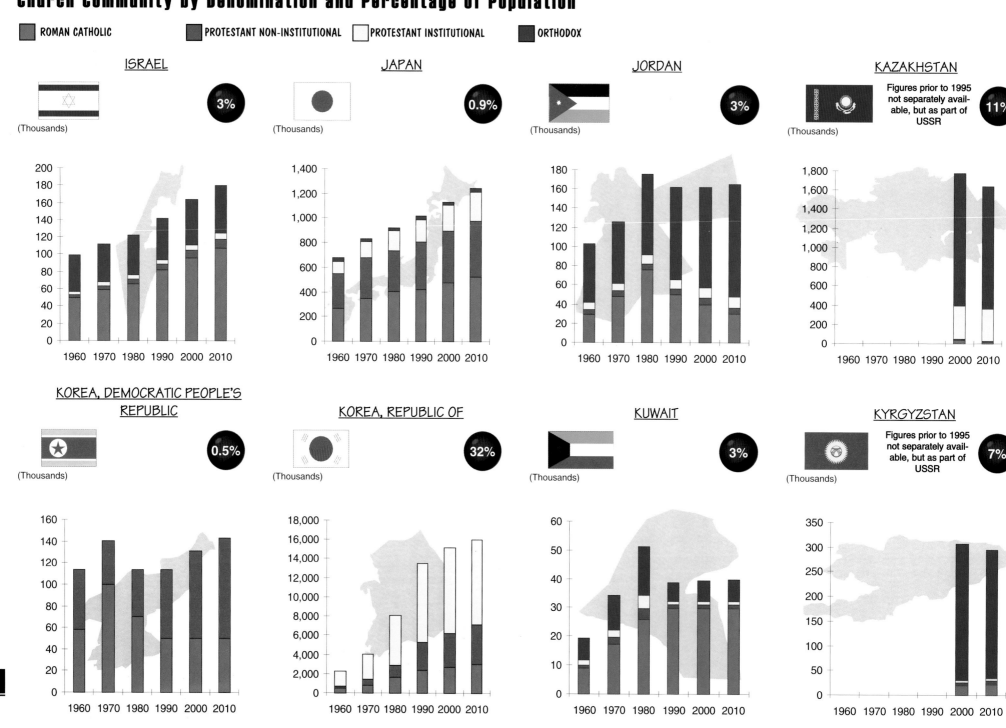

ISRAEL
(Thousands)
3%

JAPAN
(Thousands)
0.9%

JORDAN
(Thousands)
3%

KAZAKHSTAN
Figures prior to 1995 not separately available, but as part of USSR
(Thousands)
11%

KOREA, DEMOCRATIC PEOPLE'S REPUBLIC
(Thousands)
0.5%

KOREA, REPUBLIC OF
(Thousands)
32%

KUWAIT
(Thousands)
3%

KYRGYZSTAN
Figures prior to 1995 not separately available, but as part of USSR
(Thousands)
7%

Church Community by Denomination and Percentage of Population

■ ROMAN CATHOLIC　　■ PROTESTANT NON-INSTITUTIONAL　　□ PROTESTANT INSTITUTIONAL　　■ ORTHODOX

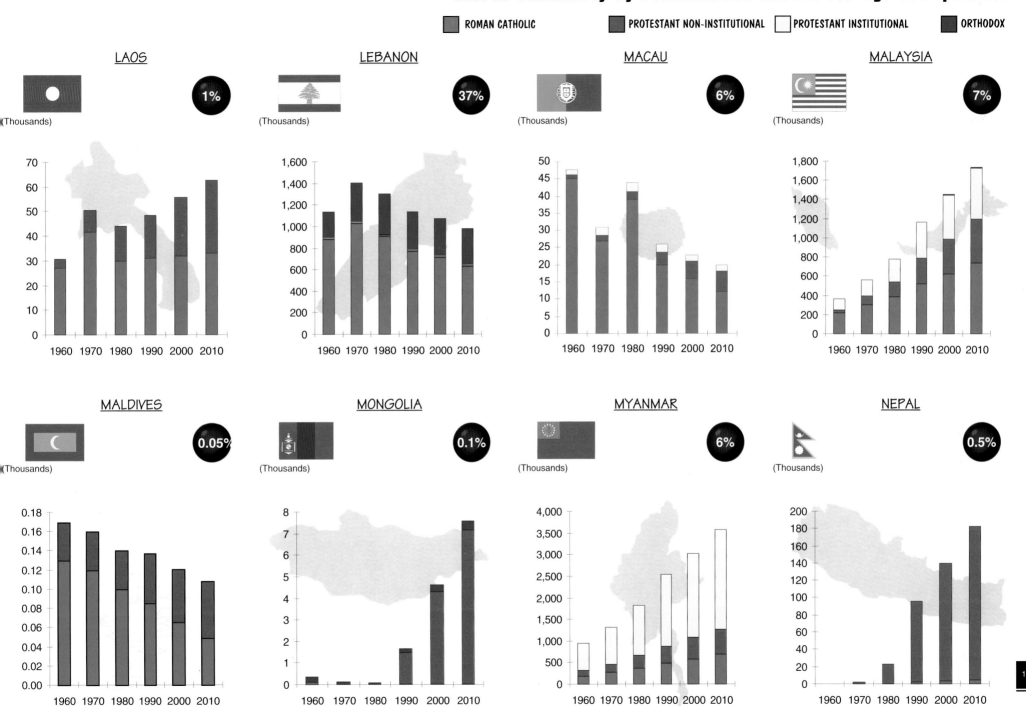

LAOS
(Thousands) — 1%

LEBANON
(Thousands) — 37%

MACAU
(Thousands) — 6%

MALAYSIA
(Thousands) — 7%

MALDIVES
(Thousands) — 0.05%

MONGOLIA
(Thousands) — 0.1%

MYANMAR
(Thousands) — 6%

NEPAL
(Thousands) — 0.5%

Church Community by Denomination and Percentage of Population

■ ROMAN CATHOLIC   ■ PROTESTANT NON-INSTITUTIONAL   □ PROTESTANT INSTITUTIONAL   ■ ORTHODOX

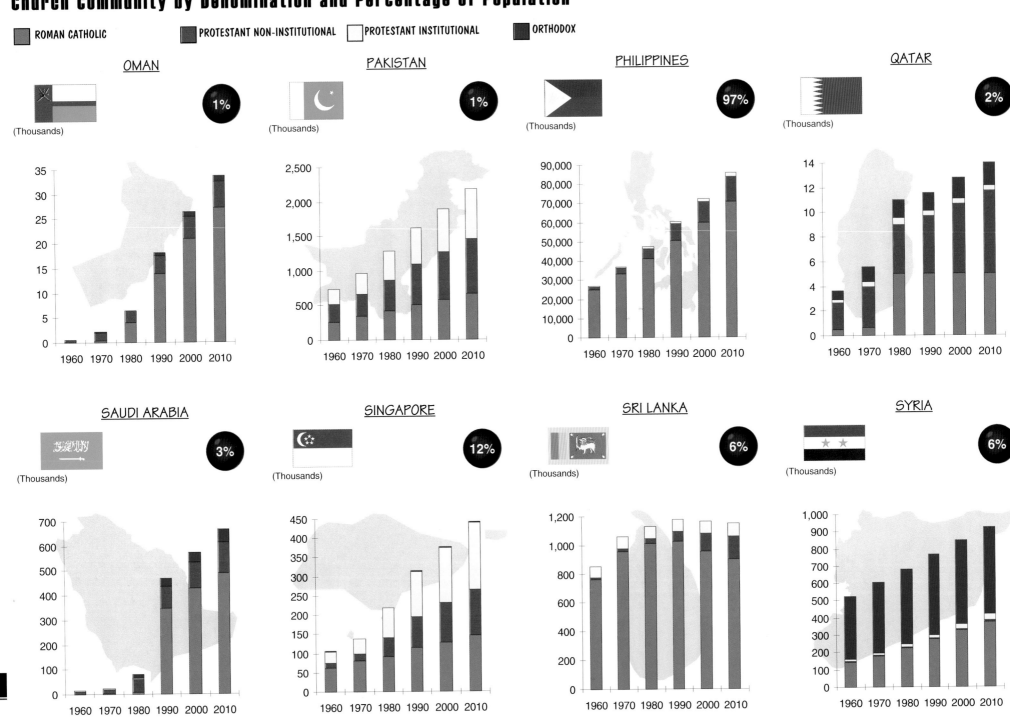

OMAN — 1%

PAKISTAN — 1%

PHILIPPINES — 97%

QATAR — 2%

SAUDI ARABIA — 3%

SINGAPORE — 12%

SRI LANKA — 6%

SYRIA — 6%

Church Community by Denomination and Percentage of Population

■ ROMAN CATHOLIC   ■ PROTESTANT NON-INSTITUTIONAL   ☐ PROTESTANT INSTITUTIONAL   ■ ORTHODOX

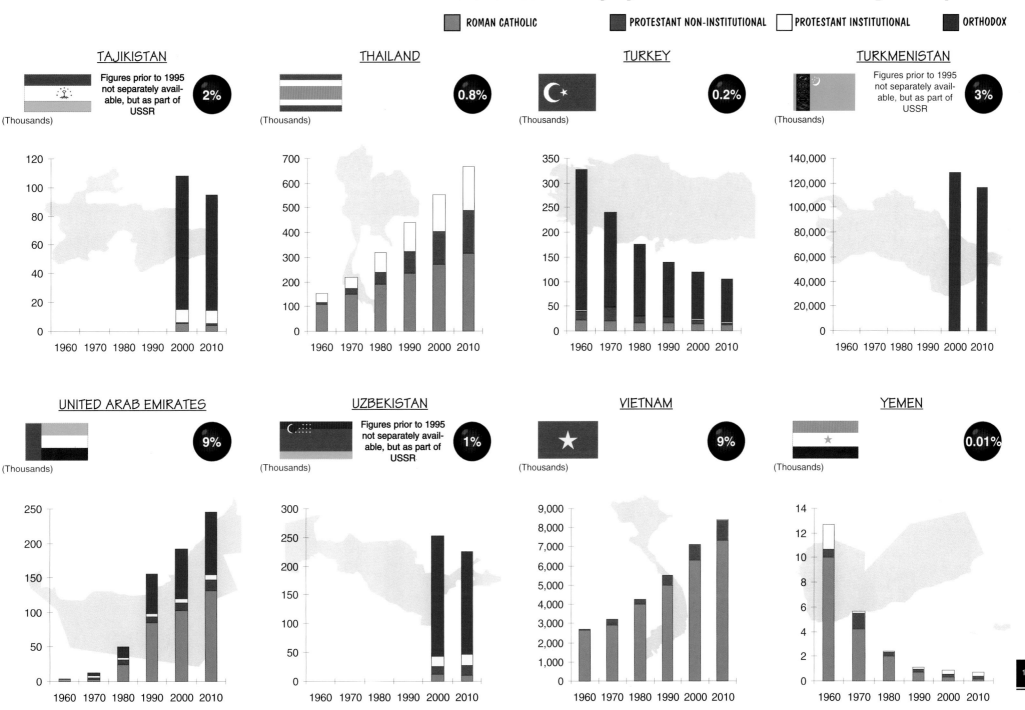

TAJIKISTAN
Figures prior to 1995 not separately available, but as part of USSR

2%

(Thousands)

THAILAND

0.8%

(Thousands)

TURKEY

0.2%

(Thousands)

TURKMENISTAN
Figures prior to 1995 not separately available, but as part of USSR

3%

(Thousands)

UNITED ARAB EMIRATES

9%

(Thousands)

UZBEKISTAN
Figures prior to 1995 not separately available, but as part of USSR

1%

(Thousands)

VIETNAM

9%

(Thousands)

YEMEN

0.01%

(Thousands)

109

Christian Community by Denominational Groups

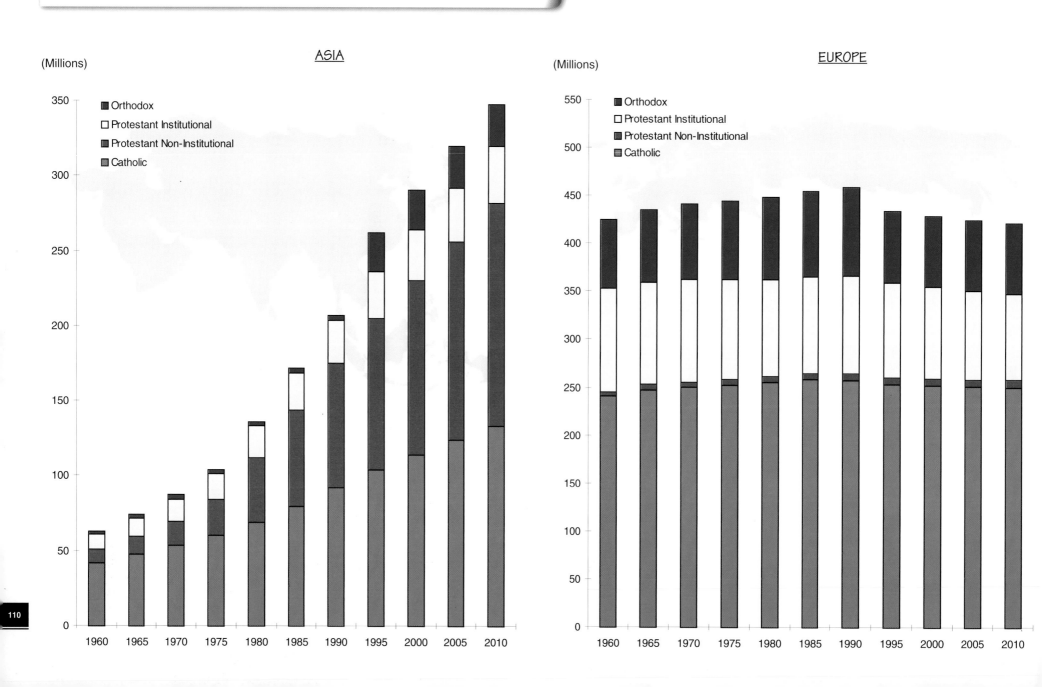

ASIA

(Millions)

- Orthodox
- Protestant Institutional
- Protestant Non-Institutional
- Catholic

EUROPE

(Millions)

- Orthodox
- Protestant Institutional
- Protestant Non-Institutional
- Catholic

Europe

Europe

Political Map

Albania (Al)
Austria
Belarus
Belgium (Bl)
Bulgaria
Cyprus
Czech Republic (Cz)
Denmark (Dk)
Estonia (Es)
Finland
France
Germany (Gr)

Greece
Hungary (Hn)
Iceland
Irish Republic
Italy
Latvia (Lt)
Lithuania (Li)
Luxembourg
Moldova, Republic of
Netherlands (NL)
Norway
Poland

Portugal
Romania
Russian Federation
Slovakia (Sv)
Spain
Sweden
Switzerland (Sw)
Ukraine
United Kingdom (UK)
Yugoslavia (Yu)

Trends in Europe

(numbers in brackets refer to page numbers of the maps)

Europe has been predominantly Christian for over a thousand years, and this is reflected in the strength of its Christian community (14) and the low number of Least Evangelized Peoples (43). However the denominational maps on pages 16-25 show that that strength is now in decline. There are no Indigenous Churches in Europe, but all the other groups except Other Churches are declining in at least one country on the continent (Anglican - Scandinavia, the UK; Baptist - Austria, the Balkans, Norway, Poland, the UK; Catholic - most of southern and western Europe; Lutheran - everywhere except Norway and Finland; Methodist - Austria, eastern Europe, France, Poland, Scandinavia, the UK; Orthodox - Belgium, eastern Europe, Finland; Pentecostal - the Balkans, Norway, Sweden; Presbyterian - the Balkans, Denmark, France, Irish Republic, Netherlands). This depressing picture is balanced by modest growth in one or more countries for each denomination. This pattern of varied growth and decline means the number of churches in Europe has remained virtually unchanged (31).

The break up of the former Soviet Union and the decline of Communism radically changed the restrictions on church growth in those areas (32). Most of the Protestant countries have experienced revival at some time (33), but since 1960 the proportion of Evangelicals has not changed significantly (36). Missionary activity originated in Europe (40) but it now receives as well as sends both Catholic and Protestant missionaries (41). Its virtually unchanged proportion of the world's parachurch agencies, 2 in 5, shows a large increase in their actual numbers (42). Europe's share of Catholic Seminaries has dropped considerably but is still more than double the proportion of Protestant Theological Institutions (44). Much of the former Soviet Union has scope for further Bible translation (45) and Christian radio broadcasts (47).

The comparative maps show this continent has a static or declining population with by far the highest percentage of people over 65 (64). The north is more urbanized than the south, but London is the only one of the "largest cities" on the continent (65). All except Romania are in the top band of the Human Development Index (66). In eastern and western Europe most of the factors which make up the index have improved from good to excellent in the second half of the 20th century. Unfortunately there are few comparative figures for the former Soviet Union. In short, Europe is rich, well educated and well provided for medically, but both its population and its churches have lost their youthful vigor!

Population per Head per Church, 1995

N

W ◆ E

S

- ○ 10,000 - 49,999
- ◌ 2,000 - 9,999
- ◉ 1,000 - 1,999
- ● Under 1,000

Source: World Churches Handbook

Strongest Religion

- ⬠ Buddhism
- ⬟ Christianity
- ⬟ Hinduism
- ⬟ Islam
- ⬡ Judaism
- ⬟ Traditional/Oriental

Source: World Christian Encyclopedia

Church Community by Denomination and Percentage of Population

- ROMAN CATHOLIC
- PROTESTANT NON-INSTITUTIONAL
- PROTESTANT INSTITUTIONAL
- ORTHODOX

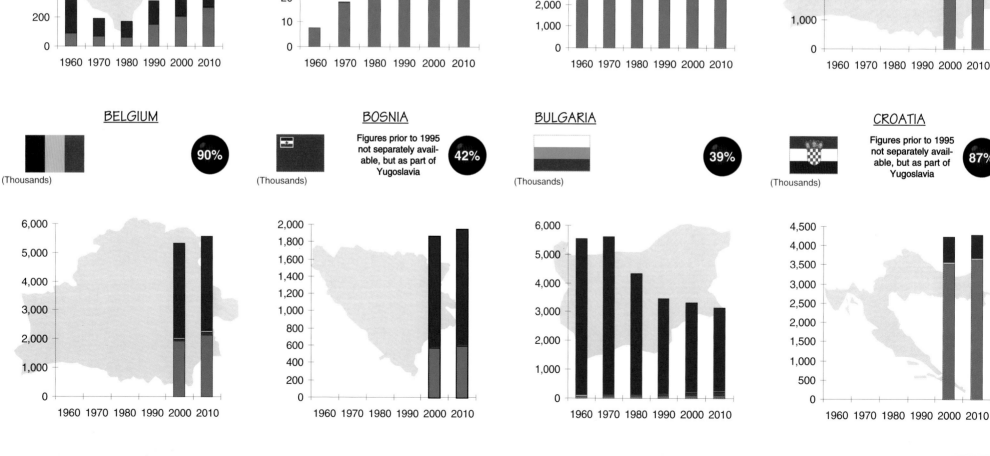

ALBANIA — 17% (Thousands)

ANDORRA — 87% (Thousands)

AUSTRIA — 81% (Thousands)

BELARUS — 34% — Figures prior to 1995 not separately available, but as part of USSR (Thousands)

BELGIUM — 90% (Thousands)

BOSNIA — 42% — Figures prior to 1995 not separately available, but as part of Yugoslavia (Thousands)

BULGARIA — 39% (Thousands)

CROATIA — 87% — Figures prior to 1995 not separately available, but as part of Yugoslavia (Thousands)

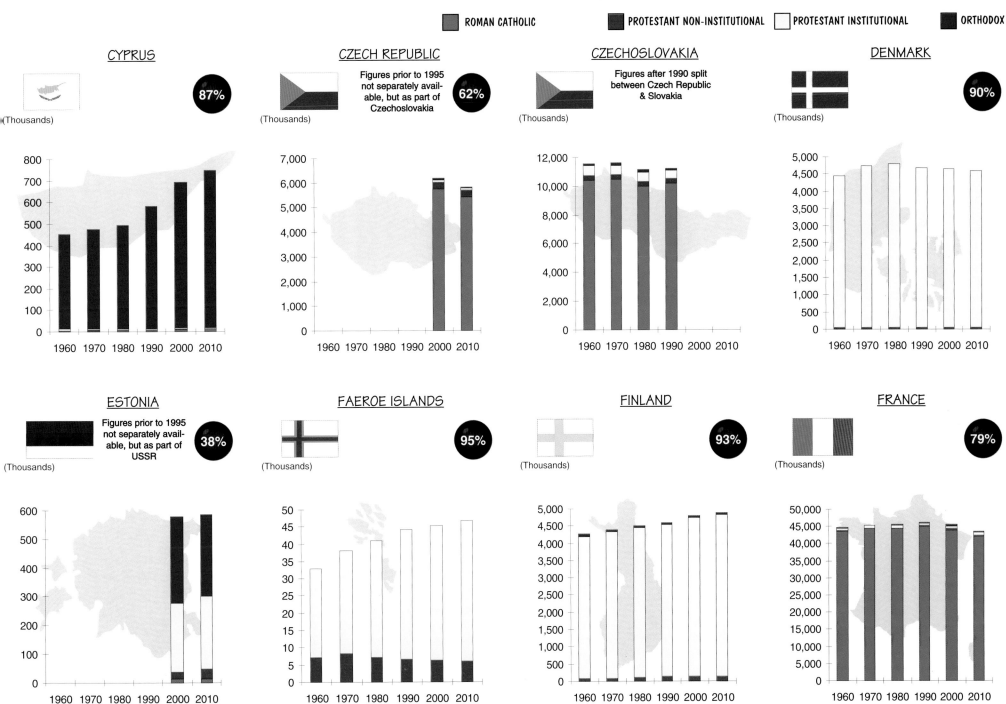

Church Community by Denomination and Percentage of Population

ROMAN CATHOLIC   PROTESTANT NON-INSTITUTIONAL   PROTESTANT INSTITUTIONAL   ORTHODOX

CYPRUS
87%
(Thousands)

CZECH REPUBLIC
Figures prior to 1995 not separately available, but as part of Czechoslovakia
62%
(Thousands)

CZECHOSLOVAKIA
Figures after 1990 split between Czech Republic & Slovakia
(Thousands)

DENMARK
90%
(Thousands)

ESTONIA
Figures prior to 1995 not separately available, but as part of USSR
38%
(Thousands)

FAEROE ISLANDS
95%
(Thousands)

FINLAND
93%
(Thousands)

FRANCE
79%
(Thousands)

115

Church Community by Denomination and Percentage of Population

■ ROMAN CATHOLIC ■ PROTESTANT NON-INSTITUTIONAL □ PROTESTANT INSTITUTIONAL ■ ORTHODOX

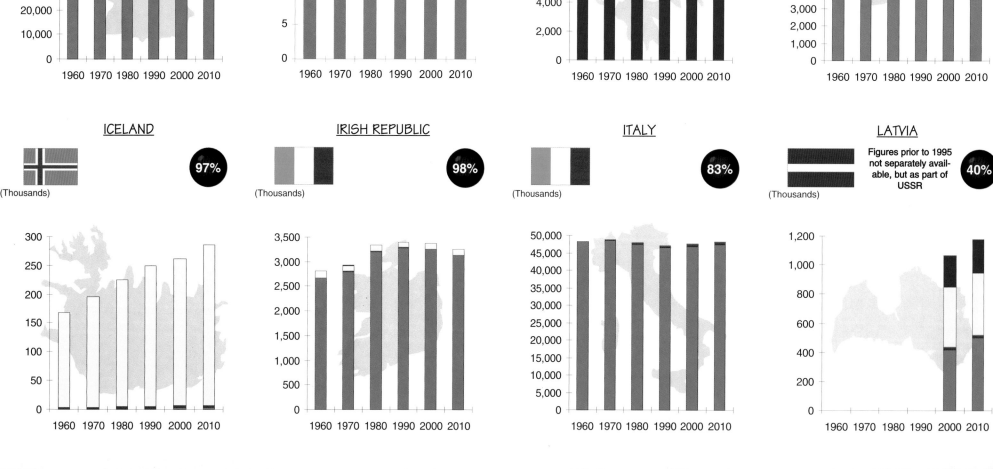

GERMANY
(Thousands) — 78%

GIBRALTAR
(Thousands) — 79%

GREECE
(Thousands) — 95%

HUNGARY
(Thousands) — 89%

ICELAND
(Thousands) — 97%

IRISH REPUBLIC
(Thousands) — 98%

ITALY
(Thousands) — 83%

LATVIA
(Thousands) — 40%
Figures prior to 1995 not separately available, but as part of USSR

Church Community by Denomination and Percentage of Population

| ROMAN CATHOLIC | PROTESTANT NON-INSTITUTIONAL | PROTESTANT INSTITUTIONAL | ORTHODOX |

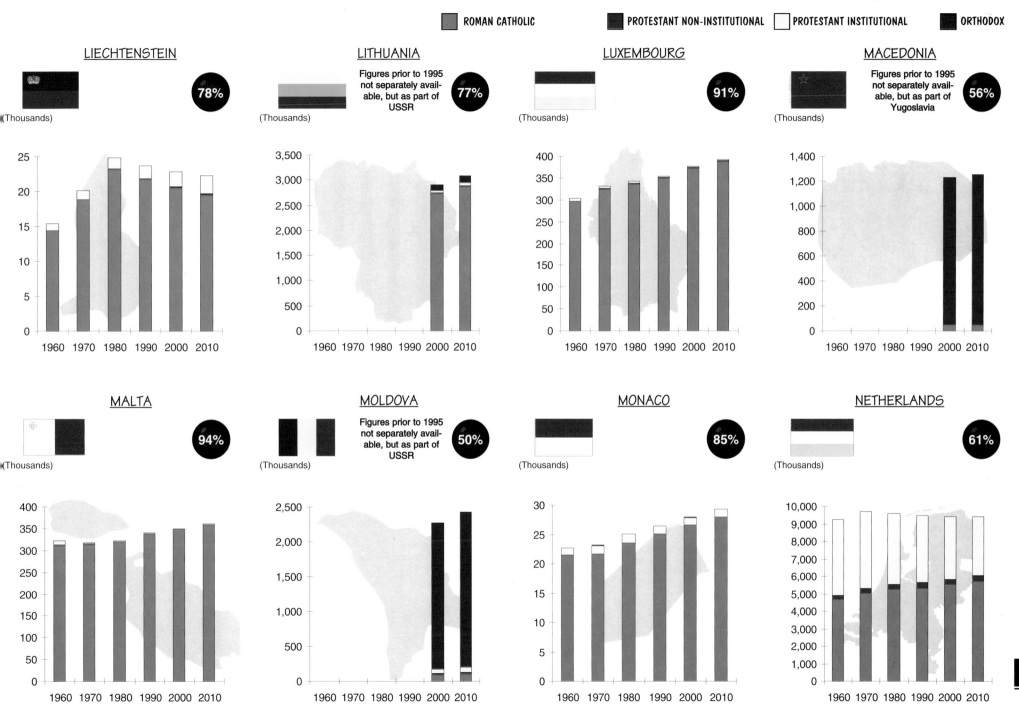

LIECHTENSTEIN
(Thousands)   78%

LITHUANIA
Figures prior to 1995 not separately available, but as part of USSR   77%
(Thousands)

LUXEMBOURG
(Thousands)   91%

MACEDONIA
Figures prior to 1995 not separately available, but as part of Yugoslavia   56%
(Thousands)

MALTA
(Thousands)   94%

MOLDOVA
Figures prior to 1995 not separately available, but as part of USSR   50%
(Thousands)

MONACO
(Thousands)   85%

NETHERLANDS
(Thousands)   61%

Church Community by Denomination and Percentage of Population

■ ROMAN CATHOLIC　　■ PROTESTANT NON-INSTITUTIONAL　　□ PROTESTANT INSTITUTIONAL　　■ ORTHODOX

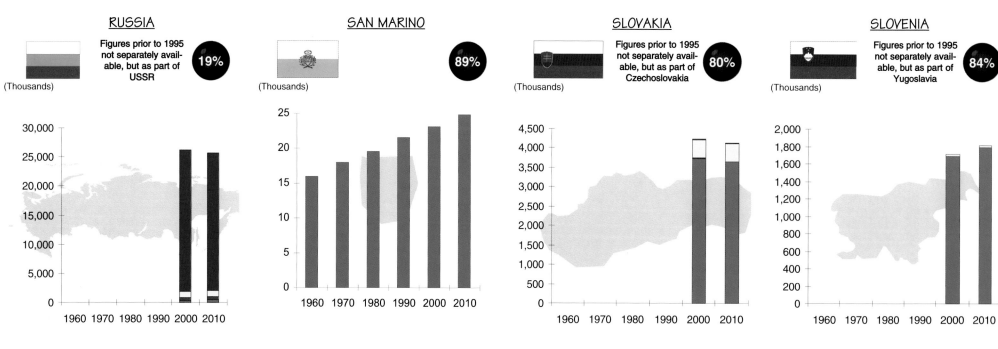

NORWAY
(Thousands)
95%

POLAND
(Thousands)
94%

PORTUGAL
(Thousands)
94%

ROMANIA
(Thousands)
93%

RUSSIA
Figures prior to 1995 not separately available, but as part of USSR
(Thousands)
19%

SAN MARINO
(Thousands)
89%

SLOVAKIA
Figures prior to 1995 not separately available, but as part of Czechoslovakia
(Thousands)
80%

SLOVENIA
Figures prior to 1995 not separately available, but as part of Yugoslavia
(Thousands)
84%

Church Community by Denomination and Percentage of Population

■ ROMAN CATHOLIC   ■ PROTESTANT NON-INSTITUTIONAL   □ PROTESTANT INSTITUTIONAL   ■ ORTHODOX

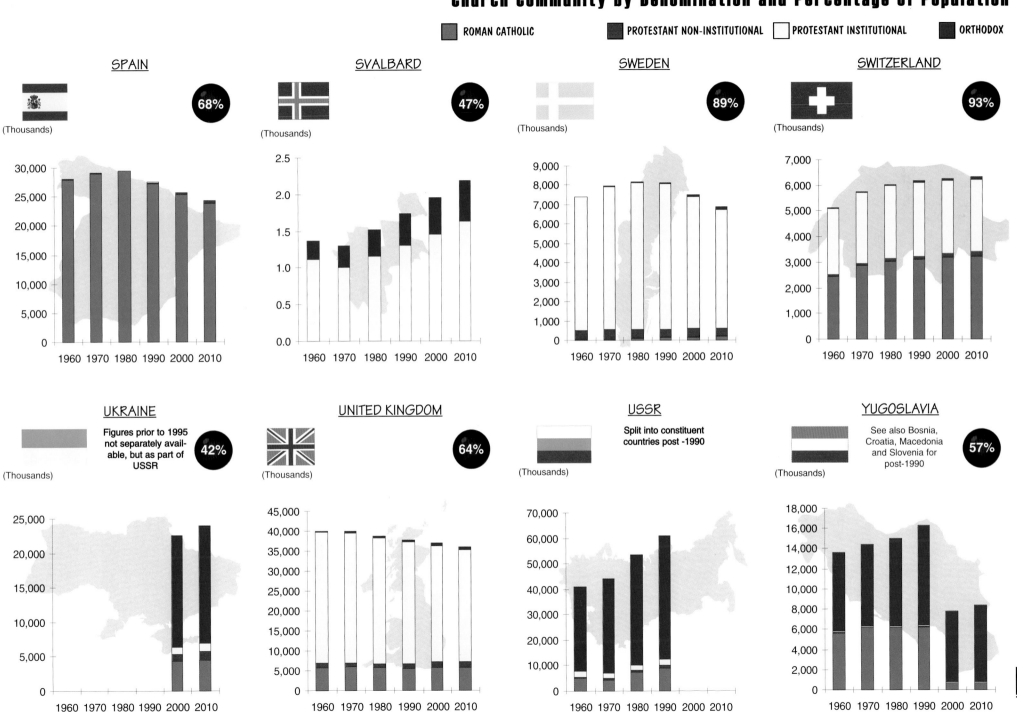

SPAIN
68%
(Thousands)

SVALBARD
47%
(Thousands)

SWEDEN
89%
(Thousands)

SWITZERLAND
93%
(Thousands)

UKRAINE
Figures prior to 1995 not separately available, but as part of USSR
42%
(Thousands)

UNITED KINGDOM
64%
(Thousands)

USSR
Split into constituent countries post -1990
(Thousands)

YUGOSLAVIA
See also Bosnia, Croatia, Macedonia and Slovenia for post-1990
57%
(Thousands)

Christian Community by Denominational Groups

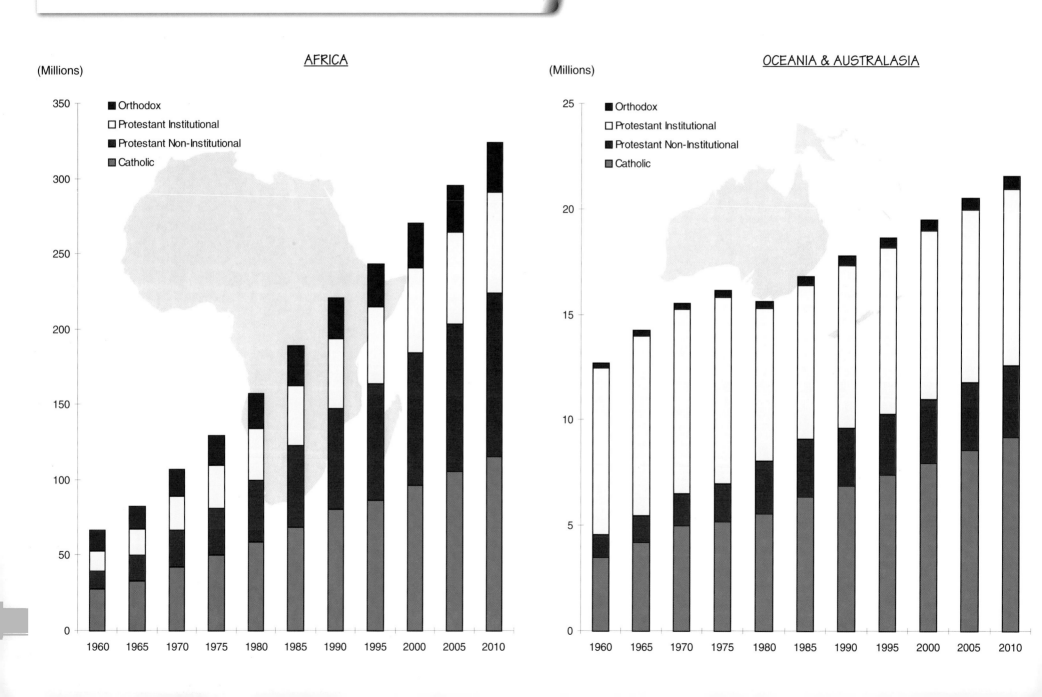

Oceania

Oceania & Australasia

Political Map

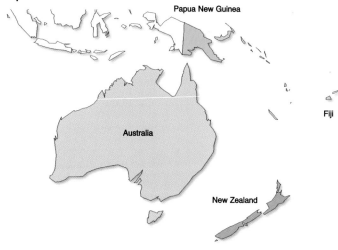

Papua New Guinea

Fiji

Australia

New Zealand

Australia
Fiji

New Zealand

Papua New Guinea

Note: also includes Pacific Islands as listed on pages 124-127

Trends in Oceania & Australasia

(numbers in brackets refer to page numbers of the maps)

This group contains many islands which are too small to show in detail on the maps in this volume and it is therefore more difficult to discern trends for the whole area than for the other continents. However even a casual glance at the next few pages shows that although the actual numbers of Christians may be small, the percentage of the population which is part of the church community is remarkably high. There is more red and yellow than green on these graphs, revealing the islands are predominantly Protestant, although there is a Catholic presence in all of them.

The following remarks relate only to Australia, Papua New Guinea and New Zealand, which are visible on the maps. The Christian community is fairly strong in each of them, but it is growing in Papua New Guinea, barely growing in Australia and declining in New Zealand. The Other Churches group is particularly strong in Australia because of the Uniting Church, and Anglicans are also strong. All other denominations except Methodists are reasonably strong in one of the three countries. With a much lower population (76) the number of churches in the region is small, but is expected to double between 1960 and 2010 (31). Papua New Guinea and New Zealand are strongly Evangelical, Australia slightly less so (36).

Australia and New Zealand send and receive both Catholic and Protestant missionaries, but while Papua New Guinea receives both it sends only a few (41). Parachurch agencies and training institutions for Oceania are included with Asia (42,44). Papua New Guinea is one of only four countries in the world in which under 25% of the population has the Bible or New Testament in their own language (others are Afghanistan, Central African Republic, Congo) (45).

The comparative maps show Australia's urbanized population to be neither particularly old nor particularly young and growing moderately (64, 65). In other respects it is very similar to Europe: in the top band of the Human Development Index (66) and with most of the factors which make up the index having improved from good to excellent in the second half of the 20th century. In contrast, Papua New Guinea is much more like its poorer neighbors in Asia with improvements in areas such as infant mortality (71), but a long way to go in others like education and literacy (68, 69). Oceania and Australasia may be a convenient geographical region, but is far from uniform in either church life or social factors.

Population per Head per Church, 1995

- 🔵 1,000 - 1,999
- 🔴 Under 1,000

Source: World Churches Handbook

Strongest Religion

- 🔵 Buddhism
- ⚫ Christianity
- 🔴 Hinduism
- 🔵 Islam
- ⚪ Judaism
- 🟣 Traditional/Oriental

Source: World Christian Encyclopedia

Church Community by Denomination and Percentage of Population

- ■ ROMAN CATHOLIC
- ■ PROTESTANT NON-INSTITUTIONAL
- □ PROTESTANT INSTITUTIONAL
- ■ ORTHODOX

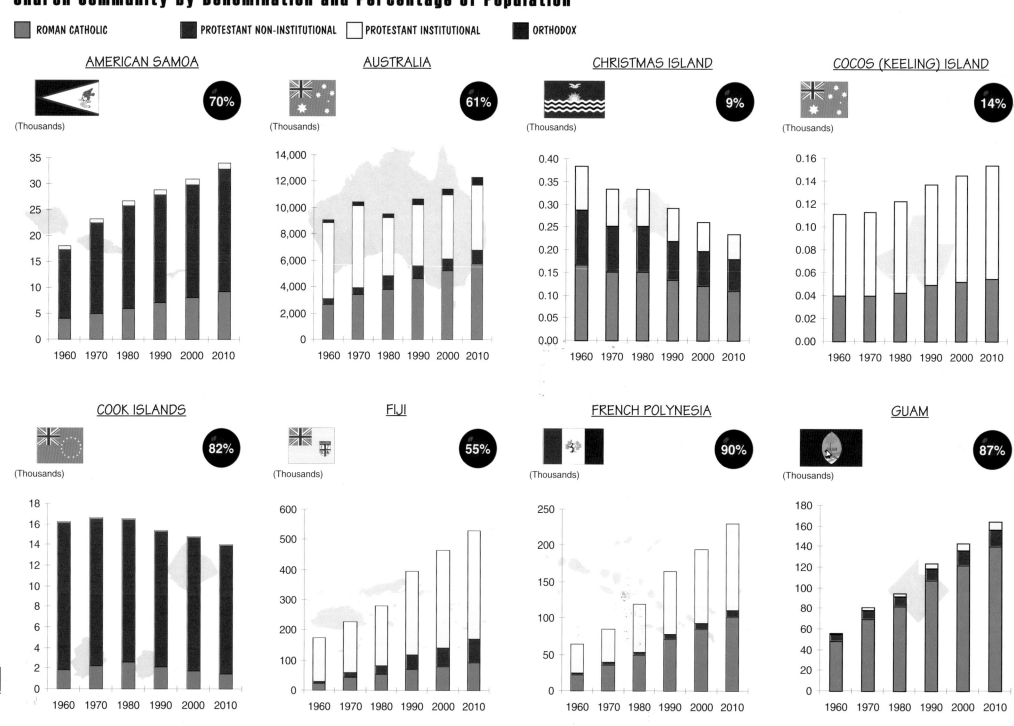

AMERICAN SAMOA — 70%
(Thousands)

AUSTRALIA — 61%
(Thousands)

CHRISTMAS ISLAND — 9%
(Thousands)

COCOS (KEELING) ISLAND — 14%
(Thousands)

COOK ISLANDS — 82%
(Thousands)

FIJI — 55%
(Thousands)

FRENCH POLYNESIA — 90%
(Thousands)

GUAM — 87%
(Thousands)

Church Community by Denomination and Percentage of Population

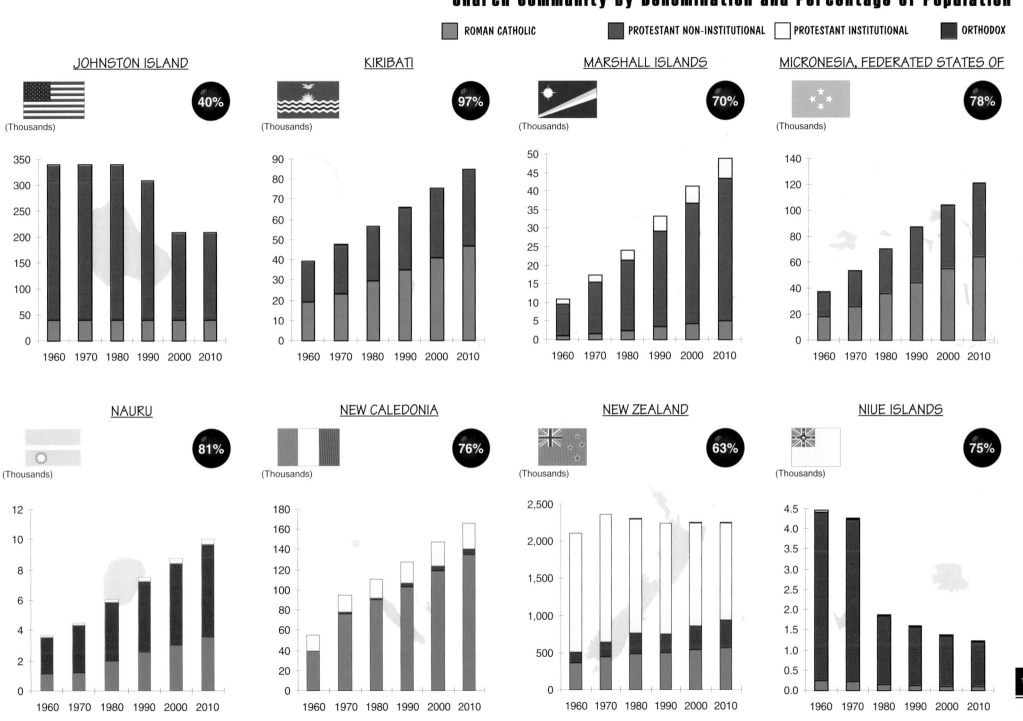

ROMAN CATHOLIC   PROTESTANT NON-INSTITUTIONAL   PROTESTANT INSTITUTIONAL   ORTHODOX

JOHNSTON ISLAND — 40%
KIRIBATI — 97%
MARSHALL ISLANDS — 70%
MICRONESIA, FEDERATED STATES OF — 78%
NAURU — 81%
NEW CALEDONIA — 76%
NEW ZEALAND — 63%
NIUE ISLANDS — 75%

125

Church Community by Denomination and Percentage of Population

- ▨ ROMAN CATHOLIC
- ▨ PROTESTANT NON-INSTITUTIONAL
- ☐ PROTESTANT INSTITUTIONAL
- ■ ORTHODOX

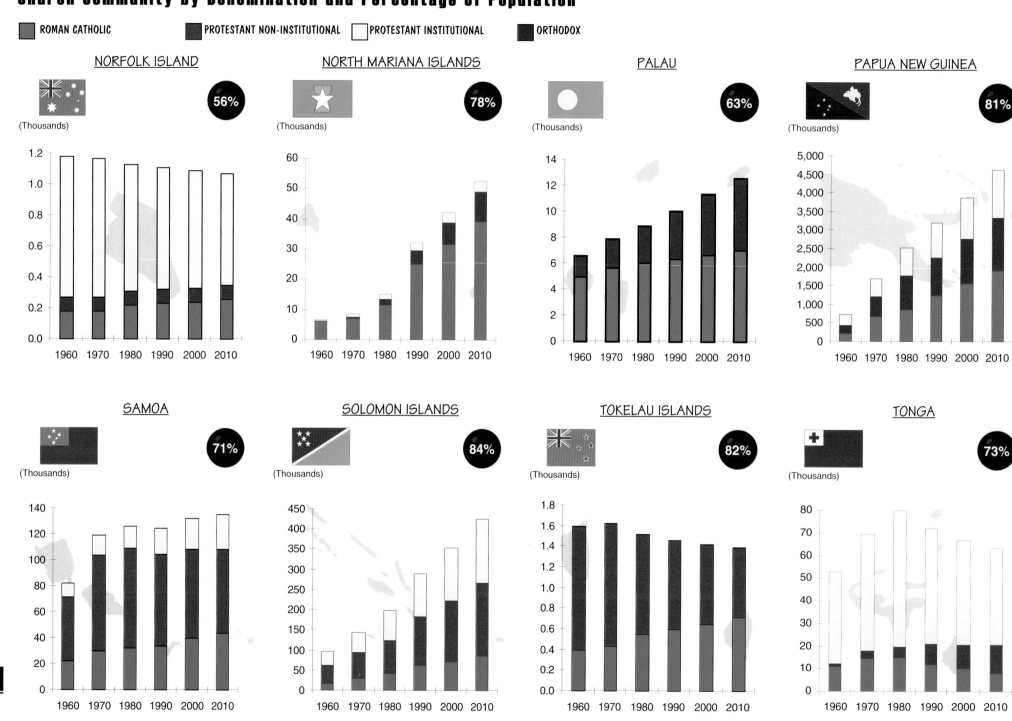

NORFOLK ISLAND
(Thousands) — 56%

NORTH MARIANA ISLANDS
(Thousands) — 78%

PALAU
(Thousands) — 63%

PAPUA NEW GUINEA
(Thousands) — 81%

SAMOA
(Thousands) — 71%

SOLOMON ISLANDS
(Thousands) — 84%

TOKELAU ISLANDS
(Thousands) — 82%

TONGA
(Thousands) — 73%

126

Church Community by Denomination and Percentage of Population

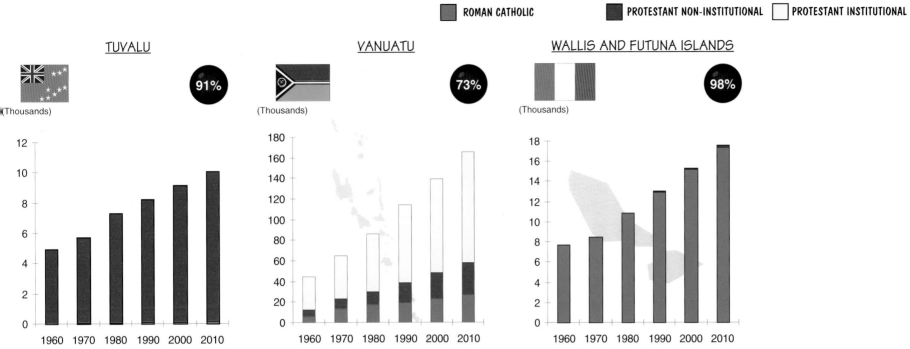

ROMAN CATHOLIC   PROTESTANT NON-INSTITUTIONAL   PROTESTANT INSTITUTIONAL   ORTHODOX

TUVALU
(Thousands)

91%

VANUATU
(Thousands)

73%

WALLIS AND FUTUNA ISLANDS
(Thousands)

98%

These tables contain the data behind some of the maps and graphs in the atlas. Only material which is not readily accessible elsewhere or which has been specially derived from other sources has been included. The column headings indicate the page number for the corresponding map/graph and its position on the page.

	14/1	14/2	14/3	14/4	16/1	16/2	16/3	16/4	17/1	17/2	17/3	17/4	18/1	18/2	18/3	18/4	19/1
Afghanistan	0.01	0.008	-47	+182	0.0006	0.0001	-67	0	0	0	n/a	n/a	0.01	0.007	-85	0	0.001
Albania	22	20	-50	+309	0	0	n/a	n/a	0	0	n/a	n/a	6	6	-25	+250	n/a
Algeria	9	0.1	-93	-38	0.007	0.0005	-25	-75	0	0	n/a	n/a	9	0.07	-94	-60	0.01
Angola	47	71	+83	+86	0.03	0.03	+73	+32	0.9	2	+172	+85	42	51	+55	+77	0.9
Argentina	98	96	+31	+32	0.04	0.06	+83	+50	0.2	0.5	+99	+117	95	87	+28	+27	0
Armenia	n/a	64	n/a	n/a	n/a	0	n/a	n/a	n/a	0.1	n/a	n/a	n/a	0.06	n/a	n/a	n/a
Australia	88	60	+5	+20	36	21	+4	+7	1	1	+48	+26	25	27	+45	+37	0
Austria	97	78	+0.4	-7	0.001	0.001	0	0	0.02	0.02	+6	+12	90	72	+0.6	-9	n/a
Azerbaijan	n/a	2	n/a	n/a	n/a	0	n/a	n/a	n/a	0.02	n/a	n/a	n/a	0.1	n/a	n/a	n/a
Bahamas, The	79	73	+70	+42	21	10	+22	+1	10	18	+205	+59	17	17	+77	+47	0.2
Bahrain	3	5	+204	+149	0.9	0.6	+150	+12	0	0	n/a	n/a	1	4	+273	+302	0
Bangladesh	0.2	0.4	+138	+65	0	0	n/a	n/a	0.06	0.1	+111	+114	0.1	0.2	+125	+57	0
Belarus	n/a	53	n/a	n/a	n/a	0	n/a	n/a	n/a	0.4	n/a	n/a	n/a	19	n/a	n/a	n/a
Belgium	92	89	+5	+3	0.1	0.1	+25	0	0.01	0.04	+161	+59	91	87	+4	+3	n/a
Belize	82	76	+69	+47	11	4	+30	-23	0.3	1	+87	+513	62	54	+59	+47	0
Benin	13	21	+136	+86	0	0	n/a	n/a	0	0.3	n/a	+957	11	16	+133	+82	1
Bermuda	82	86	+32	+14	42	28	+6	-10	0	2	n/a	+62	11	16	+55	+42	0
Bhutan	0	0.3	+1,300	+102	0	0	n/a	n/a	0	0	n/a	n/a	0	0.08	+4,200	+57	0
Bolivia	95	94	+66	+43	0	0.02	n/a	+225	0.08	0.5	+420	+180	94	85	+60	+37	0
Botswana	27	44	+180	+107	0.8	0.7	+118	+41	0	0.05	n/a	-15	0.9	4	+540	+129	6
Brazil	99	97	+67	+42	0.008	0.05	+613	+97	0.5	1	+210	+94	94	72	+52	+22	0
Brunei	7	5	+103	+34	4	2	+55	+17	0	0	n/a	n/a	3	2	+108	+40	0.3
Bulgaria	71	39	-22	-23	0	0	n/a	n/a	0.1	0.02	-82	+27	0.7	0.9	+16	+12	n/a
Burkina Faso	5	12	+245	+89	0	0	n/a	n/a	0	0.1	n/a	+204	4	8	+200	+61	0
Burundi	49	63	+85	+71	0.9	3	+276	+114	0.2	0.5	+152	+181	45	49	+73	+61	0
Cambodia	1	0.4	-90	+858	0	0.0008	n/a	n/a	0	0	n/a	n/a	0.9	0.2	-96	+1,200	0
Cameroon	27	38	+117	+79	0	0	n/a	n/a	2	2	+111	+79	17	26	+134	+79	0.3
Canada	84	59	+8	+12	7	2	-17	-35	3	1	-28	+7	46	41	+26	+21	0.3
Central African Rep	17	42	+142	+62	0	0	n/a	n/a	5	19	+512	+57	11	17	+118	+57	0.02
Chad	5	19	+322	+122	0	0	n/a	n/a	0.5	2	+323	+138	3	6	+180	+67	0.05
Chile	96	93	+45	+34	0.04	0.07	+43	+131	0.2	0.5	+177	+133	84	68	+35	+21	0.2
China, People's Rep	1	7	+536	+255	0	0	n/a	n/a	0	0	n/a	n/a	0.4	0.8	+35	+267	0.04
China, Taiwan	5	5	+56	+25	0.008	0.006	+136	-33	0.2	0.2	+67	+71	2	1	+53	+20	0.2
Colombia	99	99	+65	+48	0.01	0.01	+47	+42	0.07	0.1	+136	+63	98	95	+62	+46	0
Congo	48	60	+103	+74	0	0	n/a	n/a	0.7	0.2	-7	-24	27	38	+130	+76	11
Costa Rica	96	95	+85	+65	0.2	0.04	-27	-34	0.2	0.9	+778	+125	94	85	+76	+59	0.3
Cote d'Ivoire	22	18	+159	+86	0.01	0.01	+283	+39	0.02	0.2	+2,175	+179	15	8	+80	+71	4
Cuba	93	41	-55	+12	0.6	0.03	-90	-28	1	0.2	-62	+6	89	39	-36	-10	0
Cyprus	79	89	+10	+40	1	0.3	-33	-40	0	0	n/a	n/a	0.6	1	+116	+29	n/a
Czech Republic	n/a	60	n/a	-7	n/a	0	n/a	n/a	n/a	0.06	n/a	+32	n/a	57	n/a	-4	n/a
Democratic Rep of Congo	63	83	+176	+74	0.1	0.4	+800	0	2	3	+147	+106	35	39	+155	+61	15
Denmark	97	89	+8	-3	0.1	0.1	+7	+0.88	0.3	0.2	-12	-21	0.3	0.2	-12	-21	n/a
Djibouti	7	3	+134	-14	0	0	n/a	n/a	0	0	n/a	n/a	6	2	+144	-25	0
Dominican Rep	92	88	+71	+48	0.07	0.05	+71	+1	0.07	0.1	+212	+70	90	81	+66	+43	0
Ecuador	98	96	+81	+56	0.008	0.01	+112	+130	0	0.3	n/a	+248	97	93	+77	+54	0
Egypt	20	13	+43	+22	0.01	0.005	-58	+33	0.0007	0.003	+539	+64	0.6	0.3	-1	+19	0
El Salvador	97	94	+73	+40	0.005	0.006	+133	+50	0.3	1	+253	+197	95	76	+64	+23	0
Equatorial Guinea	73	87	+62	+31	0.6	0.8	+113	+19	0	0.1	n/a	n/a	69	83	+58	+35	0
Estonia	n/a	39	n/a	n/a	n/a	0	n/a	n/a	n/a	2	n/a	n/a	n/a	0.9	n/a	n/a	n/a
Ethiopia & Eritrea	40	38	+101	+30	0.003	0.001	+54	-30	0.6	3	+1,260	+26	0.2	0.3	+113	+92	0.003
Fiji	51	55	+59	+66	2	1	+15	+17	0	0.1	n/a	+441	7	9	+120	+53	0.2
Finland	96	92	+5	+7	0.006	0.002	-20	-38	0.1	0.07	-37	+7	0.06	0.1	+24	+93	n/a
France	98	77	+2	-0.02	0.02	0.05	+29	+132	0.008	0.04	+188	+145	96	75	+2	-0.7	n/a
French Guiana	92	55	+96	+76	0.1	0.06	+75	+43	0	1	n/a	n/a	89	49	+89	+69	0
Gabon	59	69	+128	+79	0	0	n/a	n/a	0	0	n/a	n/a	47	48	+113	+72	0.08
Gambia, The	3	2	+91	+55	0.5	0.2	+33	+26	0	0.03	n/a	n/a	2	2	+130	+55	0
Georgia	n/a	46	n/a	n/a	n/a	0	n/a	n/a	n/a	0.3	n/a	n/a	n/a	0.6	n/a	n/a	n/a
Germany	96	74	-7	-6	0.03	0.04	+34	+19	0.3	0.4	+16	+44	37	34	+8	-4	n/a

/1	14/2	14/3	14/4	16/1	16/2	16/3	16/4	17/1	17/2	17/3	17/4	18/1	18/2	18/3	18/4	19/1	
	38	+140	+90	0.7	1	+170	+52	0.07	0.2	+90	+293	11	13	+78	+94	4	Ghana
	95	+15	+6	0.04	0.03	0	+14	0	0.005	n/a	+332	0.6	0.5	-4	+16	n/a	Greece
	67	+20	+18	0	0	n/a	n/a	0	0	n/a	n/a	0.09	0.2	+100	+117	n/a	Greenland
	97	+93	+75	0.01	0.02	+179	+82	0.1	0.6	+333	+210	85	74	+73	+63	0	Guatemala
	2	+166	+80	0.02	0.02	+88	+9	0	0.002	n/a	n/a	0.7	1	+140	+71	0	Guinea
	6	+147	+53	0	0	n/a	n/a	0	0	n/a	n/a	4	6	+138	+44	0	Guinea-Bissau
	38	+31	-2	15	8	+13	-29	0.05	0.3	+849	-12	14	11	+23	-1	0.5	Guyana
	91	+86	+45	0.8	1	+68	+95	4	6	+39	+103	64	67	+74	+32	0	Haiti
	95	+89	+73	0.08	0.07	+53	+110	0.08	1	+2,285	+140	96	85	+79	+66	0	Honduras
	15	+100	+40	0.4	0.4	+84	+4	0.7	1	+128	+70	5	4	+57	-4	0.1	Hong Kong
	91	+9	-0.3	0	0	n/a	n/a	0.4	0.3	-32	-0.7770.7	58	64	+12	-2	n/a	Hungary
	96	+34	+18	0	0	n/a	n/a	0	0	n/a	n/a	0.5	1	+89	+56	n/a	Iceland
	4	+80	+54	0	0	n/a	n/a	0.3	0.4	+93	+56	1	2	+72	+62	0.04	India
	12	+162	+61	0.002	0.002	+67	+48	0.007	0.1	+1,548	+130	2	3	+175	+65	0	Indonesia
	0.2	+17	-41	0.003	0.002	+150	-14	0	0	n/a	n/a	0.1	0.01	-12	-58	0	Iran
	3	+79	+26	0.004	0.0008	+17	-43	0	0	n/a	n/a	3	2	+80	+19	0	Iraq
	97	+18	+1	4	3	-13	-5	0.02	0.04	+35	+56	94	93	+20	+2	n/a	Ireland
	3	+23	+34	0.09	0.04	+23	+15	0.02	0.05	+297	+124	2	2	+32	+45	0	Israel
	83	-1	-0.3	0.02	0.02	+10	+9	0.02	0.03	+14	+17	96	82	-2	-0.9	n/a	Italy
	54	+36	+31	8	3	-24	-15	5	5	+27	+24	8	11	+55	+43	2	Jamaica
	1	+35	+24	0.05	0.05	+30	+15	0.02	0.05	+91	+47	0.3	0.4	+51	+19	0	Japan
	3	+57	-0.3	0.3	0.1	+15	+18	0.03	0.03	+115	+57	2	0.6	+121	-38	0	Jordan
	10	n/a	n/a	n/a	0	n/a	n/a	n/a	0.6	n/a	n/a	n/a	0.2	n/a	+38	n/a	Kazakhstan
	62	+260	+97	2	6	+355	+96	0.3	2	+601	+324	11	19	+255	+95	10	Kenya
	1	+0.5	+15	0	0	n/a	n/a	0	0	n/a	n/a	0.6	0.2	+20	-29	0	Korea, Dem Rep
	32	+261	+87	0.02	0.1	+831	+44	0.1	2	+653	+280	2	6	+218	+67	0.02	Korea, Rep of
	2	+164	-23	0.3	0.01	+57	-85	0	0	n/a	n/a	3	2	+189	+15	0	Kuwait
	6	n/a	n/a	n/a	0	n/a	n/a	n/a	0.06	n/a	n/a	n/a	0.4	n/a	n/a	n/a	Kyrgyzstan
	1	+43	+26	0	0	n/a	n/a	0	0	n/a	n/a	1	0.6	+11	+7	0	Laos
	43	n/a	n/a	n/a	0	n/a	n/a	n/a	2	n/a	n/a	n/a	17	n/a	n/a	n/a	Latvia
	33	+15	-17	0.07	0.005	-51	-82	0.05	0.2	+60	+210	47	22	+4	-21	0	Lebanon
	66	+80	+42	7	5	+59	+31	0.2	0.3	+156	+70	34	37	+92	+54	4	Lesotho
	20	+222	+95	0.8	0.7	+135	+39	2	2	+180	+45	2	2	+114	+136	1	Liberia
	2	+40	+16	0.003	0.005	+400	+50	0.02	0.006	+52	0	3	0.7	-13	+19	0	Libya
	79	n/a	n/a	n/a	0	n/a	n/a	n/a	0.06	n/a	n/a	n/a	74	n/a	n/a	n/a	Lithuania
	90	+13	+10	0	0	n/a	n/a	0	0	n/a	n/a	94	89	+14	+10	n/a	Luxembourg
	39	+88	+69	0.4	1	+310	+153	0.06	0.02	-84	+645	23	17	+56	+55	0.1	Madagascar
	51	+197	+86	2	2	+106	+71	0.06	3	+385	+237	16	18	+132	+63	1	Malawi
	7	+115	+85	0.4	0.8	+186	+66	0.02	0.02	+422	-63	3	3	+75	+62	0.07	Malaysia
	2	+252	+96	0	0	n/a	n/a	0.001	0.005	+130	+334	0.5	1	+183	+82	0	Mali
	0.3	-32	+62	0	0	n/a	n/a	0	0	n/a	n/a	0.7	0.3	-32	+58	0	Mauritania
	94	+86	+46	0.01	0.02	+126	+65	0.1	0.2	+104	+89	91	90	+84	+44	0.1	Mexico
	50	n/a	n/a	n/a	0	n/a	n/a	n/a	1	n/a	n/a	n/a	2	n/a	n/a	n/a	Moldova
	0.2	-78	+568	0	0	n/a	n/a	0	0	n/a	n/a	0.008	0.002	-57	+67	0	Mongolia
	0.1	-71	-53	0.009	0.001	+500	-42	0	0.0007	n/a	+228	2	0.09	-71	-55	0	Morocco
	24	+69	+79	0.07	0.5	+1,140	+68	0.2	3	+1,673	+173	18	11	+25	+21	0.2	Mozambique
	6	+94	+65	0.006	0.006	+64	+57	3	4	+77	+67	0.8	1	+106	+54	0.03	Myanmar
	81	+120	+50	4	6	+129	+88	0	0.7	n/a	+1598	14	16	+89	+72	3	Namibia
	1	+5,809	+495	0	0	n/a	n/a	0	0	n/a	n/a	0.001	0.02	+300	+1,895	0.002	Nepal
	59	+4	-2	0.05	0.05	+38	+4	0.1	0.2	+53	+12	41	35	+12	+6	n/a	Netherlands
	60	+9	-2	35	18	-3	-15	2	2	+24	+57	15	14	+34	+9	1	New Zealand
	85	+89	+67	0.1	0.2	+193	+98	0.4	1	+408	+126	89	70	+76	+55	0	Nicaragua
	0.3	+48	+54	0	0	n/a	n/a	0.002	0.01	+896	+109	0.4	0.2	+17	+29	0.01	Niger
	34	+298	+107	1	5	+789	+67	0.3	1	+620	+85	5	8	+122	+105	3	Nigeria
	94	+9	+7	0.05	0.04	+11	-26	0.4	0.3	-9	-13	0.2	0.9	+121	+217	n/a	Norway
	1	+1,037	+305	0	0	n/a	n/a	0	0	n/a	n/a	0.04	0.8	+1,900	+428	0	Oman
	1	+76	+48	0	0	n/a	n/a	0	0.003	+2,149	+132	0.5	0.4	+62	+38	0	Pakistan
	95	+73	+41	2	0.6	-7	+8	1	1	+42	+76	90	79	+67	+31	0	Panama

	14/1	14/2	14/3	14/4	16/1	16/2	16/3	16/4	17/1	17/2	17/3	17/4	18/1	18/2	18/3	18/4	19/1
Papua New Guinea	37	81	+243	+58	3	5	+200	+64	0.5	3	+365	+169	11	32	+314	+79	2
Paraguay	95	94	+81	+74	0.05	0.3	+941	+105	0.1	0.5	+369	+157	93	88	+76	+70	0
Peru	97	95	+71	+49	0.006	0.01	+341	+52	0.04	0.3	+720	+134	96	88	+67	+44	0
Philippines	97	97	+76	+53	0.2	0.1	+95	+10	0.2	1	+535	+130	83	81	+65	+47	3
Poland	92	94	+21	+11	0	0	n/a	n/a	0.02	0.01	+66	-42	90	92	+20	+12	n/a
Portugal	98	94	+7	-0.4	0.06	0.08	+39	+6	0.03	0.1	+206	+74	97	92	+7	-1	n/a
Puerto Rico	96	93	+34	+17	0.4	0.4	+31	+27	0.7	2	+208	+93	89	62	+16	-3	0
Qatar	8	2	+202	+17	0.5	0.07	+150	-31	0	0	n/a	n/a	1	0.8	+900	0	0
Romania	94	93	+20	+1	0.001	0.001	-20	+55	0.5	4	+176	+248	7	10	+41	+29	n/a
Russia	n/a	18	n/a	n/a	n/a	0	n/a	n/a	n/a	0.5	n/a	n/a	n/a	0.3	n/a	n/a	n/a
Rwanda	28	32	+332	-14	2	3	+568	-25	0.1	0.8	+220	-20	22	22	+286	-14	0.002
Saudi Arabia	0.4	3	+394	+630	0.03	0.009	+208	-50	0	0	n/a	n/a	0.07	2	+400	+340	0.001
Senegal	4	5	+102	+81	0.003	0.002	+80	+33	0	0.007	n/a	+125	4	5	+102	+79	0
Sierra Leone	5	8	+138	+59	0.7	0.6	+69	+18	0.001	0.3	+4,809	+860	2	2	+64	+41	0.01
Singapore	6	13	+108	+72	0.5	1	+98	+63	0.09	0.6	+245	+245	4	4	+49	+41	0
Slovakia	n/a	78	n/a	-7	n/a	0	n/a	n/a	n/a	0	n/a	n/a	n/a	68	n/a	-4	n/a
Somalia	0.3	0.02	-61	-18	0.007	0.0003	-65	-58	0	0	n/a	n/a	0.3	0.02	-74	-5	0
South Africa	49	44	+67	+43	5	5	+86	+47	0.3	0.5	+108	+87	5	8	+159	+45	0.7
Spain	92	64	+5	-13	0.02	0.05	+242	+30	0.02	0.05	+87	+49	92	63	+5	-14	n/a
Sri Lanka	9	6	+32	+3	0.4	0.3	+15	+8	0.03	0.02	-9	+13	8	5	+33	-5	0
Sudan	5	11	+176	+129	0.7	34	+501	+91	0	0.003	n/a	+1620	4	7	+112	+156	0.009
Suriname	45	36	+13	+10	0.3	0.2	+10	-22	0.06	0.3	+439	+53	21	21	+27	+22	0.03
Swaziland	41	65	+132	+104	0.6	2	+250	+109	0	0.09	n/a	n/a	6	5	+79	+32	15
Sweden	99	84	+11	-8	0.04	0.03	+6	-7	1	0.8	-16	+7	0.4	2	+277	+81	n/a
Switzerland	96	92	+18	+4	0.1	0.2	+57	+18	0.07	0.05	+1	-0.3330.3	46	47	+24	+4	n/a
Syria	12	5	+30	+24	0	0	n/a	n/a	0	0	n/a	n/a	3	2	+57	+45	0
Tajikistan	n/a	2	n/a	n/a	n/a	0	n/a	n/a	n/a	0.007	n/a	n/a	n/a	0.08	n/a	n/a	n/a
Tanzania	29	32	+109	+109	0.9	4	+568	+123	0.01	0.5	+2,900	+400	23	17	+59	+83	0.2
Thailand	1	1	+107	+74	0.002	0.001	-27	+50	0.02	0.08	+472	+107	0.4	0.4	+75	+42	0
Togo	21	25	+120	+79	0	0	n/a	n/a	0.007	0.6	+4,440	+543	16	19	+127	+79	0.6
Trinidad & Tobago	66	58	+22	+19	18	11	+3	-0.1110.1	1	0.8	-12	+6	39	27	+7	+7	0
Tunisia	2	0.1	-74	-45	0.001	0.001	+200	-7	0	0	n/a	n/a	2	0.1	-74	-47	0
Turkey	1	0.2	-46	-33	0	0	n/a	n/a	0	0	n/a	n/a	0.08	0.02	-25	-16	0
Turkmenistan	n/a	3	n/a	n/a	n/a	0	n/a	n/a	n/a	0.004	n/a	n/a	n/a	0	n/a	n/a	n/a
Uganda	40	63	+220	+85	13	22	+239	+91	0	0.1	n/a	+66	26	38	+215	+73	0.6
Ukraine	n/a	44	n/a	n/a	n/a	0	n/a	n/a	n/a	2	n/a	n/a	n/a	8	n/a	n/a	n/a
United Arab Emirates	6	9	+1,235	+189	0.8	0.2	+328	+64	0	0	n/a	n/a	1	5	+2,400	+308	0
United Kingdom	77	63	-4	-4	53	42	-3	-7	1	0.8	-17	-4	11	10	+0.5	+0.9	0
Uruguay	78	84	+21	+16	0.03	0.04	+25	+28	0.1	0.4	+106	+112	75	79	+18	+15	0
USA	74	69	+19	+20	2	0.8	-7	-26	16	17	+27	+19	38	23	+27	+17	0
Uzbekistan	n/a	1	n/a	n/a	n/a	0	n/a	n/a	n/a	0.04	n/a	n/a	n/a	0.05	n/a	n/a	n/a
Venezuela	95	92	+98	+58	0.009	0.001	+43	-70	0.03	0.3	+667	+229	93	86	+95	+53	0.4
Vietnam	8	9	+57	+66	0.002	0.003	+200	+49	0	0.01	+3,407	+80	8	8	+51	+57	0
Yemen	0.2	0.005	-81	-63	0.04	0.001	-94	+58	0	0.001	n/a	n/a	0.2	0.002	-80	-83	0
Yugoslavia	73	67	+10	+12	n/a	0	n/a	n/a	0.04	0.01	-26	-30	30	26	+9	+6	n/a
Zambia	22	43	+313	+60	1	0.2	-30	-36	0.4	2	+285	+297	10	14	+438	-5	3
Zimbabwe	29	44	+143	+108	2	2	+112	+59	0.2	0.8	+399	+180	6	6	+165	+22	8

	15/1	31/1	31/2	31/3	31/4	31/5	31/6	34/1	34/2	34/3	34/4	35/1	35/2	35/3	35/4	76/1	76/2	76/3
1960	30.39	126,200	346,300	35,100	103,500	301,900	20,900	342,531,498	98,666,000	47,272,000	61,970,071	561,452	211,313	55,772	95,726	281,000,000	270,000,000	147,000,000
1965	29.67							372,604,255	100,329,000	53,046,000	65,193,686	612,753	218,288	65,190	100,790	320,000,000	296,000,000	167,000,000
1970	28.99	212,400	377,500	80,200	159,200	315,300	29,000	399,818,080	102,624,000	64,392,000	69,719,376	660,850	228,478	82,468	107,888	364,000,000	321,000,000	191,000,000
1975	28.4							427,265,022	104,156,000	77,402,000	72,990,352	710,514	237,200	104,267	113,500	412,000,000	348,000,000	214,000,000
1980	28.49	321,800	426,100	128,600	317,000	318,700	32,400	457,183,919	107,233,000	97,294,000	77,083,020	762,658	246,238	143,998	120,770	476,000,000	374,000,000	240,000,000
1985	28.71							488,581,498	111,185,000	124,285,000	80,927,245	818,531	257,703	194,456	127,629	548,000,000	402,000,000	267,000,000
1990	29.32	476,000	493,600	220,000	528,600	325,300	37,600	516,501,880	115,432,000	150,666,000	83,728,437	865,478	271,151	243,498	131,869	643,000,000	424,000,000	293,000,000
1995	28.12							543,435,641	118,083,000	170,201,000	91,899,239	912,636	278,456	284,432	139,544	744,000,000	455,000,000	320,000,000
2000	27.68	584,700	549,900	269,100	692,600	320,800	40,700	572,482,613	119,993,000	189,787,000	92,230,594	963,192	285,063	322,730	139,468	851,000,000	484,000,000	346,000,000
2005	27.27							599,031,861	121,614,000	209,644,000	92,551,568	1,009,470	290,706	361,452	141,546	963,000,000	511,000,000	372,000,000
2010	26.92	697,800	599,900	321,000	848,000	322,400	43,300	625,709,030	123,550,000	230,075,000	94,034,041	1,055,458	297,856	400,449	143,475	1,088,000,000	538,000,000	397,000,000

9/2	19/3	19/4	20/1	20/2	20/3	20/4	21/1	21/2	21/3	21/4	22/1	22/2	22/3	22/4	
007	+776	+311	0	0	n/a	n/a	0	0	n/a	n/a	0	0	n/a	n/a	Afghanistan
a	n/a	n/a	0	0	n/a	n/a	0	0	n/a	n/a	16	14	-56	+338	Albania
04	-38	+1,150	0	0	n/a	n/a	0.004	0.008	+227	+70	0.04	0.002	-44	-77	Algeria
	+401	+134	0	0.1	n/a	+347	0.6	2	+217	+117	0	0	n/a	n/a	Angola
	n/a	n/a	0.7	0.2	-19	-21	0.1	0.1	-8	+86	0.5	0.4	+25	+18	Argentina
a	n/a	n/a	n/a	0	n/a	n/a	n/a	0	n/a	n/a	n/a	63	n/a	n/a	Armenia
	n/a	n/a	1	2	+100	+52	9	0.02	-99	+281	2	3	+52	+55	Australia
	n/a	n/a	6	5	-3	-7	0.02	0.03	+33	+22	0.1	0.7	+68	+428	Austria
	n/a	n/a	n/a	0	n/a	n/a	n/a	0	n/a	n/a	n/a	2	n/a	n/a	Azerbaijan
1	+80	+17	0	0	n/a	n/a	5	4	+51	+43	0.4	0.1	-19	+17	Bahamas, The
	n/a	n/a	0	0	n/a	n/a	0	0	n/a	n/a	0.2	0.4	+307	+127	Bahrain
	n/a	n/a	0.0019	0.008	+1,835	+22	0	0	n/a	n/a	0	0	n/a	n/a	Bangladesh
a	n/a	n/a	n/a	0.01	n/a	n/a	n/a	0	n/a	n/a	n/a	33	n/a	n/a	Belarus
a	n/a	n/a	0.08	0.05	-16	-14	0	0	n/a	n/a	0.5	0.5	+21	-12	Belgium
	n/a	n/a	0	0	n/a	n/a	4	2	+62	-19	0	0	n/a	n/a	Belize
	+148	+74	0	0	n/a	n/a	1	1	+131	+69	0	0	n/a	n/a	Benin
	n/a	n/a	0	0	n/a	n/a	15	15	+29	+7	0	0	n/a	n/a	Bermuda
	n/a	n/a	0	0	n/a	n/a	0	0	n/a	n/a	0	0	n/a	n/a	Bhutan
	n/a	n/a	0.05	0.3	+249	+380	0.1	0.2	+258	+26	0	0.04	n/a	+39	Bolivia
8	+595	+141	1	2	+147	+84	2	0.6	-2	+13	0.009	0.006	+60	+46	Botswana
	n/a	n/a	0.9	0.7	+35	+30	0.1	0.2	+108	+44	0.2	0.1	+46	+28	Brazil
.2	+83	+25	0	0	n/a	n/a	0.07	0.04	+67	+10	0	0	n/a	n/a	Brunei
/a	n/a	n/a	0	0	n/a	n/a	0.02	0.05	+43	+80	69	37	-23	-26	Bulgaria
.1	n/a	+364	0	0	n/a	n/a	0	0	n/a	n/a	0	0	n/a	n/a	Burkina Faso
.3	n/a	+308	0	0	n/a	n/a	0.4	1	+114	+295	0.04	0.01	-11	-7	Burundi
	n/a	n/a	0	0	n/a	n/a	0	0	n/a	n/a	0	0	n/a	n/a	Cambodia
.7	+205	+105	0.4	1	+187	+204	0	0	n/a	n/a	0.01	0.008	+25	+23	Cameroon
.3	+26	+13	2	1	-38	+40	0.09	0.05	-13	-4	3	2	+23	+0.6	Canada
.5	+900	+338	0.3	0.8	+317	+57	0	0	n/a	n/a	0	0	n/a	n/a	Central African Rep
.5	+967	+134	0.2	0.7	+439	+103	0	0	n/a	n/a	0	0	n/a	n/a	Chad
.4	+180	+102	1	0.08	-70	-17	0.2	0.1	+47	-16	0.3	0.2	+13	+14	Chile
.3	+220	+335	0	0	n/a	n/a	0	0	n/a	n/a	0	0	n/a	n/a	China, People's Rep
.2	+94	+38	0.2	0.09	+8	+19	0.04	0.06	+160	+23	0	0	n/a	n/a	China, Taiwan
	n/a	n/a	0.02	0.02	+66	+42	0.005	0.01	+283	+77	0.02	0.02	+83	+54	Colombia
	-15	+57	0	0	n/a	n/a	0	0	n/a	n/a	0.02	0.02	+135	+30	Congo
.3	+91	+51	0.04	0.02	+29	-4	0.2	0.3	+94	+182	0	0	n/a	n/a	Costa Rica
	+366	+83	0	0.0003	n/a	n/a	2	1	+104	+52	0.04	0.1	+700	+158	Cote d'Ivoire
	n/a	n/a	0	0	n/a	n/a	0.3	0.09	-47	+5	0.04	0.008	-40	-43	Cuba
/a	n/a	n/a	0	0	n/a	n/a	0	0	n/a	n/a	77	87	+9	+41	Cyprus
/a	n/a	n/a	n/a	0.5	n/a	-12	n/a	0.07	n/a	+7	n/a	0.6	n/a	-46	Czech Republic
2	+115	+41	0	0.1	n/a	+365	0.7	2	+151	+269	0.07	0.02	-10	+28	Democratic Rep of Congo
/a	n/a	n/a	95	98	+8	-3	0.1	0.04	-50	-22	0.004	0.008	+50	+47	Denmark
	n/a	n/a	0	0	n/a	n/a	0	0	n/a	n/a	0.8	0.5	+108	+91	Djibouti
	n/a	n/a	0	0	n/a	n/a	0.2	0.3	+96	+75	0	0	n/a	n/a	Dominican Rep
	n/a	n/a	0.006	0.01	+188	+115	0	0.0007	n/a	n/a	0.01	0.02	+112	+47	Ecuador
	n/a	n/a	0	0	n/a	n/a	0.05	0.06	+105	+58	19	12	+41	+21	Egypt
	n/a	n/a	0.02	0.3	+560	+376	0	0	n/a	n/a	0	0	n/a	n/a	El Salvador
	n/a	n/a	0	0	n/a	n/a	0.3	0.2	+5	+7	0	0	n/a	n/a	Equatorial Guinea
/a	n/a	n/a	n/a	14	n/a	n/a	n/a	0.3	n/a	-5	n/a	20	n/a	n/a	Estonia
0.02	+567	+206	0.1	2	+1,854	+129	0	0	n/a	n/a	39	30	+74	+32	Ethiopia & Eritrea
.3	+120	+41	0	0	n/a	n/a	40	37	+36	+65	0	0	n/a	n/a	Fiji
/a	n/a	n/a	92	89	+6	+6	0.07	0.03	-29	-23	2	1	-24	-6	Finland
/a	n/a	n/a	0.6	0.4	-9	+0.3	0.02	0.02	-10	+53	0.4	0.5	+47	+23	France
	n/a	n/a	0	0	n/a	n/a	0	0	n/a	n/a	0	0	n/a	n/a	French Guiana
8	+2,176	+536	0	0	n/a	n/a	0	0	n/a	n/a	0	0	n/a	n/a	Gabon
	n/a	n/a	0	0	n/a	n/a	0.5	0.2	+13	+16	0	0	n/a	n/a	Gambia, The
	n/a	n/a	n/a	0.4	n/a	n/a	n/a	0	n/a	n/a	n/a	45	n/a	n/a	Georgia
/a	n/a	n/a	56	38	-17	-8	0.2	0.1	+38	+12	0.6	0.8	+28	+15	Germany

	19/2	19/3	19/4	20/1	20/2	20/3	20/4	21/1	21/2	21/3	21/4	22/1	22/2	22/3	22/4
Ghana	9	+291	+86	0	0.06	n/a	+470	3	2	+97	+27	0	0	n/a	n/a
Greece	n/a	n/a	n/a	0	0	n/a	n/a	0	0	n/a	n/a	98	94	+15	+6
Greenland	n/a	n/a	n/a	85	65	+19	+17	0	0	n/a	n/a	0	0	n/a	n/a
Guatemala	0	n/a	n/a	0.07	0.03	-5	+42	0.05	0.1	+326	+93	0	0	n/a	n/a
Guinea	0	n/a	n/a	0	0	n/a	n/a	0	0	n/a	n/a	0	0	n/a	n/a
Guinea-Bissau	0	n/a	n/a	0	0	n/a	n/a	0	0	n/a	n/a	0	0	n/a	n/a
Guyana	0.7	+80	+35	3	3	+48	+9	4	1	+14	-42	0.7	1	+85	+37
Haiti	0	n/a	n/a	0	0.02	n/a	+167	0.8	1	+71	+88	0	0	n/a	n/a
Honduras	0	n/a	n/a	0	0.002	n/a	-34	0.1	0.03	-35	+36	0.2	0.1	+98	+41
Hong Kong	0.4	+219	+94	0.8	0.8	+56	+23	0.2	0.6	+192	+67	0.002	0.0004	-33	-56
Hungary	n/a	n/a	n/a	4	5	-0.5	+10	0.04	0.08	+47	+23	0.7	0.4	-35	-1
Iceland	n/a	n/a	n/a	93	93	+34	+18	0	0	n/a	n/a	0	0	n/a	n/a
India	0.06	+94	+63	0.1	0.1	+75	+47	0.1	0.07	+61	-20	0.3	0.2	+37	+21
Indonesia	0	n/a	n/a	1	2	+114	+48	0.01	0.3	+691	+0.7	0.00008	0.00006	+25	+20
Iran	0	n/a	n/a	0	0	n/a	n/a	0	0	n/a	n/a	0.9	0.2	+22	-42
Iraq	0	n/a	n/a	0	0	n/a	n/a	0	0	n/a	n/a	0.9	0.7	+84	+49
Ireland	n/a	n/a	n/a	0.01	0.02	+120	-22	0.2	0.1	-17	-8	0.02	0.02	+6	0
Israel	0	n/a	n/a	0.07	0.004	-53	-66	0	0	n/a	n/a	2	0.9	+7	+13
Italy	n/a	n/a	n/a	0.009	0.02	+56	+47	0.07	0.07	+2	+5	0.07	0.06	+8	+5
Jamaica	3	+42	+27	0	0	n/a	n/a	4	3	+14	-0.2	0.2	0.1	+22	-4
Japan	0	n/a	n/a	0.01	0.03	+98	+40	0.004	0.004	+6	+6	0.04	0.02	-30	+7
Jordan	0	n/a	n/a	0.09	0.02	+7	-1	0	0	n/a	n/a	4	2	+36	+25
Kazakhstan	0	n/a	n/a	n/a	1	n/a	n/a	0	0	n/a	n/a	n/a	8	n/a	n/a
Kenya	8	+116	+37	0.01	0.1	+1,900	+143	0.1	0.8	+1,285	+64	2	2	+146	+61
Korea, Dem Rep	0	n/a	n/a	0	0	n/a	n/a	0	0	n/a	n/a	0	0	n/a	n/a
Korea, Rep of	0.3	+1,725	+89	0.001	0.007	+427	+109	1	3	+155	+104	0	0	n/a	n/a
Kuwait	0	n/a	n/a	0	0	n/a	n/a	0	0	n/a	n/a	3	0.4	+126	-57
Kyrgyzstan	0	n/a	n/a	n/a	0	n/a	n/a	n/a	0	n/a	n/a	n/a	5	n/a	n/a
Laos	0	n/a	n/a	0	0	n/a	n/a	0	0	n/a	n/a	0	0	n/a	n/a
Latvia	n/a	n/a	n/a	n/a	15	n/a	n/a	n/a	0	n/a	n/a	n/a	9	n/a	n/a
Lebanon	0	n/a	n/a	0	0	0	n/a	0	0	n/a	n/a	13	11	+57	-7
Lesotho	11	+484	+42	0	0	0	n/a	2	1	+24	+17	0	0	n/a	n/a
Liberia	5	+633	+101	0.5	2	+620	+104	3	2	+91	+27	0	0	n/a	n/a
Libya	0	n/a	n/a	0	0	n/a	n/a	0	0	n/a	n/a	2	0.8	+142	+10
Lithuania	n/a	n/a	n/a	n/a	1	n/a	n/a	n/a	0	n/a	n/a	n/a	4	n/a	n/a
Luxembourg	n/a	n/a	n/a	2	0.5	-56	-16	0	0	n/a	n/a	0	0	n/a	n/a
Madagascar	0.3	+350	+102	4	7	+135	+111	0	0	n/a	n/a	0.008	0.003	+44	-6
Malawi	11	+598	+327	0	0.2	n/a	+494	0.08	0.5	+424	+350	0.02	0.005	+6	-28
Malaysia	0.07	+73	+61	0.05	0.3	+793	+113	0.7	0.8	+29	+132	0.02	0.01	+17	+28
Mali	0	n/a	n/a	0	0.002	n/a	n/a	0	0	n/a	n/a	0	0	n/a	n/a
Mauritania	0.001	n/a	+200	0	0	n/a	n/a	0	0	n/a	n/a	0	0	n/a	n/a
Mexico	0.2	+99	+61	0.02	0.005	+67	-57	0.2	0.09	+2	+26	0.09	0.1	+108	+52
Moldova	n/a	n/a	n/a	n/a	0	n/a	n/a	n/a	0	n/a	n/a	n/a	47	n/a	n/a
Mongolia	0	n/a	n/a	0	0	n/a	n/a	0	0	n/a	n/a	0.03	0.01	-83	+500
Morocco	0	n/a	n/a	0	0	n/a	n/a	0	0	n/a	n/a	0.03	0.003	-67	-25
Mozambique	4	+1,095	+284	0	0	n/a	n/a	0.5	0.4	+111	-9	0.02	0.002	-81	0
Myanmar	0.03	+95	+63	0.001	0.002	+74	+150	0.06	0.2	+242	+98	0	0	n/a	n/a
Namibia	7	+208	+102	38	38	+109	+32	2	0.9	+82	-25	0	0	n/a	n/a
Nepal	0.5	+10,390	+507	0	0	n/a	n/a	0	0	n/a	n/a	0	0	n/a	n/a
Netherlands	n/a	n/a	n/a	0.5	0.1	-36	-57	0	0	n/a	n/a	0.009	0.07	+59	+550
New Zealand	1	+52	+44	0.09	0.1	+19	+101	7	3	-14	-33	0.1	0.1	+15	+17
Nicaragua	0	n/a	+n/a	0.03	0	-92	-100	0	0	n/a	n/a	0	0	n/a	n/a
Niger	0.02	+211	+67	0	0	n/a	n/a	0	0.001	n/a	+65	0	0	n/a	n/a
Nigeria	7	+240	+112	0.07	0.4	+649	+100	0.6	2	+296	+103	0.005	0.003	+64	+40
Norway	n/a	n/a	n/a	94	88	+9	+6	0.5	0.3	-2	-22	0.003	0.05	+1,400	+54
Oman	0	n/a	n/a	0	0	n/a	n/a	0	0	n/a	n/a	0	0.03	n/a	+620
Pakistan	0	n/a	n/a	0	0	n/a	n/a	0.02	0.03	+266	+47	0	0	n/a	n/a
Panama	0	n/a	n/a	0.02	0.07	+135	+267	0.2	0.7	+167	+255	0.07	0.05	+60	+30

9/2	19/3	19/4	20/1	20/2	20/3	20/4	21/1	21/2	21/3	21/4	22/1	22/2	22/3	22/4	
	+117	+47	11	15	+148	+36	0	0	n/a	n/a	0	0	n/a	n/a	Papua New Guinea
n/a	n/a	n/a	0.06	0.4	+1,195	+61	0.01	0.03	+475	+70	0.1	0.2	+205	+63	Paraguay
n/a	n/a	n/a	0.02	0.001	-42	-69	0.09	0.1	+19	+165	0	0	n/a	n/a	Peru
	+257	+87	0.01	0.04	+328	+66	1	0.7	-4	+94	0	0	n/a	n/a	Philippines
n/a	n/a	n/a	0.4	0.2	-28	+11	0.08	0.02	-53	-43	1	1	+90	-8	Poland
n/a	n/a	n/a	0.001	0.003	+53	+92	0.02	0.07	+95	+65	0.01	0.01	+22	+20	Portugal
n/a	n/a	n/a	0.2	0.1	-24	-10	0.8	0.5	+51	-37	0.04	0.03	+19	+20	Puerto Rico
a	n/a	n/a	0	0	n/a	n/a	0	0	n/a	n/a	2	0.3	+100	+21	Qatar
a	n/a	n/a	1	0.6	-14	-31	0	0	n/a	n/a	81	72	+17	-6	Romania
a	n/a	n/a	n/a	0.2	n/a	n/a	n/a	0	n/a	n/a	n/a	17	n/a	n/a	Russia
.08	+510	+167	0	0	n/a	n/a	0.2	0.6	+275	+167	0.004	0.02	+800	+113	Rwanda
06	+44,900	+44	0	0	n/a	n/a	0	0	n/a	n/a	0.02	0.2	+1,789	+127	Saudi Arabia
.005	n/a	+400	0	0.03	n/a	+112	0	0	n/a	n/a	0	0	n/a	n/a	Senegal
.2	+900	+159	0	0.03	n/a	n/a	2	3	+189	+37	0	0.007	n/a	+75	Sierra Leone
a	n/a	n/a	0.04	0.2	+292	+98	0.8	2	+168	+67	0.04	0.09	+157	+53	Singapore
a	n/a	n/a	n/a	6	n/a	-12	n/a	0	n/a	n/a	0	0.7	n/a	-46	Slovakia
	n/a	n/a	0	0	n/a	n/a	0	0	n/a	n/a	0	0	n/a	n/a	Somalia
	+438	+64	3	2	+2	+37	11	6	+7	+34	0.2	0.1	+61	+38	South Africa
	n/a	n/a	0	0	n/a	n/a	0	0	n/a	n/a	0.001	0.007	+417	+84	Spain
	n/a	n/a	0.004	0.004	+49	+30	0.2	0.1	+7	+5	0	0	n/a	n/a	Sri Lanka
.02	+140	+195	0	0	n/a	n/a	0	0	n/a	n/a	0.8	0.7	+74	+43	Sudan
.2	+450	+64	2	0.8	-5	-11	0.2	0.3	+98	+29	0	0	n/a	n/a	Suriname
5	+257	+151	1	0.6	+14	+43	6	2	+14	+3	0	0	n/a	n/a	Swaziland
a	n/a	n/a	90	75	+11	-10	0.3	0.09	-68	-4	0.3	1	+171	+79	Sweden
a	n/a	n/a	0.07	0.2	+233	+3	0.4	0.2	-15	-26	0.3	1	+164	+142	Switzerland
	n/a	n/a	0	0	n/a	n/a	0	0	n/a	n/a	8	3	+20	+11	Syria
	n/a	n/a	n/a	0.1	n/a	n/a	n/a	0	n/a	n/a	n/a	1	n/a	n/a	Tajikistan
.6	+350	+152	3	5	+188	+140	0	0	n/a	n/a	0.07	0.02	+88	-26	Tanzania
	n/a	n/a	0	0.002	n/a	+739	0	0	n/a	n/a	0	0	n/a	n/a	Thailand
.7	+138	+71	0	0.1	n/a	+6,180	0.3	0.2	+50	+40	0	0	n/a	n/a	Togo
	n/a	n/a	0	0	n/a	n/a	2	0.9	-33	+16	0.3	0.6	+134	+53	Trinidad & Tobago
.001	+294	+87	0	0	n/a	n/a	0.002	0	-58	-100	0.005	0.003	+19	+20	Tunisia
	n/a	n/a	0	0	n/a	n/a	0	0	n/a	n/a	1	0.1	-49	-34	Turkey
	n/a	n/a	0	n/a	n/a	n/a	n/a	0	n/a	n/a	n/a	3	n/a	n/a	Turkmenistan
.9	+100	+176	0	0	n/a	n/a	0	0	n/a	n/a	0.05	0.2	+439	+93	Uganda
a	n/a	n/a	n/a	0.06	n/a	n/a	n/a	0.001	n/a	+410	n/a	32	n/a	n/a	Ukraine
	n/a	n/a	0	0	n/a	n/a	0	0	n/a	n/a	3	3	+1,180	+125	United Arab Emirates
a	n/a	n/a	0.06	0.03	-30	-2	3	2	-15	-10	0.6	1	+20	+52	United Kingdom
	n/a	n/a	0.1	0.2	+57	+4	0.1	0.02	+300	-93	0.7	0.9	+28	+30	Uruguay
	n/a	n/a	8	5	+3	-4	8	5	-11	-8	3	3	+24	+0.2	USA
	n/a	n/a	n/a	0	n/a	n/a	n/a	0	n/a	n/a	n/a	0.8	n/a	n/a	Uzbekistan
.05	-33	-35	0.03	0.05	+154	+86	0	0.002	n/a	+661	0.1	0.8	+88	+27	Venezuela
.08	n/a	+344	0	0	n/a	n/a	0	0	n/a	n/a	0	0	n/a	n/a	Vietnam
	n/a	n/a	0	0	n/a	n/a	0	0	n/a	n/a	0	0	n/a	n/a	Yemen
a	n/a	n/a	0.5	0.3	-10	-5	0.02	0.02	+12	+15	42	41	+11	+18	Yugoslavia
5	+249	+106	0.001	0.05	+2,827	-35	0.9	0.9	+110	+51	0.2	0.03	-17	-29	Zambia
4	+177	+107	0.3	0.6	+140	+126	3	3	+131	+52	0.2	0.01	-33	-60	Zimbabwe

	30/3
Anglican Churches	130
Baptist Churches	210
Catholic Churches	1,410
Indigenous Churches	150
Lutheran Churches	480
Methodist Churches	140
Orthodox Churches	1,030
Pentecostal Churches	100
Presbyterian Churches	215
Other Churches	110

	60A	60B	76/4	76/5	76/6
1960	1,022,794,000	3,660,000	1,671,000,000	657,000,000	16,000,000
1965	1,120,207,000	53,372,000	1,865,000,000	693,000,000	18,000,000
1970	1,245,445,500	62,863,000	2,109,000,000	721,000,000	19,000,000
1975	1,427,841,300	80,436,000	2,361,000,000	748,000,000	21,000,000
1980	1,567,931,000	95,385,000	2,591,000,000	768,000,000	23,000,000
1985	1,662,794,000	103,767,000	2,842,000,000	788,000,000	25,000,000
1990	1,757,306,000	94,851,000	3,116,000,000	790,000,000	27,000,000
1995	1,335,847,000	87,083,000	3,396,000,000	796,000,000	29,000,000
2000	1,410,211,000	99,008,000	3,666,000,000	800,000,000	31,000,000
2005			3,931,000,000	801,000,000	33,000,000
2010			4,188,000,000	802,000,000	35,000,000

	23/1	23/2	23/3	23/4	24/1	24/2	24/3	24/4	25/1	25/2	25/3	25/4	26/1	26/2	26/3	26/4	30/1	30/2	32/1	32/2	36/1	36/2	36/3
Afghanistan	0	0	n/a	n/a	0	0	n/a	n/a	0.001	0.0008	+11	+26	0.0001	0.00002	-57	-17	8	10	47	57.5	0.002	0.005	0.003
Albania	0.03	0.04	-67	+900	0	0	n/a	n/a	0.05	0.08	-77	+1,303	0.01	0.04	-29	+922	7	10	79	3	0.02	0.01	0.002
Algeria	0.009	0.0004	-92	+50	0	0	n/a	n/a	0.04	0.005	-67	-0.5	0.003	0.0005	-77	+127	30	40	42	57	0.04	0.02	0.01
Angola	0.1	2	+1,272	+147	0.02	0.3	+1,100	+195	2	9	+327	+104	0.0006	0.4	+26,900	+539	29	20	0	n/a	2	3	5
Argentina	0.8	6	+399	+166	0.04	0.02	+15	-23	1	2	+72	+59	0.1	1	+571	+159	143	190	n/a	0	2	2	4
Armenia	n/a	1	n/a	n/a	n/a	0	n/a	n/a	n/a	0	n/a	n/a	n/a	0.05	n/a	n/a	n/a	5	n/a	10.5	0.002	0.1	0.1
Australia	0.2	1	+317	+253	8	0.9	-81	-0.2	4	4	+115	-28	0.8	1	+67	+109	240	390	0	0	17	16	15
Austria	0.01	0.04	+50	+113	0.4	0.1	-55	-35	0.2	0.3	+11	+53	0.2	0.7	+96	+63	61	80	0	0	0.4	0.4	0.4
Azerbaijan	n/a	0	n/a	n/a	n/a	0	n/a	n/a	n/a	0.003	n/a	n/a	n/a	0	n/a	n/a	n/a	9	n/a	21	0	0	0.01
Bahamas, The	6	8	+103	+78	0.5	0.4	+47	+22	19	16	+47	+45	0.5	2	+202	+174	38	50	0	0	33	36	31
Bahrain	0	0.2	n/a	+144	0.3	0.2	+116	+22	0.5	0.3	+125	-13	0	0.005	n/a	+100	16	20	46.5	47.5	0.7	1	1
Bangladesh	0.002	0.005	+71	+330	0.005	0.006	+108	+74	0.05	0.08	+179	+40	0	0.0001	n/a	+471	31	60	n/a	30.5	0.04	0.06	0.06
Belarus	n/a	0.7	n/a	n/a	n/a	0	n/a	n/a	n/a	0.1	n/a	n/a	n/a	0.07	n/a	n/a	n/a	21	n/a	7	0.2	0.2	0.4
Belgium	0.03	0.1	+249	+19	0.1	0.2	+38	+28	0.4	0.6	+42	+17	0.4	0.8	+53	+36	82	110	0	0	0.2	0.2	0.3
Belize	0.8	4	+455	+184	0.05	0.2	+458	+68	4	10	+269	+90	0.6	2	+210	+161	32	40	0	0	5	6	9
Benin	0.3	0.9	+148	+248	0	0	n/a	n/a	0.06	0.2	+335	+138	0.2	0.2	+22	+82	31	40	n/a	0.5	0.4	0.8	0.8
Bermuda	1	4	+136	+62	0.9	1	+46	+52	12	20	+80	+37	0.6	2	+208	+86	70	100	0	0	1	2	2
Bhutan	0	0	n/a	n/a	0	0	n/a	n/a	0	0.2	n/a	+122	0	0	n/a	n/a	8	10	63	52.5	0	0.1	0.2
Bolivia	0.1	3	+2,713	+159	0.02	0.08	+331	+128	0.9	5	+369	+158	0.03	1	+2,007	+459	114	160	n/a	n/a	1	3	5
Botswana	0.5	3	+676	+145	4	1	-21	+62	12	6	+24	+34	0.1	0.2	+41	+269	104	180	n/a	n/a	4	4	4
Brazil	2	21	+657	+215	0.4	0.3	+68	+18	0.6	2	+203	+125	0.1	0.9	+480	+224	460	660	n/a	n/a	4	7	10
Brunei	0	0	n/a	n/a	0	0.03	n/a	+32	0.2	0.9	+7,725	+64	0	0.03	n/a	+186	7	10	44	47	0.4	1	1
Bulgaria	0.1	1	+93	+363	0	0	n/a	n/a	0.2	0.4	+9	+104	0.009	0.02	-15	+202	21	20	68.5	16.5	0.4	0.5	0.4
Burkina Faso	0.2	2	+1,142	+197	0.01	0.03	+180	+111	0.05	0.9	+1,001	+323	0	0.02	n/a	+335	15	12	n/a	0.5	0.2	0.8	2
Burundi	2	7	+245	+113	0	0	n/a	n/a	0.5	1	+233	+99	0.0001	0.01	+10,900	+127	21	40	n/a	n/a	4	5	11
Cambodia	0	0.07	n/a	n/a	0	0	n/a	n/a	0.09	0.1	-30	-309	0	0	n/a	n/a	4	8	65	28	0.1	0.1	0.1
Cameroon	0.2	0.6	+351	+114	6	6	+54	+61	0.6	1	+146	+91	0.2	0.2	+176	+46	59	80	n/a	n/a	2	3	4
Canada	1	2	+84	+60	2	1	-13	+1	20	8	-20	-10	0.9	1	+64	+43	300	430	0	0	11	9	8
Central African Rep	0.6	3	+515	+90	0.004	0.03	+471	+153	0.2	1	+884	+108	0.2	0.1	+191	-37	20	30	n/a	n/a	5	22	24
Chad	0.007	0.3	+5,230	+113	0	0	n/a	n/a	1	9	+619	+176	0.001	0.01	+925	+166	23	30	n/a	26.5	2	7	8
Chile	10	22	+129	+95	0.1	0.1	-58	+375	0.7	2	+186	+80	0.07	3	+2,720	+248	240	340	n/a	n/a	11	15	19
China, People's Rep	0	0	n/a	n/a	0	0	n/a	n/a	0.2	6	+1,676	+250	0	0	n/a	n/a	14	10	85.5	68	0.2	0.2	0.2
China, Taiwan	0.1	0.2	+75	+64	1	0.9	+14	+21	1	1	+112	+25	0.05	0.2	+168	+160	135	210	n/a	0	2	2	2
Colombia	0.6	2	+302	+142	0.04	0.1	+264	+57	0.4	2	+409	+99	0.03	0.6	+1,598	+228	105	160	n/a	40	0.7	2	2
Congo	0	0.4	n/a	n/a	0	0	n/a	n/a	10	16	+175	+74	0.3	0.3	+97	+5	27	30	n/a	n/a	9	13	16
Costa Rica	0.4	5	+1,107	+200	0	0.01	n/a	n/a	0.8	3	+427	+114	0.8	2	+243	+162	66	100	0	0	1	3	6
Cote d'Ivoire	0.1	1	+1,777	+275	0	0.0005	n/a	n/a	0.8	2	+633	+120	3	1	+87	+49	60	37	n/a	8.5	1	1	3
Cuba	0.7	1	+79	+69	0.2	0.06	-43	-15	0.5	0.8	+69	+73	0.3	0.1	-54	+25	60	60	62	44	2	3	2
Cyprus	0.01	0.08	+108	+292	0.01	0.1	+813	+65	0.3	0.3	-4	+10	0.6	1	+77	+39	21	20	n/a	n/a	0.4	0.4	0.4
Czech Republic	n/a	0.1	n/a	+90	n/a	0	n/a	n/a	n/a	3	n/a	-11	n/a	0.05	n/a	-45	26	30	57.5	n/a	2	2	2
Democratic Rep of Congo	2	8	+364	+212	1	2	+267	+74	7	16	+346	+91	0.03	0.8	+2,107	+316	540	590	n/a	n/a	8	15	16
Denmark	0.2	0.3	+8	+36	0.03	0.007	-44	-58	0.4	0.4	-2	+6	0.4	0.8	+46	+35	51	70	0	0	8	7	6
Djibouti	0	0	n/a	n/a	0.2	0.02	-29	-41	0.1	0.04	+43	+26	0	0	n/a	n/a	4	6	35	31	0.04	0.03	0.02
Dominican Rep	0.7	3	+407	+163	0	0.2	n/a	+8,104	0.8	3	+256	+137	0.06	0.6	+1,089	+132	40	50	n/a	n/a	1	2	3
Ecuador	0.07	0.9	+1,804	+102	0	0	n/a	n/a	0.4	2	+572	+153	0.06	2	+186	+415	120	170	n/a	n/a	0.4	1	2
Egypt	0.08	0.08	+74	+43	0.3	0.6	+231	+55	0.2	0.1	+60	+3	0.004	0.002	+18	+43	58	70	49	64	0.5	0.6	0.8
El Salvador	2	15	+497	+291	0	0.007	n/a	n/a	0.3	2	+545	+176	0.09	2	+1,713	+202	43	60	0	0	2	5	9
Equatorial Guinea	0	0.5	n/a	n/a	2	2	+164	-50	0.3	0.6	+61	+111	0.6	0.9	+92	+43	9	10	n/a	n/a	1	2	1
Estonia	n/a	1	n/a	n/a	n/a	0	n/a	n/a	n/a	0.4	n/a	n/a	n/a	0.5	n/a	n/a	8	12	n/a	n/a	8	7	7
Ethiopia & Eritrea	0.006	1	+13,547	+308	0.03	0.2	+1,043	+24	0.05	0.5	+1,188	+136	0.0008	0.004	+690	+80	50	70	n/a	28	0.8	3	7
Fiji	0.4	4	+862	+189	0.3	0.07	-9	-26	1	3	+231	+52	0.2	1	+570	+114	22	30	0	0	5	6	7
Finland	1	2	+19	+29	0	0	n/a	n/a	0.6	0.8	+36	+11	0.4	0.8	+73	+53	36	50	0	0	16	16	16
France	0.1	0.4	+143	+70	0.9	0.8	-6	+14	0.1	0.2	+50	+49	0.2	0.6	+117	+60	294	400	0	0	0.3	0.4	0.5
French Guiana	0.1	2	+2,400	+182	0.9	0.5	+153	+24	1	2	+306	+144	0.05	2	+3,757	+178	8	10	n/a	n/a	3	3	3
Gabon	0.2	1	+606	+243	11	13	+143	+65	1	3	+325	+93	13	8	+25	+75	7	10	n/a	n/a	2	6	6
Gambia, The	0	0.04	n/a	+629	0	0	n/a	n/a	0	0.08	n/a	+466	0	0.007	n/a	+182	5	10	n/a	0.5	0.1	0.1	0.1
Georgia	n/a	0.2	n/a	n/a	n/a	0	n/a	n/a	n/a	0.004	n/a	n/a	n/a	0.01	n/a	n/a	n/a	4	n/a	21.5	0.1	0.2	0.2
Germany	0.1	0.3	+60	+48	0.02	0.06	+121	+67	1	1	+7	-12	0.4	0.6	+26	+33	282	320	57.5	0	5	5	5

3/1	23/2	23/3	23/4	24/1	24/2	24/3	24/4	25/1	25/2	25/3	25/4	26/1	26/2	26/3	26/4	30/1	30/2	32/1	32/2	36/1	36/2	36/3	
	5	+287	+118	4	5	+94	+69	0.6	3	+360	+197	0.7	1	+189	+95	520	750	n/a	3.5	3	5	7	Ghana
.03	0.08	+105	+58	0.06	0.04	-25	+3	0.04	0.06	+58	+19	0.1	0.5	+156	+64	53	70	28	26	0.1	0.1	0.1	Greece
7	2	+150	+60	0	0	n/a	n/a	0.7	0.9	+85	+26	0.03	0.4	+1,580	+43	9	10	0	0	5	4	3	Greenland
	14	+938	+218	0.4	1	+216	+177	1	6	+449	+138	0.2	1	+417	+328	77	100	n/a	n/a	3	6	13	Guatemala
.002	0.04	+2,023	+63	0	0	n/a	n/a	0.1	0.5	+301	+120	0.002	0.01	+620	+57	8	10	n/a	0	0.1	0.2	0.4	Guinea
	0.02	n/a	+100	0	0	n/a	n/a	0.1	0.8	+345	+186	0	0.004	n/a	n/a	5	10	n/a	3	0.1	0.4	0.4	Guinea-Bissau
.2	5	+2,229	+79	1	1	+14	+16	8	6	+21	+5	3	0.9	-34	-26	70	90	n/a	n/a	5	6	9	Guyana
	5	+230	+75	0	0.008	n/a	n/a	2	11	+514	+130	0.08	0.4	+332	+134	210	310	0	0	7	10	14	Haiti
.4	5	+1,477	+188	0.2	0.1	+82	+17	1	4	+353	+64	0.1	0.9	+635	+269	60	90	0	0	2	3	7	Honduras
.3	1	+289	+94	0.2	0.3	+86	+90	2	5	+174	+64	0.07	0.5	+503	+120	196	270	0	0	4	5	6	Hong Kong
.1	0.6	+147	+90	20	20	+2	+0.5	0.4	0.3	-16	-7	0.1	0.2	-2	+128	25	30	42	n/a	3	4	4	Hungary
.3	0.8	+38	+233	0	0	n/a	n/a	1	0.6	+0.8	-12	0.09	0.3	+180	+91	15	20	0	0	3	3	3	Iceland
.07	0.3	+338	+96	0.06	0.06	+53	+48	0.8	0.9	+85	+51	0.007	0.009	+73	+69	306	420	n/a	32.5	0.5	0.6	0.8	India
.8	3	+341	+80	2	3	+95	+42	0.2	0.9	+72	+93	0.05	0.1	+165	+88	240	370	n/a	33	1	3	3	Indonesia
.008	0.005	+90	+22	0.03	0.003	-33	-48	0.02	0.007	-28	+103	0.002	0.0003	-34	-13	40	70	29.5	75	0.05	0.05	0.03	Iran
	0.002	n/a	+165	0.03	0.009	-41	+67	0.04	0.009	+16	-29	0	0.0001	n/a	+114	21	30	31.5	32	0.06	0.04	0.03	Iraq
.002	0.02	+260	+137	0.6	0.4	-13	-13	0.3	0.3	-5	+53	0.03	0.07	+96	+78	34	40	0	0	1	0.9	0.8	Ireland
.005	0.007	+96	+94	0	0	n/a	n/a	0.1	0.1	+108	+67	0.006	0.02	+385	+88	65	80	26	25	0.2	0.2	0.1	Israel
.05	0.8	+968	+84	0	0	n/a	n/a	0.1	0.3	+86	+51	0.03	0.8	+1,030	+157	225	250	0	0	0.3	0.4	0.6	Italy
	11	+143	+48	0	0	n/a	n/a	15	18	+35	+38	0.8	0.8	+2	+46	135	190	0	0	13	16	17	Jamaica
.01	0.03	+63	+78	0.02	0.04	+81	+57	0.3	0.3	+17	+21	0.08	0.9	+599	+106	192	230	n/a	1.5	0.2	0.3	0.3	Japan
.03	0.02	+67	+48	0	0	n/a	n/a	0.3	0.08	+3	+0.1	0.01	0.002	-34	+2	26	30	19.5	22.5	0.3	0.3	0.3	Jordan
/a	0.03	n/a	n/a	n/a	0.01	n/a	n/a	n/a	0.03	n/a	n/a	n/a	0.04	n/a	n/a	n/a	15	n/a	17	1	1	1	Kazakhstan
	5	+472	+1,164	0.5	3	+888	+128	6	16	+342	+80	0.08	0.1	+213	+112	246	470	n/a	n/a	10	20	25	Kenya
	0	n/a	n/a	0	0	n/a	n/a	0.5	0.3	-20	+84	0	0	n/a	n/a	7	0	n/a	n/a	0.5	0.3	0.2	Korea, Dem Rep
.09	3	+1,491	+325	5	14	+261	+57	0.9	4	+267	+117	0.6	1	+399	-13	173	250	66	65	4	7	11	Korea, Rep of
.06	0.03	+777	-63	0.4	0.04	+200	-70	0.3	0.04	+194	-68	0.008	0.003	+26	+72	15	40	44.5	50	0.6	0.4	0.4	Kuwait
/a	0.1	n/a	n/a	n/a	0	n/a	n/a	n/a	0.006	n/a	n/a	n/a	0.01	n/a	n/a	n/a	22	n/a	14	0.05	0.08	0.1	Kyrgyzstan
	0	n/a	n/a	0	0	n/a	n/a	0.2	0.4	+266	+68	0	0	n/a	n/a	10	10	43	48	0.2	0.3	0.3	Laos
	0.5	na	n/a	0	0	n/a	n/a	n/a	0.2	n/a	n/a	n/a	0.06	n/a	n/a	n/a	6	n/a	n/a	5	5	5	Latvia
.04	0.02	+105	-42	0.4	0.08	-15	-55	0.6	0.2	-6	-27	0.2	0.2	+76	+48	48	60	n/a	15.5	0.6	0.7	0.5	Lebanon
.3	0.8	+267	+99	23	10	+4	+12	0.6	0.7	+77	+61	0.04	0.2	+444	+122	293	460	n/a	n/a	2	3	4	Lesotho
	3	+260	+120	0.1	0.1	+80	+82	1	3	+184	+199	0.1	0.2	+231	+41	130	210	n/a	22	3	6	5	Liberia
	0	n/a	n/a	0.04	0.09	+679	+48	0.2	0.03	-73	+189	0.007	0.001	-85	+438	9	4	60	63	0.02	0.1	0.1	Libya
/a	0.2	n/a	n/a	n/a	0.1	n/a	n/a	n/a	0.02	n/a	n/a	n/a	0.06	n/a	n/a	n/a	4	n/a	n/a	0.2	0.2	0.2	Lithuania
	0.03	n/a	n/a	0	0	n/a	n/a	0.5	0.7	+41	+16	0.2	0.7	+212	+94	27	40	0	0	0.1	0.1	0.1	Luxembourg
.3	0.9	+284	+163	0	0.2	n/a	+315	12	13	+114	+61	0.003	0.05	+1,569	+303	34	60	n/a	n/a	3	5	5	Madagascar
.2	2	+752	+307	9	9	+255	+5	3	5	+187	+133	1	0.4	+24	+9	120	170	n/a	9	4	7	8	Malawi
.09	0.3	+235	+152	0.05	0.04	0	+126	0.3	1	+494	+139	0.008	0.02	+180	+131	50	60	n/a	32	0.6	1	2	Malaysia
	0.03	n/a	n/a	0	0.00006	n/a	n/a	0.1	0.7	+490	+108	0	0.003	n/a	+198	9	10	n/a	11.5	0.2	0.5	0.6	Mali
	0.005	n/a	n/a	0	0	n/a	n/a	0.001	0.003	+121	+126	0	0.0003	n/a	n/a	n/a	n/a	57	58	0.002	0.003	0.002	Mauritania
.6	1	+127	+128	0.2	0.5	+161	+121	0.9	2	+183	+74	0.3	2	+321	+243	260	380	37	43	2	2	3	Mexico
/a	0.4	n/a	n/a	n/a	0	n/a	n/a	n/a	0.2	n/a	n/a	n/a	0.05	n/a	n/a	n/a	7	n/a	n/a	0.7	0.9	1	Moldova
	0	n/a	n/a	0	0	n/a	n/a	0	0.2	n/a	n/a	0	0.02	n/a	+400	4	3	62.5	21	0	0	0	Mongolia
.0007	0.0003	-19	+12	0.05	0.001	-80	-71	0.01	0.003	-26	-4	0.005	0.0004	-53	-59	29	40	62.5	63.5	0.01	0.009	0.006	Morocco
.3	3	+596	+316	0.2	0.7	+294	+107	0.9	1	+79	+116	0.02	0.4	+2,859	+50	138	170	n/a	22.5	0.8	3	4	Mozambique
.1	0.2	+270	+22	0.02	0.08	+449	+73	0.5	0.7	+92	+92	0.003	0.01	+463	+94	48	36	n/a	29	3	3	3	Myanmar
.9	2	+254	+100	6	7	+175	+17	0.9	4	+308	+177	0.07	0.2	+192	+106	77	100	n/a	n/a	9	11	14	Namibia
	0	n/a	n/a	0	0	n/a	n/a	0.002	0.02	+1,201	+199	0.0004	0.002	+250	+207	12	20	60.5	35.5	0.003	0.01	0.2	Nepal
.4	0.6	+119	+2	37	22	-6	-11	2	1	+1	+21	0.8	0.7	+13	+21	235	260	0	0	7	7	6	Netherlands
.4	2	+301	+139	23	14	-3	-2	5	5	+76	-9	1	3	+85	+60	90	120	0	0	20	23	24	New Zealand
	10	+799	+244	0	0	n/a	n/a	3	4	+169	+74	0.08	0.2	+677	+48	81	120	n/a	n/a	2	4	8	Nicaragua
	0.02	n/a	+70	0	0	n/a	n/a	0.006	0.06	+1,154	+172	0	0.003	n/a	+154	16	20	n/a	18	0.008	0.05	0.06	Niger
.8	6	+826	+167	0.2	0.07	-43	+83	2	5	+387	+104	0.2	0.4	+179	+85	910	1,160	28	51.5	3	8	12	Nigeria
2	2	-4	+11	0	0	n/a	n/a	2	3	+23	+30	0.3	0.5	+70	+30	43	50	0	0	13	11	11	Norway
	0.02	n/a	+119	0	0	n/a	n/a	0.07	0.2	+494	+81	0	0	n/a	n/a	11	20	41	64	0.02	0.09	0.1	Oman
.01	0.4	+351	+183	0.4	0.4	+94	+48	0.5	0.4	+64	+49	0.02	0.01	+35	+36	53	70	42.5	53.5	0.2	0.2	0.2	Pakistan
	9	+303	+144	0	0	n/a	n/a	2	4	+163	+111	0.4	2	+226	+208	52	70	0	0	4	5	8	Panama

	23/1	23/2	23/3	23/4	24/1	24/2	24/3	24/4	25/1	25/2	25/3	25/4	26/1	26/2	26/3	26/4	30/1	30/2	32/1	32/2	36/1	36/2	36/3
Papua New Guinea	2	8	+450	+123	0	0	n/a	n/a	8	15	+267	+20	0.1	0.3	+241	+135	105	150	0	0	7	14	19
Paraguay	0.2	2	+613	+296	0	0.08	n/a	+95	0.9	2	+205	+151	0.06	0.4	+747	+151	47	60	n/a	n/a	0.9	2	3
Peru	0.2	2	+1,341	+125	0.08	1	+869	+239	0.7	3	+270	+242	0.1	2	+1,068	+255	100	150	n/a	45.5	0.8	2	3
Philippines	0.5	3	+427	+144	0	0.02	n/a	+407	2	4	+191	+84	0.5	1	+136	+145	460	610	n/a	26.5	2	3	4
Poland	0.03	0.2	+315	+76	0.01	0.01	+14	0	0.06	0.09	+32	+54	0.05	0.7	+353	+266	48	50	37.5	n/a	0.2	0.2	0.2
Portugal	0.1	1	+244	+174	0.02	0.05	+78	+15	0.1	0.3	+131	+30	0.02	1	+2,212	+263	40	50	0	0	0.2	0.5	0.6
Puerto Rico	2	23	+490	+167	0.4	0.5	+70	+15	2	4	+264	-4	0.9	4	+301	+88	95	130	n/a	n/a	5	7	14
Qatar	0	0.1	n/a	+927	0	0	n/a	n/a	5	0.8	+78	+26	0	0	n/a	n/a	24	60	62.5	65	2	0.9	0.8
Romania	0.3	2	+313	+58	4	3	+11	+3	0.9	1	+44	+31	0.3	0.4	+33	+42	35	40	65.5	6	3	3	4
Russia	n/a	0.2	n/a	n/a	n/a	0.004	n/a	n/a	n/a	0.08	n/a	n/a	n/a	0.1	n/a	n/a	146	180	66.5	14.5	0.3	0.3	0.4
Rwanda	0.1	1	+4,852	-32	0.1	2	+1,238	+200	4	2	+225	-38	0	0.007	n/a	+9	14	20	n/a	n/a	3	9	15
Saudi Arabia	0	0	n/a	n/a	0	0	n/a	n/a	0.3	0.4	+233	+125	0	0	n/a	n/a	20	60	83.5	86	0.1	0.1	0.3
Senegal	0.005	0.04	+250	+670	0.06	0.004	-64	-45	0.008	0.02	+235	+181	0.003	0.03	+1,445	+113	18	30	n/a	7.5	0.02	0.04	0.03
Sierra Leone	0.2	0.9	+489	+94	0	0.04	n/a	n/a	0.5	1	+109	+142	0.04	0.04	+139	-11	40	60	n/a	9	0.8	1	2
Singapore	0.2	0.9	+437	+99	0.4	1	+179	+94	0.7	3	+236	+112	0.07	0.2	+185	+83	64	90	n/a	10.5	2	2	4
Slovakia	n/a	0.04	n/a	+90	n/a	3	n/a	-19	n/a	0.2	n/a	-11	n/a	0.05	n/a	-45	n/a	15	n/a	2	2	2	2
Somalia	0	0	n/a	n/a	0	0	n/a	n/a	0.007	0.006	+440	-41	0	0	n/a	n/a	5	10	33.5	60.5	0.006	0.02	0.02
South Africa	3	7	+165	+153	17	10	+47	+2	4	4	+80	+71	0.4	0.5	+65	+80	3,350	4,080	n/a	9.5	14	14	14
Spain	0.1	0.6	+1,713	+213	0.0002	0.003	+436	+199	0.09	0.2	+103	+63	0.02	0.8	+1,902	+166	148	170	0	0	0.1	0.2	0.4
Sri Lanka	0.05	0.5	+239	+430	0.07	0.007	-66	-44	0.1	0.1	+51	+34	0.007	0.03	+209	+138	37	50	26.5	36.5	0.2	0.2	0.2
Sudan	0	0.02	n/a	+138	0.02	0.4	+2,140	+157	0.04	0.5	+890	+271	0.0008	0.003	+270	+164	21	30	n/a	73.5	0.5	2	2
Suriname	0.06	0.6	+281	+296	6	1	-61	-12	17	12	+17	-6	0.2	0.7	+170	+83	25	30	n/a	n/a	2	2	3
Swaziland	2	4	+271	+59	0.3	0.1	+17	-3	10	6	+29	+52	0.3	0.4	+71	+119	87	100	n/a	n/a	11	12	12
Sweden	2	2	+43	-3	0	0	n/a	n/a	5	3	-24	-10	0.4	0.7	+61	+44	107	150	0	0	9	8	7
Switzerland	0.06	0.6	+567	+91	48	41	+9	+0.7	1	2	+48	+33	1	1	+10	+11	145	170	0	0	5	5	5
Syria	0.001	0.002	+418	+24	0.3	0.2	+16	+65	0.06	0.04	+95	+50	0.004	0.003	+71	+58	27	30	29.5	30	0.1	0.1	0.1
Tajikistan	n/a	0.01	n/a	n/a	n/a	0	n/a	n/a	n/a	0	n/a	n/a	n/a	0.004	n/a	n/a	n/a	5	n/a	26	0.04	0.04	0.03
Tanzania	0.4	1	+358	+122	0	0	n/a	n/a	1	4	+334	+188	0.02	0.03	+253	+124	77	110	n/a	24.5	2	5	7
Thailand	0.006	0.07	+925	+183	0.1	0.2	+75	+70	0.02	0.1	+474	+196	0.004	0.01	+214	+188	42	60	n/a	4	0.1	0.1	0.2
Togo	0.6	0.7	+165	+47	4	3	+70	+61	0.01	0.08	+825	+109	0.05	0.3	+449	+255	42	70	n/a	2	0.9	1	1
Trinidad & Tobago	1	8	+402	+75	1	4	+205	+48	3	6	+116	+73	0.5	1	+91	+98	69	80	0	0	5	7	9
Tunisia	0.0007	0.0002	0	-41	0.01	0.0009	-88	+55	0.02	0.0004	-87	-60	0.002	0.0005	-6	-38	15	20	49.5	49.5	0.01	0.009	0.004
Turkey	0	0	n/a	n/a	0.001	0.002	+100	+59	0.07	0.01	-26	-42	0.008	0.006	+61	+9	34	40	49.5	56	0.02	0.02	0.008
Turkmenistan	n/a	0.004	n/a	n/a	n/a	0	n/a	n/a	n/a	0.0006	n/a	n/a	n/a	0.006	n/a	n/a	n/a	3	n/a	27	0	0	0.01
Uganda	0.8	2	+171	+250	0	0	n/a	n/a	0.3	1	+161	+389	0.0009	0.02	+913	+887	61	90	n/a	n/a	12	14	15
Ukraine	n/a	2	n/a	n/a	n/a	0.4	n/a	n/a	n/a	0.3	n/a	n/a	n/a	0.3	n/a	n/a	n/a	39	n/a	6.5	0.8	1	1
United Arab Emirates	0	0	n/a	n/a	0	0	n/a	n/a	0.9	0.6	+724	+100	0	0	n/a	n/a	19	50	50.5	50.5	0.5	0.9	0.4
United Kingdom	0.2	1	+226	+125	5	4	+0.2	-10	2	1	-46	-9	0.6	2	+134	+55	500	650	0	0	6	7	8
Uruguay	0.3	2	+345	+63	0	0	n/a	n/a	2	3	+44	+39	0.6	3	+172	+112	58	70	n/a	n/a	0.7	1	2
USA	2	10	+137	+151	3	3	+35	+9	8	6	-11	+10	2	5	+60	+79	1,860	2,790	0	0	24	24	27
Uzbekistan	n/a	0.06	n/a	n/a	n/a	0.03	n/a	n/a	n/a	0	n/a	n/a	n/a	0.006	n/a	n/a	n/a	7	n/a	49	0.1	0.1	0.1
Venezuela	0.3	4	+635	+347	0.02	0.005	+178	-67	0.4	1	+370	+100	0.1	1	+659	+393	93	120	0	0	1	2	2
Vietnam	0	0.2	n/a	+5,388	0	0	n/a	n/a	0.2	0.7	+229	+124	0.0004	0.0006	+49	+184	42	30	65	58	0.2	0.5	0.5
Yemen	0	0	n/a	n/a	0	0	n/a	n/a	0.01	0.001	-52	-26	0	0	n/a	n/a	9	10	'48[1]	61.5	0.02	0.02	0.005
Yugoslavia	0.06	0.05	-21	+26	0.2	0.05	-35	-42	0.1	0.08	-9	-14	0.02	0.06	+156	+95	70	80	41	n/a	0.2	0.2	0.2
Zambia	0.4	3	+884	+165	1	2	+239	+64	6	16	+220	+192	6	2	-17	+51	127	150	n/a	n/a	4	6	8
Zimbabwe	2	10	+273	+422	4	1	-31	+43	3	6	+170	+129	1	1	+132	+91	206	290	n/a	0.5	5	7	7

[1] This figure is for N Yemen; S Yemen is 53.5

54

	1900	1920	1930	1940	1950	1960	1970	1980	1990	2000
Trinitarian Christians	558,056,300	633,400,000	704,800,000	775,545,000	860,100,000	924,262,500	1,079,684,000	1,273,665,000	1,511,996,000	1,710,454,000
Muslims	200,102,200	238,080,000	275,310,000	316,500,000	368,800,000	464,022,500	608,084,000	788,722,000	1,034,838,000	1,340,743,000
Hindus	203,033,300	234,360,000	262,890,000	289,180,000	320,800,000	384,494,000	473,050,000	583,546,000	716,455,000	865,565,000
Buddhists	127,159,000	143,220,000	157,320,000	168,500,000	147,500,000	159,853,000	178,880,000	207,121,000	242,687,000	272,950,000
Oriental Religions	394,020,000	428,358,000	461,610,000	439,235,000	459,785,000	478,365,900	445,881,000	436,457,000	370,222,000	444,745,000
Other Religions	134,367,100	163,982,000	175,364,000	184,575,000	192,195,000	206,931,500	225,271,000	263,676,000	297,854,000	343,397,000
Non-religious/ Atheists	3,148,900	18,600,000	32,706,000	103,465,000	176,820,000	422,682,700	713,543,000	917,893,000	1,118,375,000	1,200,143,000

6/4	41/1	41/2	41/3	41/4	43	44/1	44/2	44/3	45	46/1	46/2	50/1	50/2	72/2	73/1	73/2	74/1	75/1	75/2	75/3	75/4	
.01	n/a	n/a	10	0	100	n/a	n/a	0	10	0.42	0	1.6	0	0.32	0	0	n/a	2	9	1	n/a	Afghanistan
.06	182	0	17	0	86	n/a	n/a	0	95	2.62	3	32	0	0	0	2	n/a	8	28	25	1	Albania
.07	n/a	n/a	108	50	100	n/a	n/a	0	90	0.09	0	0	5.5	0.1	7.5	60	6	16	19	14	1	Algeria
	115	7	768	54	5	4	12	1	85	0.73	2	6	0.9	2.14	40.5	109	3	2	10	5	0.5	Angola
	913	51	7,611	915	2	30	49	8	90	0.04	0	0.3	0	1.13	206	1,318	53	30	65	36	12	Argentina
.6	10	0	0	0	4	n/a	n/a	0	97	3.46	3	0	0	0	0.14	0	n/a	n/a	n/a	n/a	n/a	Armenia
3	743	2,062	1,993	1,054	0.2	33	15	28	97	0.52	4	7.9	0	0	298	571	527	65	149	52	25	Australia
.5	593	37	430	907	0.3	6	11	2	100	n/a	2	12	0	0	68	164	67	40	115	57	20	Austria
.02	n/a	n/a	0	0	88	n/a	n/a	0	97	0.51	1	0	0	0	0	1	n/a	n/a	n/a	n/a	n/a	Azerbaijan
44	68	0	64	0	n/a	n/a	n/a	n/a	100	n/a	2	1.4	0	0	78	261	7	47	74	31	n/a	Bahamas, The
.7	n/a	n/a	14	0	100	n/a	n/a	0	100	n/a	0	0	0	0.01	0.78	6	n/a	26	54	32	14	Bahrain
.1	316	0	304	0	31	n/a	1	4	90	0.08	1	6	0	1.02	n/a	n/a	n/a	n/a	6	3	0.5	Bangladesh
	6	0	0	0	1	n/a	n/a	0	100	0.45	2	0	0	0	0.6	2	n/a	n/a	29	25	n/a	Belarus
.3	572	22	1,040	7,702	3	32	12	5	98	n/a	2	1.6	0	0	99	181	176	48	78	45	37	Belgium
1	105	1	56	0	30	n/a	n/a	0	90	n/a	2	8.2	0	0.01	0.35	18	n/a	n/a	45	23	16	Belize
.3	171	3	274	20	31	1	1	n/a	45	1.30	2	8	3.2	1.10	33	200	n/a	3	8	2	1	Benin
	13	0	11	0	n/a	n/a	n/a	n/a	100	n/a	2	7.6	0	0	15	28	5	64	100	71	43	Bermuda
.3	72	0	10	0	100	n/a	n/a	0	40	1.87	0	0	0	0.71	0	0	n/a	1	4	n/a	n/a	Bhutan
	1,010	7	342	1,610	2	7	17	3	90	0.75	3	7.8	9.6	1.67	5	12	n/a	18	46	13	n/a	Bolivia
8	249	0	51	0	11	n/a	1	1	80	4.67	2	2.4	0	0.01	77	677	1	1	17	2	n/a	Botswana
	3,397	832	3,567	970	0.2	62	210	15	90	0.87	3	5.9	0	6.10	3,095	9,261	42	14	46	26	3	Brazil
	0	0	5	0	95	n/a	n/a	0	45	n/a	0	0	0	0.01	0.3	0.3	2	9	29	21	11	Brunei
	77	0	0	0	11	n/a	n/a	1	95	2.31	1	3.8	0	0	1	6	15	22	68	38	9	Bulgaria
14	364	136	579	56	32	n/a	3	n/a	55	n/a	2	3.7	4.8	0.69	206	836	n/a	2	5	0.5	0.5	Burkina Faso
0.1	95	2	407	30	n/a	1	3	n/a	95	0.55	2	0	19.4	0.01	483	87	3	2	7	0.5	0.5	Burundi
	105	0	1	0	74	n/a	1	0	90	1.16	2	7.6	0	3.21	n/a	29	3	9	15	1	n/a	Cambodia
3	689	2	1,640	162	35	1	7	1	40	0.26	2	2	9.6	1.98	157	1,059	8	7	16	5	1	Cameroon
24	408	3,636	570	2,959	1	38	20	55	98	0.83	3	5.6	21.2	0	631	1,093	322	94	154	63	25	Canada
14	208	2	531	3	19	n/a	n/a	3	20	n/a	2	2.2	12.2	7.52	282	171	n/a	4	10	1	n/a	Central African Rep
27	197	2	406	2	82	n/a	1	0	60	n/a	1	6.4	9.3	5.65	42	957	1	1	12	0.5	n/a	Chad
0.5	565	39	135	550	3	4	23	n/a	95	n/a	2	3.1	0	0.01	52	18	28	21	36	22	4	Chile
2	n/a	n/a	5	0	20	n/a	n/a	0	90	0.54	0	32.5	0	1.51	1	21	n/a	2	25	21	1	China, People's Rep
18	1,209	22	731	60	0.3	4	8	11	95	n/a	4	2.6	1.6	0.05	n/a	n/a	n/a	13	47	38	21	China, Taiwan
10	947	34	792	1,466	0.2	23	75	1	90	n/a	2	3.2	30.4	1.42	265	683	19	23	43	17	5	Colombia
5	116	1	337	6	100	8	5	n/a	20	n/a	2	1.7	5.3	4.12	376	835	6	3	14	4	n/a	Congo
3	452	99	21	234	n/a	1	5	4	90	n/a	3	3.0	0	0.79	31	131	n/a	22	24	17	2	Costa Rica
0.4	900	6	805	135	31	1	4	2	40	n/a	2	4.2	4.5	1.62	107	3,527	5	10	15	6	1	Cote d'Ivoire
	2	2	211	0	n/a	1	3	0	100	2.19	0	0	0	0.94	13	67	6	22	33	23	n/a	Cuba
20	137	0	75	0	28	n/a	n/a	n/a	100	n/a	2	5	0	0	2	4	11	26	59	32	14	Cyprus
5	87	1	0	13	n/a	5	5	1	97	1.25	2	1.3	0	0	2	12	110	28	61	49	11	Czech Republic
0.04	1,470	33	4,366	830	7	n/a	58	4	65	0.30	1	1.1	3.9	1.77	1,583	1,324	14	2	9	4	0.5	Democratic Rep of Congo
5	31	342	677	16	n/a	n/a	n/a	2	98	0.61	3	22	0	0	83	208	142	50	136	58	27	Denmark
4	28	0	50	0	84	n/a	n/a	0	65	5.83	1	0	18	0.01	22	153	n/a	n/a	8	4	n/a	Djibouti
0.7	216	5	1,561	60	n/a	1	3	n/a	95	n/a	2	4.5	0	1.54	149	285	1	12	15	10	n/a	Dominican Rep
20	1,151	3	304	120	1	8	32	3	95	n/a	4	3.6	14.5	0.51	19	75	n/a	16	33	28	4	Ecuador
1	n/a	n/a	1,135	75	88	n/a	6	1	90	0.10	1	7.3	0	0.78	4	19	42	17	29	16	3	Egypt
8	113	38	829	80	n/a	2	1	n/a	90	n/a	1	19	0	0.01	31	273	4	26	38	13	2	El Salvador
13	42	0	213	10	n/a	2	n/a	n/a	85	n/a	2	9.5	7.5	0.01	1	264	1	2	25	1	n/a	Equatorial Guinea
10	45	4	0	0	n/a	n/a	n/a	1	100	1.33	2	0	0	0	0.2	1	n/a	n/a	55	43	4	Estonia
16	623	5	263	0	11	5	6	3	90	0.50	0	4.3	7.6	1.76	376	4,850	13	2	10	1	0.5	Ethiopia & Eritrea
0.6	78	73	97	5	67	2	5	2	60	n/a	3	5.5	0	0.01	0.3	1	16	10	54	8	7	Fiji
4	20	1,278	58	5	0.8	n/a	n/a	4	94	0.38	3	13.9	0	0	9	31	61	45	83	67	24	Finland
0.6	1,048	293	12,409	22,754	6	65	56	7	98	0.81	2	6.5	0	0	1,806	4,361	351	45	111	54	23	France
4	18	0	129	0	n/a	n/a	n/a	n/a	60	n/a	2	0	0	0.01	0.22	58	n/a	8	57	16	n/a	French Guiana
0.2	68	2	213	10	12	n/a	1	n/a	45	n/a	2	10.4	100	18.48	28	199	1	12	23	6	5	Gabon
0.4	109	2	51	0	77	n/a	n/a	n/a	20	n/a	2	0.8	7.8	0.01	17	44	2	9	16	n/a	n/a	Gambia, The
5	8	0	0	0	7	n/a	n/a	n/a	85	1.02	2	0	0	0	0.1	8	n/a	n/a	n/a	n/a	n/a	Georgia
5	1,247	2,861	4,506	21,487	2	38	40	12	97	3	3	7.4	0	0	696	1,307	639	50	97	53	21	Germany

	36/4	41/1	41/2	41/3	41/4	43	44/1	44/2	44/3	45	46/1	46/2	50/1	50/2	72/2	73/1	73/2	74/1	75/1	75/2	75/3	75/4
Ghana	9	400	128	540	62	13	1	3	7	85	0.38	2	2.1	2.2	1.26	735	1,868	7	10	24	5	1
Greece	0.1	144	8	180	0	2	n/a	n/a	1	98	0.19	2	0.5	0	0	53	165	17	21	58	39	14
Greenland	4	50	2	2	0	n/a	n/a	n/a	0	100	n/a	3	9.8	0	0	0	8	n/a	20	42	27	n/a
Guatemala	23	612	36	97	140	0.3	6	13	5	90	n/a	3	3.7	16.4	0.23	26	114	8	12	22	11	3
Guinea	0.5	199	0	45	0	91	n/a	n/a	n/a	40	n/a	2	6.7	0	5.03	48	335	4	2	7	1	1
Guinea-Bissau	0.9	72	1	74	2	50	n/a	n/a	n/a	20	n/a	2	12.3	0	2.57	20	209	n/a	0.8	5	n/a	n/a
Guyana	15	47	4	36	2	81	n/a	n/a	1	90	n/a	3	1.8	0	0.01	28	103	11	31	40	6	n/a
Haiti	21	473	3	792	5	n/a	2	6	3	95	3.24	3	6.3	0	1	358	n/a	2	8	22	0.5	n/a
Honduras	11	384	23	113	50	n/a	1	1	2	90	n/a	3	3.3	0	0.01	175	659	3	12	26	11	2
Hong Kong	7	767	171	591	60	0.3	3	1	9	99	n/a	3	7	6.4	0	5	25	37	23	77	47	26
Hungary	5	213	7	0	38	1	8	11	2	98	2.77	2	4.7	0	0	8	27	15	29	88	44	14
Iceland	3	20	22	44	0	n/a	n/a	n/a	1	100	n/a	2	10.3	0	0	2	4	9	49	57	32	19
India	1	775	171	2,377	5,561	87	38	121	66	80	0.56	2	30.2	4.3	6.10	19	618	351	3	10	5	1
Indonesia	4	1,599	68	1,269	205	63	12	22	39	75	0.52	3	2.3	3.2	2.07	2	16	9	3	15	9	2
Iran	0.03	n/a	n/a	107	0	54	n/a	n/a	0	70	0.42	0	0	0	0.22	4	19	15	9	23	13	2
Iraq	0.03	n/a	n/a	56	20	100	3	1	0	75	0.25	0	87	0	0.01	1	10	2	13	21	9	4
Ireland	0.9	274	39	15	4,498	n/a	28	19	2	100	n/a	2	2.8	0	0	25	47	325	27	72	35	13
Israel	0.2	434	0	350	8	80	3	4	1	85	0.14	1	8.5	0	0.01	17	33	34	26	48	33	14
Italy	1	462	42	8,200	26,450	0.1	224	277	3	97	1.54	3	2.5	0	0	1,223	4,440	176	30	100	62	12
Jamaica	20	209	23	167	40	n/a	1	1	5	95	n/a	2	25	1.7	0	31	294	9	30	54	22	n/a
Japan	0.3	3,015	271	1,731	186	97	n/a	4	14	95	0.41	3	9.7	0.03	0	38	175	18	83	96	68	24
Jordan	0.2	106	20	70	15	n/a	n/a	n/a	n/a	95	n/a	1	3.6	0	0.01	2	5	n/a	21	37	21	9
Kazakhstan	0.7	n/a	n/a	0	0	46	n/a	n/a	0	90	0.24	1	0	0	0	0	2	n/a	17	24	24	3
Kenya	36	2,322	118	2,200	52	8	1	9	18	85	n/a	3	4.5	6.1	0.28	2,645	6515	13	7	18	3	0.5
Korea, Dem Rep	0.4	0	0	0	0	98	n/a	n/a	0	100	8.24	0	0	0	0	2	4	n/a	5	17	4	n/a
Korea, Rep of	21	409	2,032	432	211	2	2	5	51	100	0.53	4	4.6	10.4	0.25	0.8	7	n/a	8	66	29	10
Kuwait	0.1	n/a	n/a	37	0	100	n/a	n/a	0	95	n/a	0	0	0	0.01	0.6	3	n/a	36	69	43	21
Kyrgyzstan	0.2	n/a	n/a	0	0	73	n/a	n/a	0	90	n/a	0	0	0	0	n/a	n/a	n/a	n/a	n/a	n/a	n/a
Laos	0.7	36	0	215	0	100	n/a	n/a	0	90	5.71	0	25	0	0.01	0.1	4	n/a	3	15	1	n/a
Latvia	6	29	2	0	0	0.1	n/a	1	0	100	1.87	2	3.4	0	0	0.3	2	n/a	51	36	5	
Lebanon	0.4	42	15	779	150	2	6	12	1	97	n/a	3	5.3	0	0.01	3	18	20	25	62	30	11
Lesotho	4	142	4	140	10	n/a	1	1	1	95	1.67	2	9.1	5	0.01	14	166	4	0.6	21	2	n/a
Liberia	8	353	1	212	0	28	n/a	1	n/a	60	n/a	3	0.7	4.2	1.70	2	81	4	12	21	2	n/a
Libya	0.1	n/a	n/a	110	0	100	n/a	n/a	0	95	n/a	0	0	0	0.77	0.8	2	6	10	27	12	n/a
Lithuania	0.3	4	0	0	0	0.3	1	7	0	100	1.46	2	50	0	0	0.3	1	n/a	n/a	48	40	4
Luxembourg	0.1	10	1	20	90	n/a	1	2	0	95	n/a	2	0	0	0	4	14	9	53	79	39	18
Madagascar	6	192	7	1,222	100	2	2	10	2	95	0.74	3	2.6	2.3	4.91	0.4		11	7	17	1	0.5
Malawi	10	385	94	578	30	19	1	4	4	90	0.13	3	2.4	1.3	0.94	1,925	4,345	5	4	13	n/a	n/a
Malaysia	3	189	145	370	0	93	1	4	6	85	0.35	0	2.2	0	0.81	6	61	32	10	21	18	6
Mali	0.8	315	0	257	1	88	n/a	1	0	60	n/a	3	3.1	0	4.74	94	427	3	2	7	1	0.5
Mauritania	0	32	0	50	0	n/a	n/a	n/a	n/a	65	n/a	0	18	22.6	1.87	5	22	n/a	5	14	2	n/a
Mexico	5	1,891	84	112	2,020	2	49	90	7	95	5.33	2	5.9	100	0.68	1,008	4,183	17	12	39	19	4
Moldova	2	0	0	0	0	8	n/a	n/a	0	75	n/a	3	0	0	0	0.3	1	n/a	n/a	n/a	n/a	n/a
Mongolia	0.1	89	0	0	0	100	n/a	n/a	0	85	0.76	1	36	0	0.01	n/a	n/a	n/a	17	15	5	n/a
Morocco	0.05	n/a	n/a	412	0	91	n/a	n/a	0	70	0.35	0	6.6	0	0.41	9	51	8	9	31	16	5
Mozambique	10	285	5	648	60	55	3	3	1	85	1.32	1	5.6	3.1	6.17	47	384	3	2	5	0.5	0.5
Myanmar	4	22	39	155	25	85	1	3	4	80	2.78	0	0	19.3	4.72	3	174	n/a	2	8	0.2	n/a
Namibia	12	190	17	281	0	3	n/a	n/a	3	90	n/a	3	1	5.3	0.01	259	1,479	n/a	n/a	10	6	4
Nepal	0.6	584	2	118	0	100	n/a	n/a	2	60	0.42	0	1.7	0	6.05	1	12	n/a	0.6	6	2	1
Netherlands	5	367	866	1,559	5,044	3	n/a	4	13	97	n/a	4	15	0	0	185	383	278	37	105	52	24
New Zealand	26	218	1,347	553	295	n/a	4	n/a	11	97	9.67	4	9.7	0	0	28	41	153	44	98	37	21
Nicaragua	16	108	9	36	70	n/a	1	3	n/a	90	n/a	2	8.2	0	0.01	4	21	5	15	25	15	2
Niger	0.09	264	1	138	0	89	n/a	n/a	1	55	0.38	1	16.3	14	3.29	58	307	2	2	6	1	n/a
Nigeria	15	768	243	923	80	40	4	18	24	85	0.13	2	2.2	1.2	1.96	50	295	19	3	19	9	2
Norway	10	52	1,498	476	20	n/a	n/a	n/a	6	98	0.47	3	22	0	0	22	57	169	49	124	51	23
Oman	0.2	n/a	n/a	1	0	83	n/a	n/a	0	90	n/a	0	0	0	0.01	2	8	n/a	1	47	33	17
Pakistan	0.2	736	6	455	0	93	2	3	4	85	0.16	0	2.7	0.7	0.48	2	8	48	3	8	7	1
Panama	12	228	1	141	350	3	n/a	3	n/a	85	n/a	2	1.2	5.7	0.01	34	156	6	47	39	22	8

6/4	41/1	41/2	41/3	41/4	43	44/1	44/2	44/3	45	46/1	46/2	50/1	50/2	72/2	73/1	73/2	74/1	75/1	75/2	75/3	75/4	
9	2,278	40	1,157	5	8	n/a	4	8	20	3.18	3	3.2	12	3.14	5	23	3	0.7	10	1	n/a	Papua New Guinea
	520	10	51	180	n/a	4	13	n/a	90	n/a	3	7.6	0	2.75	7	26	n/a	21	25	15	1	Paraguay
.2	1,043	58	581	250	1	11	30	1	95	0.73	3	1.5	17.8	0.12	123	328	9	15	26	17	3	Peru
	2,958	178	247	855	9	34	100	50	80	0.16	4	2.9	4	1.70	7	42	8	8	18	9	1	Philippines
.2	77	6	1	1,029	n/a	54	89	4	95	0.59	3	8.6	0	0	9	72	7	16	57	41	14	Poland
	333	129	260	2,309	n/a	35	23	2	98	0.35	2	1.3	0	0	104	424	60	21	46	35	14	Portugal
4	141	61	1,650	520	n/a	1	10	4	95	n/a	4	3.4	0	0.01	n/a	n/a	n/a	39	68	26	7	Puerto Rico
.5	n/a	n/a	2	0	39	n/a	n/a	0	95	n/a	0	0	0	0.01	4	6	n/a	9	51	37	26	Qatar
	165	2	0	0	1	1	5	6	90	1.18	3	19.8	0	0	165	431	8	12	42	35	4	Romania
.6	505	0	0	0	11	1	1	1	90	1.38	4	6.5	0	0	9	30	152	21	24	41	1	Russia
1	150	0	753	70	1	2	2	2	95	n/a	2	0	9.2	0.01	677	1,220	4	1	6	n/a	n/a	Rwanda
.3	n/a	n/a	85	0	97	n/a	n/a	0	95	0.41	0	0	0	0.58	4	28	n/a	10	34	28	17	Saudi Arabia
.07	468	1	644	70	80	1	2	n/a	55	n/a	3	3.4	0	0.95	46	308	7	9	18	7	1	Senegal
2	233	2	234	0	25	n/a	1	6	60	n/a	1	4.4	8	1.25	6	25	3	9	20	1	0.5	Sierra Leone
	385	567	165	2	100	n/a	1	10	95	n/a	1	5.7	0	1.61	4	31	7	19	71	39	21	Singapore
.01	10	1		0	2	n/a	6	0	97	3.80	1	20	0	0	0.5	2	n/a	n/a	56	47	7	Slovakia
	n/a	n/a	67	0	79	n/a	n/a	0	95	0.72	0	8	4.4	1.14	1	0	4	3	6	1	n/a	Somalia
6	1,294	651	2,589	100	3	4	6	41	95	1.97	3	5.1	1.4	0.09	148	2,113	244	21	31	11	3	South Africa
0.8	1,109	62	1,280	21,020	0.03	123	151	4	98	0.56	2	5.5	0	0	1,443	4,804	100	25	64	38	15	Spain
0.4	117	3	1,208	30	8	4	5	3	97	0.71	1	0.4	0.08	1.03	1	10	n/a	5	16	4	1	Sri Lanka
3	162	4	371	55	100	n/a	3	0	85	0.74	0	8.6	3.5	2.09	49	188	4	5	13	8	1	Sudan
13	156	1	107	10	45	n/a	n/a	n/a	85	n/a	2	1.9	1.8	5.92	10	25	n/a	20	55	14	n/a	Suriname
7	220	26	222	0	n/a	n/a	n/a	2	100	3.50	3	5.7	0.9	0.01	18	114	1	2	15	3	n/a	Swaziland
5	88	1,652	347	20	0.2	n/a	1	3	95	0.66	3	15.4	0	0	57	159	162	63	161	63	26	Sweden
	219	1,083	845	1,804	12	7	5	9	98	n/a	2	16.6	0	0	250	433	203	41	83	78	40	Switzerland
0.1	n/a	n/a	81	36	63	4	1	0	95	n/a	0	0	0	0.17	2	2	1	16	28	14	5	Syria
0.02	n/a	n/a	0	0	82	n/a	n/a	0	95	0.09	1	0	0	0	0	0	n/a	n/a	n/a	n/a	n/a	Tajikistan
0	1,367	44	1,908	92	14	5	6	6	80	1.43	1	3.2	4.9	1.45	3,063	3,454	6	5	16	1	0.5	Tanzania
0.3	1,293	4	401	5	100	n/a	1	13	85	0.38	3	5.2	2.9	0.53	153	6,665	19	9	19	15	3	Thailand
2	275	3	249	32	42	n/a	1	2	60	n/a	1	3.8	0	1.18	153	1,156	6	2	15	1	n/a	Togo
11	94	9	85	33	3	1	1	5	95	n/a	3	2.5	0	0	88	220	10	23	61	29	n/a	Trinidad & Tobago
0.003	n/a	n/a	430	0	1	n/a	n/a	0	90	n/a	0	0	0	0.21	9	42	19	16	28	15	3	Tunisia
0.006	n/a	n/a	240	0	99	n/a	n/a	0	95	0.15	0	14.2	0	0	7	25	15	11	16	17	n/a	Turkey
0.01	n/a	n/a	0	0	72	n/a	n/a	0	95	n/a	1	0	0	0	0.01	0	n/a	n/a	8	18	1	Turkmenistan
25	382	20	779	110	5	2	6	9	70	n/a	3	3.7	8.3	0.73	2,754	3,784	4	4	17	2	0.5	Uganda
3	48	30	0	0	3	n/a	4	0	97	0.29	3	5.5	0	0	1	12	n/a	n/a	23	29	2	Ukraine
0.3	n/a	n/a	34	0	57	2	n/a	0	90	n/a	0	0	0	0.01	0.6	0	n/a	10	51	36	18	United Arab Emirates
2	1,021	5,368	3,074	1,432	2	21	14	46	97	9.92	4	10.7	0	0	545	1,288	n/a	65	148	71	30	United Kingdom
	217	28	1,447	350	5	4	5	n/a	95	n/a	1	1.7	0	0.01	17	108	11	38	57	25	3	Uruguay
30	2,484	39,951	10,582	5,595	14	189	116	105	98	4.13	4	2.6	0	0.02	23,698	56,513	776	146	223	77	31	USA
0.1	n/a	n/a	0	0	81	n/a	n/a	0	95	0.07	0	0	0	0	0.01	0.3	n/a	n/a	8	18	0	Uzbekistan
5	637	12	150	480	0.3	4	12	1	90	n/a	3	2.3	4	1.92	227	595	8	24	49	21	6	Venezuela
0.8	19	3	1	340	15	4	5	0	90	1.08	0	26	0	0.70	n/a	97	n/a	8	9	7	1	Vietnam
0.004	n/a	n/a	60	0	100	n/a	n/a	0	95	n/a	0	7.2	0	0.51	0.3	5	2	5	13	4	2	Yemen
0.1	53	2	71	526	37	12	n/a	n/a	100	0.37	2	0	0	0	20	76	12	18	38	23	9	Yugoslavia
13	626	44	1,066	30	18	1	4	8	90	n/a	4	2.2	5.3	1.46	1,993	1,531	3	9	19	8	1	Zambia
14	630	45	905	10	4	n/a	1	13	95	1.55	3	3.1	6.9	0.11	1,338	7,519	61	8	14	3	0.5	Zimbabwe

	55/1900	55/1980	55/2000	56/1900	56/1980	56/2000	57/1900	57/1980	57/2000	58/1900	58/1980	58/2000	59/1900	59/1980	59/2000
Africa	3,400	12,140	21,980	279,320	1,148,900	1,536,437	34,531,292	149,728,390	341,716,748	1,900	8,600	16,562	62,685,265	63,872,800	67,059,763
America, North	40,140	198,450	560,896	1,000	545,000	998,138	10,050	2,038,000	5,875,154	75,120	116,000	560,896	144,000	70,000	81,927
America, South	5,930	461,430	418,710	163,160	609,150	804,088	57,710	581,570	1,429,444	1,600	67,500	56,265	2,244,540	1,173,250	1,575,830
Asia and USSR	127,102,701	272,856,200	271,592,520	202,576,400	579,699,830	861,341,600	162,717,260	521,886,535	969,912,256	381,633,440	206,036,850	443,958,323	39,978,790	24,745,030	61,876,785
Europe	0	170,480	209,027	50	482,890	562,674	2,772,600	8,634,580	21,400,207	0	54,000	69,835	n/a	n/a	n/a
Oceania and Australia	6,530	16,890	67,230	13,400	264,150	322,052	13,372	87,429	409,690	12,678	18,796	82,751	1,287,000	102,370	127,000

[1] Estimate

bibliography

* = key source, used for more than one page

Annuarium Statisticum Ecclesical (Statistical Yearbook of the Church), the Vatican, 1970, 1993

Books in Print, Whitaker, London, UK, various years

* *Demographic Yearbook*, United Nations, New York, USA, various years

Evangelical Awakenings in Africa, J Edwin Orr, Bethany Fellowship, Minneapolis, 1975

Evangelical Awakenings in Eastern Asia, J Edwin Orr, Bethany Fellowship, Minneapolis, 1975

Evangelical Awakenings in Southern Asia, J Edwin Orr, Bethany Fellowship, Minneapolis, 1975

Great Revivals, Colin Whittaker, Marshall Morgan & Scott, Basingstoke, UK, 1984

* *Human Development Report 1995,* United Nations Development Programme, Oxford University Press, UK, 1995

Independent, The (newspaper), London, UK, 30 May 1996

Least Evangelized Peoples of the World, The, Peoples Information Network, Dallas, USA, 1995

* *Operation World,* Patrick Johnstone, OM Publishing, Carlisle, UK, 1993

* *Operation World data base,* Patrick Johnstone, WEC International, Gerrards Cross, UK, 1993

Revival Fire, Wesley Duewel, Zondervan Publishing House, Grand Rapids, USA, 1995

Revival - God's Spotlight, H H Osborn, Highland Books, Guildford, UK, 1996

Signs of Revival, Dr Patrick Dixon, Kingsway Publications, Eastbourne, UK, 1994

Statistical Yearbook of the Church - see Annuarium Statisticum Ecclesical

Target Earth, Frank Kaleb Jansen (editor), University of the Nations, Hawaii and Global Mapping International, Pasadena, USA, 1989

Tear Times, Tear Fund, Teddington, UK, Spring 1993

* *A Third World Guide, The World, 1995/96,* Instituto del Tercer Mundo, Oxfam UK & Ireland, 1995

UK Christian Handbook 1996/97, Peter Brierley & Heather Wraight (editors), Christian Research, London, UK, 1995

Willing's Press Guide, Thomas Skinner Directories, East Grinstead, UK, various years

* *World Christian Encyclopedia,* David B Barrett (editor), Oxford University Press, UK, 1982

* *World Churches Handbook,* Peter Brierley (editor), Christian Research, London, UK, and Lausanne Committee for World Evangelization, Edinburgh, UK, 1997

World Directory of Theological Institutions, Bong Rin Ro, World Evangelical Fellowship Theological Commission, Wheaton, USA, 1995

World Health Organisation Weekly Epidemiological Record, World Health Organisation, Geneva, Switzerland, No 20, 17 May, 1996

* *World Population Data Sheet,* Population Reference Bureau Inc., Washington, USA, 1995

* *World Population Prospects,* United Nations, New York, USA, 1992

* *World Population Prospects,* The 1994 Revision, United Nations, New York, USA, 1994

World Radio & Television Receivers, International Broadcasting Research, BBC, London, UK, 1971, 1981, 1995

OTHER SOURCES

CAFOD (Catholic Fund for Overseas Development), Romero Close, Stockwell Road, London SW9 9TY, UK

Catholic Central Library and Information Centre, 47 Francis Street, London SW1P 1QR, UK

Catholic Relief Services, 209 W Fayette Street, Baltimore, Maryland 21201, USA

Christian Aid, PO Box 100, London SE1 7RT, UK

Frank Gray, FEBC Radio International, c/o FEBA Radio, Ivy Arch Road, Worthing, BN14 8BX, UK

International Broadcasting Research, see World Radio & Television Receivers in Bibliography

Leprosy Mission, International Office, 80 Windmill Road, Brentford TW8 0QH, UK

Lutheran World Relief, 390 Park Avenue South, New York 10016, USA

Open Doors, PO Box 318, 3850 AH Ermelo, The Netherlands

SIL Ethnologue, SIL, Horsleys Green, High Wycombe HP14 3XL, UK

Tear Fund, 100 Church Road, Teddington TW11 8QE, UK

United Bible Societies World Service Centre, Reading Bridge House, Reading RG1 8PJ, UK

World by 2000 Project, see Frank Gray

World Vision International, 800 W Chestnut Avenue, Monrovia, California 91016-3198, USA

World Vision UK, 599 Avebury Boulevard, Milton Keynes MK9 3PG, UK